Organizational Assessment

Organizational Assessment

A STEP-BY-STEP GUIDE TO EFFECTIVE CONSULTING

Harry Levinson

AMERICAN PSYCHOLOGICAL ASSOCIATION
WASHINGTON, DC

Published by
American Psychological Association
750 First Street, NE
Washington, DC 20002
www.apa.org

First printing May 2002
Second printing March 2004

To order
APA Order Department
P.O. Box 92984
Washington, DC 20090-2984
Tel: (800) 374-2721;
Direct: (202) 336-5510
Fax: (202) 336-5502;
TDD/TTY: (202) 336-6123
Online: www.apa.org/books/
Email: order@apa.org

In the U.K., Europe, Africa, and the Middle East, copies may be ordered from American Psychological Association
3 Henrietta Street
Covent Garden, London
WC2E 8LU England

Typeset in Goudy by World Composition Services, Inc., Sterling, VA

Printer: Phoenix Color, Hagerstown, MD
Cover Designer: Berg Design, Albany, NY
Production Editor: Catherine Hudson
Project Manager: Debbie Hardin, Carlsbad, CA

The opinions and statements published are the responsibility of the authors, and such opinions and statements do not necessarily represent the policies of the American Psychological Association.

Library of Congress Cataloging-in-Publication Data
Levinson, Harry.
   Organizational assessment : a step-by-step guide to effective consulting / Harry Levinson.
     p. cm.
   Includes bibliographical references and index.
   ISBN 1-55798-921-4
   1. Organizational effectiveness—Evaluation.   2. Business consultants. I. Title.
   HD58.9.L48 2002
   001—dc21

2002018251

British Library Cataloguing-in-Publication Data
A CIP record is available from the British Library.

Printed in the United States of America
First Edition

To Miriam,
whose love, affection, and insightful support
make her a cherished, invaluable, if silent
partner in all aspects of my work. I owe her
more than I shall ever be able to express.

CONTENTS

PREFACE

Two colleagues, one a sociologist and the other a psychiatrist, and I had undertaken a study of what was then the Kansas Power and Light Company. While my sociologist colleague and I were in other parts of a community, interviewing and observing the employees, our psychiatric colleague was doing the same with one of the line crews. He was riding with the crew in its truck while its driver was trying to avoid some children who were playing with their dog in the street. Unfortunately, despite his effort, that truck hit and killed the dog. The children started to scream and cry. Their mother came running out of her house, yelling and cursing at the foreman of the crew. Already dismayed and not knowing how else to cope with that catastrophe, his voice quivering, he introduced a rider on his truck, "Here's a psychiatrist. Talk to him." My nonplused colleague comforted the astonished mother and her children. No public utility had ever before (and probably none since) offered such a spontaneous service. Later the company bought them a new dog.

Not long afterward, we were interviewing and observing in another community. A gas line across the Kansas River had blown up. A gas crew was rowing toward the point of the explosion when they suddenly became aware of my sociologist colleague observer in the boat. In surprised astonishment, they wanted to know what on earth he was doing there. "Observing," he replied. But that did not really explain his presence.

In both instances, and ultimately in 840 interviews (Levinson, Munden, Price, Mandl, & Solley, 1962), we were immersing ourselves in the organization. We wanted to learn about the impact of work on mental health, but apart from attitude surveys there was no accepted method for the psychological study of whole organizations. The rest of the industrial/organizational (I/O) psychology literature was largely (and still is) odds and ends of small researches. How we wound up on those trucks interviewing employees over two thirds of Kansas is a story in itself.

I took my clinical psychology training in a doctoral program conducted jointly by the University of Kansas, The Menninger Foundation, and the Topeka Veterans Administration Hospital. The clinical component in the VA hospital was supervised by the late David Rapaport, a psychologist and psychoanalyst, who was director of research at The Menninger Foundation. Rapaport wisely (I always thought of him as a Hungarian genius) rotated my 19 colleagues and myself on the hospital wards, where we spent four years immersed in clinical phenomena while concurrently taking our academic courses. That immersion enabled us to experience phenomena that often were not in textbooks and to experience firsthand the limits and inadequacies of the literature.

In that immersion, there were two fundamental components that long had been the clinical basis for the Menninger reputation. The first was a heavy emphasis on diagnosis (Menninger, 1962). The second was the use of the whole hospital environment as the therapeutic milieu rather than psychotherapy or other specific therapies alone (W. C. Menninger, 1936). In addition, the orientation was to open-system thinking, drawn from biology (Bertalanffy, 1950; Goldstein, 1939; Kohler, 1940). As Karl Menninger summarized it,

> The open system exchanges energy with its environment, its components are materially in flux, and not only does it maintain itself as a whole with a relative degree of constancy, but it may also change to different levels of organization, as an organism does when it grows. The combination of these and other features of open systems have some bearing on the form of equilibrium that can be attributed to it under the principle of constancy. (Menninger, Mayman, & Pruyser, 1963, p. 92)

Before my training was completed, I became heavily involved in the reform of the Topeka State Hospital. That led to my concern not only with the whole institution but also others in the Kansas state hospital system and interaction with the press and the state legislature. When the reform effort was moving along well, William C. Menninger, following his experience as chief of U.S. Army psychiatry in World War II, where his responsibility was to sustain the mental health of the soldiers, asked me to undertake a project on how to keep well people functioning well. That public health task meant working with large numbers of people. Where else but where they worked?

Initially, my concern was with the symptoms and problems of the individual at work. My early focus, for example, was on accidents, absenteeism, and alcoholism as reflections of the psychological problems of individuals. It became increasingly evident to me that the way an organization was managed had considerable import for the mental health of the people who worked in it. Logically, then, an important mode of preventing emotional distress was to understand organizational malfunctioning, and the symptoms that resulted, and to evolve ways of ameliorating both simultaneously.

Although there is a long history of idiographic research (Hormuth, 1986; Rosenzweig, 1951), the intensive study of the single patient, there were then and even now no generally accepted systematic ways of examining organizations to assess their psychological well-being and to decide what, if anything, needed to be done to help them improve it. Our own initial efforts to formulate an examination procedure were crude. We found other methods to be too limited or too mechanistic. As my early colleagues went their own professional ways, I continued to work on evolving a diagnostic procedure.

It became evident that the very factors and forces that made our and other diagnostic efforts inadequate dictated what an adequate diagnostic process should be. An organization is a living system. It has components that, taken together, make up its whole. The components interact with each other and the whole with other wholes and its own environment. It grows and develops, has a history, experiences crises, and adapts. Like people, organizations die. They fail or are adopted (acquired by others). An organization, then, is like any other living system. Therefore, modes of systematically studying and evaluating other systems might be extrapolated to the study of organizations.

When confronted with an issue similar to trying to understand a new patient—namely how, without formal guidelines, to understand an organization—I fell back on the same method in which I had been trained. My colleagues and I immersed ourselves in the Kansas Power and Light Company. Why that one? As Margaret Mead once said when she was asked why she chose a given tribe, "It was the first one I came to."

Our immersion was without a formal research design. We knew of none that fit our task. I counted on our psychoanalytically oriented clinical training to help us understand and integrate what we were learning. In the words of Geertz (1973, p. 20), we were "guessing at meanings, assessing the guesses, and drawing explanatory conclusions from the better guesses." But it was a difficult struggle to make sense out of all the interviews and other data. I yearned for a systematic method for gathering data on a whole organization. I constructed some rough outlines. I began with a crudely extrapolated outline that I used for teaching fellows in The Menninger School of Psychiatry. My intention was to have them extend their basic examination method in which they were trained to the study of organizations. I did not then think of using the same method myself. I constructed revised forms of the outline in my teaching at the Sloan School of Management at Massachusetts Institute of Technology, at the University of Kansas School of Business, and at the Harvard Graduate School of Business Administration. In addition, clergy who were participants in the Pastoral Care and Counseling Program of The Menninger Foundation helped me formulate revisions as they undertook to study church institutions. But these efforts were not enough.

In the course of this work it became clear to me that the organization, not business, hospital, school, church, or some other institution, was the subject. Experience demonstrated that the kind of organization was irrelevant to the method for studying it, just as the psychological assessment method may be applied with equal facility to a young child, an old man, a menopausal woman, a delinquent adolescent, a depressed executive, or a candidate for submarine training.

The most highly systematized examinational procedure for a living system is that used for the physical and psychiatric examination of the individual person. For years, physicians have been examining people for the purpose of assessing their health and treating their illnesses. The psychiatric examination is a direct extension of the medical examination, with a heavier emphasis on the person's understanding of the problems that prevent the person's successful adaptation to his or her environment.

Then surprise! Perhaps the most detailed psychiatric examination outline, and most highly elaborated diagnostic system, both of which lean heavily on an open-system theory from biology, is that of Karl Menninger (1962; Menninger et al., 1963). There it was, right in my own front yard. What easier way than to extrapolate from the centuries-long efforts to study the individual person?

That is what I did. *Organizational Diagnosis* was in print for 23 years, for 14 of which I used it for teaching the seminar on that topic for Harvard graduate students. In practice, the outline was used with equal success in monasteries, public schools, hospitals, churches, and businesses. The original volume was reprinted eight times over the 23 years it was in print. However, the volume was too thick to carry around while one was working in an organization and was buttressed with a plethora of references, many of which soon became obsolete. That suggested a handier, more practical volume, a manual. References in this book have been kept to a minimum to keep this book short. "Particularly relevant" refers to cites the reader should read as contrasted with those for added information. In addition, examples from one kind of organization do not always make sense to those who are more knowledgeable about another. The manual is intended to be used by assessors who are not necessarily psychologists. Yet to offer multiple examples for each topic, as in the original volume, would make the book too long as a manual. Therefore, the reader frequently will have to develop his or her own examples. The press, particularly the business press, is full of them. (It would be a good exercise for students to compile such a body of examples.) The checklists will help as the assessor evolves his or her analysis. Part I is a guide to getting started and entering an organization, together with an illustrative case summary. Part II describes the data to be gathered and how to classify, interpret, and summarize them. The appendixes include examples of questionnaires, both objective and subjective, a sample report, and other material that may help the reader use the outline more effectively. The detailed outline of the whole process makes up appendix D. It is this with which the reader most frequently will work after he or she has become experienced.

Meanwhile, organizations and management practices have changed drastically since the original volume was published in 1972, along with experiences in the fields of practice. When I started to learn about the organizational world, some of my clinical colleagues complained that I was lending myself to management to exploit their employees. I/O psychologists, heavily into statistics, were then hostile to clinical insights. Now, 30 years later, despite the managerial and organizational changes, much about both remains the same. All organizations necessarily are built on authority and accountability, and yet, despite cultural differences, much human behavior is the same the world over. Practices in psychology, sociology, anthropology, and economics have served to broaden the involvement of organizational participants in decisions about their governance and in the adaptive innovations of their organizations. Given the problems of managed care, many clinical psychologists are moving into organizational consultation, and given the limits of statistical generalizations, many I/O psychologists as well as students of business, sociology, entrepreneurs, and others are becoming more interested in clinical insights. The interests of both clinical and nonclinical assessors overlaps in the recent and increasing attention to executive coaching. All of these factors combine to make this volume even more timely than the original. In addition, it is shorter, easier to use while working in organizations, and more illustrative.

In these days of pressure for fast decisions and rapid change, there is some skepticism about, if not resistance to, efforts to understand organizations that take time and careful work, even though many mergers and other forms of reorganization have not yielded the positive results that their progenitors had hoped for. Nevertheless, to avoid management by impulse and the tendency to adopt fads (Rigby, 2001; Shapiro, 1995) and to abandon structure, methods, and techniques, it is necessary to understand and have a psychological logic for solving many managerial problems and especially for dealing with change.

To be comprehensive, this manual is necessarily detailed. Its detail will help the reader understand more clearly the multiple dimensions of an organization. I assume the reader who attains some skill in organizational consultation will abstract from and condense the outline to meet his or her own needs. However, the purpose of writing an assessment is to specify the data one is using so that one may check the sources of one's diagnostic inferences and hypotheses—in short, to be as scientific in one's orientation as one can. If one eliminates these data, one risks vitiating the purpose for using this outline.

My intention in preparing this manual is twofold: (a) to help formalize and professionalize the organizational consultation role, whether for consultation or internal organizational study and change efforts. Originally, I wrote it for organizational consultants and graduate students who intended to become consultants and (b) to assist managers who want to sharpen their assessment skills or who must undertake an effort to resolve an organizational problem or to integrate a new unit into theirs or to help the members of a newly acquired unit understand their own organization. Duncan, Ginter, and Swayne (1998) pointed out that internal organizational assessment is less well-developed than other areas of organizational assessment and suggest that conducting such assessment enhances organizations' competitive edge.

Society needs people who can help its organizations do their work more effectively. I hope this volume will be a contribution toward meeting that need.

ACKNOWLEDGMENTS

I owe an important debt to many colleagues and students who helped me in myriad ways to evolve this volume and to the many organizations that lent themselves for research and study, as well as those who supported the initial work. I will not here acknowledge that debt further. I expressed my deepest appreciation to them in the original edition. I owe special appreciation to Jean Senecal who did most of the typing and retyping of *Organizational Assessment*. Marilyn Farinato not only retyped this revision but also gave exquisitely careful attention to many editorial details. Her 23 years as my secretary is a history of that invaluable, patient support that has contributed significantly to assuring the continuity and clarity of all that I have written and to my relationships with clients, colleagues, and staff. Andrew G. Spohn and Janice Molinari made important contributions to the original volume. Leslie Pratch did a thorough job of reviewing and editing the manuscript from her experience as a consulting psychologist, clinical psychologist, and editor. Bea Mah Holland and especially Celia Morris carefully did the subsequent editing. Judy Nemes, development editor in the Books Department at the American Psychological Association, and four anonymous reviewers, did a final extremely helpful critique. To the many individuals, financial supporters, organizations, and to the administrators of The Menninger Foundation, Harvard Graduate School of Business, and the Levinson Institute who facilitated this work, I extend my appreciative thanks.

I
INTRODUCTION

1

OVERVIEW

Most human beings are interdependent. They need each other. That has led them to form ever-larger agglomerates of people: families, kinship communities, tribes. As specific complementary family and occupational roles become defined, groups of people become members of work organizations. Those organizations specify rights and responsibilities, codes of behavior, value systems and rituals, and leadership.

Larger social units—communities, states, nations—require organizations, rather than individuals, to carry out their adaptive tasks, particularly as technical developments lead to specialization of functions and the physical techniques and facilities for carrying them out. There is a vast proliferation of software. A ship requires a crew, a school needs a faculty (even though it might provide distance learning), a manufacturing company must carry out its work in a plant. This functional specialization, in turn, increases work-group interdependence, no longer limited by geography. Sales is necessarily dependent on manufacturing, manufacturing on engineering, engineering on research, research on sales. The special education program of a public school aspires to move its students into the educational mainstream. A monastery in which silence governs may nevertheless offer products that some monks may produce and others sell.

Thus, organizations comprise interdependent groups having different immediate goals, different ways of working, different formal training, and different personality types. An accounting department does work that is different in style, method, and goal than sales. Accountants as a group are different people than sales people. Nurses differ from physicians, although both take care of patients. These differences make for different styles of functioning within groups. Each group has its own process—its own way of carrying through its work from beginning to end—based on whatever training it has and the specialized technology it uses. This process may be regarded as a *system*, a series of interrelated steps, functions, and activities yielding a palpable result. Both the process and the result may be explained, measured, controlled, and interrelated with other systems.

Perforce, an organization as a whole is a system of interrelated subsystems. In its turn, it is also a component of larger systems—an industry,

3

a community, an economy. It affects and is affected by other systems. We speak of an organization therefore as being an *open system*, a concept drawn from biology (Bertalanffy, 1950; Goldstein, 1939; Kohler, 1940). This concept calls attention to the need for studying living organisms in their contexts and to the limitations and difficulty of understanding information about living organisms when that information is taken out of context.

A conception of an organism—whether an amoeba, a person, or an organization—as an open system requires thinking of such a system as having a major three-fold task to survive: It must maintain equilibrium (a) among its internal subsystems, (b) between itself as a system and other systems, and (c) between itself and the larger systems of which it is a part. Failure to maintain an adequately adaptive equilibrium results in collapse or destruction. But any system is more than the sum of its subsystems. To pursue the analogy, individual people are not merely interconnected gastrointestinal, cardiovascular, motor, and nervous systems. They have uniqueness, personality, and the capacity to act on their environment in a host of spontaneous ways. They are, of course, a product of their history, as well as their capacities. So it is with organizations. They achieve uniqueness in their ways of performing their functions despite the similarities of their organizational structures, marketplaces, personnel, and techniques.

Organisms have energy. They are not merely acted on. They can act forcibly on their environments. They adapt—that is, they master the environment for their own survival—by modifying or controlling their own behavior, as well as the external influences on them.

Like all other organisms, organizations have their problems in adaptation. Sometimes their internal subsystems do not function well together; sometimes their environments change so significantly that former modes of adaptation no longer work effectively. Subsystems can become so specialized as to be almost foreign to other subsystems. A data-processing department in a public utility is a total stranger to most of the operating units. An organization plan that is highly defined to let each person know his or her job, reporting responsibility, and goals is fine for a stable organization. Although clear accountability is necessary in all organizations and for all roles and tasks, rigid definition is less helpful for an organization that must evolve new roles and processes to adapt quickly to changes in an unstable environment.

Subsystems tend to develop their own autonomy and to have internal norms or shared beliefs, goals, and values. They become behavioral settings for the people who work in them, shaping their thoughts, aspirations, and feelings about themselves, their work, and the organization.

Organizations, too, suffer insult and injury from their environments or conflict because of contradictory goals and purposes. Like individuals, they can be self-destructive (Weaver, 1988). At times, it becomes necessary to assess both the nature and degree of dysfunction.

There are many processes for assessing part-functions of organizations (Howard, 1994). The social psychologist may examine an organization's bureaucracy. The accountant may compute its bank balances. The financial analyst may judge its economic health. The marketing consultant may analyze marketing strategies. Each specialty has its own remedies for ameliorating or resolving the problems it perceives. Often efforts to resolve problems in one area create new ones for the organization as a whole or for other areas. This is especially true if examination of the environmental context of the organization is limited to that part of the environment in which the consultant's specialty operates—for example, the consumer market or the nonexempt (from governmental regulations concerning wages and hours) component of the workforce.

Traditional efforts to look at the whole organization tend to concentrate on its bureaucratic structure: What are the organizational units required to do its task, and how do they relate to each other (Kotter, 1978)? Or on its role structure: What roles are required to do the organizational task, and what are their requirements? Or on status arrangements and communications systems. Or, with survey methods, on attitudes (Rogers & Fong, 2000). These highly intellectualized analyses, however useful for other purposes, do not easily lend themselves to understanding the organization as an active, unique, living entity.

A comprehensive method of assessing organizations, specifically their points and nodes of dysfunction, should cover a number of major areas. It should include an evaluation of the relationship of the organization as an open system with other systems with which it interacts. It should be an ordered, systematic gathering of information as a basis for consultation or organizational change efforts.

Before undertaking an assessment, an assessor should be familiar with the ethical and moral principles that should govern his or her effort. All of the topics discussed in chapters 4 through 9 assume adherence to them. These therefore are elaborated in chapters 2 and 3 as preparation for undertaking the assessment.

To understand an organization, it will be important to understand the organization's *purpose*—in other words, what it stands for. For example, a hospital may stand for providing the highest quality health care for children who have cancer. Organizational purpose is akin to the underlying standard of behavior toward which an individual is always striving. Churches and synagogues differentiate themselves by their creeds. Organizational purpose also implies a mind picture of the organization by the people who work in it or who adhere to it. This picture, in turn, is or should be related to what the organization does and how it does it. For instance, to ensure its continued profitability, Ford Motor Company strives to maintain good labor relations. Ideally, the organization should also be structured to move effectively toward its purpose. Most are not (Jaques, 1996). It should also be directed to the future, because any concept of *purpose* implies the future.

To be directed toward the future, it must have a clear *vision*, a picture of the arena in which it competes. A pharmaceutical company must have a grasp of health and illness the world over. It must then narrow its focus by formulating its *mission*, that part of the market toward which it intends to address itself, followed by a *strategy*, the manner in which it proposes to fulfill its mission. Strategy, in turn, requires *goals*, which are long-term steps toward purpose, and objectives, or short-term steps. The leadership of an organization is crucial to its adaptation, and its style of management says much about how the organization will adapt. These, too, need careful scrutiny.

An assessor should have a sense of what organizations are about before starting to assess them. The fundamentals in any textbook on management are clearly organized. That fact may be a significant advantage.

If the reason for the assessment is consultation or internal study, such an analytic or diagnostic method should require a consultant or manager to describe fully an organization's concept of itself and its aspirations, its plans, its view of itself in its competitive world, as well as its relationships with others, and its leadership. It must enable the consultant to understand systems of communications, coordination, guidance, control, and support. It must help the consultant to delineate relevant environments and behavior settings. It must be a guide to unfolding the rationale of the organization, explaining its activities, and critically evaluating the organization's adaptive adequacy, followed by a reasoned series of recommendations.

An organization assessment method should be equally useful to consultants in a wide range of disciplines and to those with varying points of view within a given discipline. Instructors are likely to come from varied disciplines and orientations. They likely will want those who are learning to integrate their learning according to those orientations. Also, they probably want the learners to focus on areas in which they themselves have special interests: small group functioning, human resources practices, conflict resolution, executive coaching. The instructors will be the best sources of references for those specialized needs.

Ideally, such a method should make it possible to specify the data on the basis of which anyone intends to act to change the organization or from which to choose from among action possibilities. Because any assessment is hypothesis, it becomes important to be able to return continuously to the information on which the hypothesis is based if the assessment proves to be incorrect or inadequate or if the mode of intervention fails to produce the anticipated results.

An assessment method should also be a basis to train people for organizational consultation or to assess their own organizations. It should provide students of organizations with a basic professional tool for gathering information, putting it in some reasonably sequential order, and making inferences and interpretations.

Anyone trying to understand an organization or an organization problem necessarily moves from *fact* to *inference* to *interpretation*. The basic data are facts. Inferences are the extrapolations drawn from the facts. Interpretations are the meanings formulated from the inferences, based on a person's theoretical frame of reference. For organizational assessment, one must keep these separate.

A formal assessment process also serves as a device for training managers and executives to better understand their organizations and to continuously assess their managerial efforts. It should be capable of modification and refinement, based on experience, and of including within its purview more specialized analytic devices (accounting, marketing, engineering analyses), just as a physician will make use of X-ray, blood tests, and more highly specialized measures as necessary.

Such an assessment procedure is outlined in this book. Written in the form of a manual, this volume is an information-gathering guide. It serves to sharpen perceptions and to organize them into a systematic whole. One would therefore do well first to read it quickly to get an overview. Then one should review the outline itself, Appendix D, interjecting one's own examples as they come to mind.

Then, as one proceeds with assessment, one will have in mind the kinds of information required. That makes it possible to complete various parts of the outline while gathering information, rather than waiting until the end of the data-gathering process to integrate this information. To facilitate that effort, one should put the detailed outline on a computer and then fill in the data under the outline headings as one goes along. Failure to do so results in a mass of information that later must be sorted and organized. While doing so, one will be formulating and testing hypotheses mentally about how the organization operates and will more easily be able to follow up new leads, develop fresh ideas, and confirm or reject impressions.

Although the outline is intended to be encompassing, many topics are redundant because they depend on the same source material. Rather than rigidly following all categories in detail, one will need to be appropriately selective. The outline is a systematically organized checklist. How much detail one will pursue depends on the complexity of the problem and one's own time constraints. However, one should be careful to note that although many items touch on the same material, each approaches the material from a slightly different point of view. The subtleties of difference should not be taken lightly, because the capacity to understand and make use of subtlety distinguishes the sophisticated consultant from the herd. Any fool can tell that a river flows. Only one who understands its cross-currents, its eddies, the variations in its speed, the hidden rocks, and its action in drought and flood is the master of its functioning. So it is with organizations. The person who uses this manual to sharpen his or her awareness of subtlety and the bases of inferences will find it helpful. If one uses it in rote fashion, it will be just a chore or, at best, an exercise.

Nothing is more comforting to consultants than to be able to specify and demonstrate how they arrived at their conclusions. This enables both consultants and those to whomever they are accountable to weigh appropriately the emphasis to be given to a particular point, the need for more information, the gaps in the assessment, and the weaknesses of the data. The outline helps to keep assessors honest with themselves and their clients.

Ideally, with enough experience, consultants will build the outline into their mode of working as a personal device, a way of looking at organizations almost automatically. This will also help them to organize their reading and weigh new concepts and ideas, to have a psychological hook on which to hang them, and to provide a basis for critical judgment.

One of the disadvantages of much social science theory is that it is composed of first-order inferences and limited, unrelated concepts. The inadequacies of such limited conceptual thinking become apparent when one has to work with it to solve problems. The kind of outline and diagnostic manual that I have set forth requires that one evolve one's own overall theory, one's own way of tying together what one knows, and that one rise to the level of being an organizational generalist. In short, it should compel one to raise one's sights, broaden one's purview, and see oneself in a more comprehensive role. Such a conception and the study method to go with it become two legs of a professional role, the third being conceptually based modes of intervention or what in medicine are called treatments of choice.

This manual, then, outlines a mode of gathering information. It speaks to the question: What do you gather, and how do you order it? It also focuses on the relationship of the consultant to the organization while getting and communicating that information and some suggestions for dealing with the problems of doing so. It provides structure related to personality theory in a professional field that otherwise depends primarily on ad hoc actions. This method provides a cross-sectional view of the organization at a given point in time against the context of its history and environment. But it is not by itself a source of answers for, What do you do about it? It is not a comprehensive reference on organizational consultation and change. I expect those who teach organizational consultation to focus their conceptual perspectives for their students and then to draw on the literature that complements those perspectives for methods of change that are consistent with their point of view. Although my own orientation, and indeed the conception of this manual, arises from a psychoanalytic clinical point of view, it is not my intention to make a case for that orientation.

However, this orientation dictates the structure of the method. It begins with a genetic or historical base: How did the organization get to be the way it is? What forces have affected it and how? How did it grow and what directions did it take? This is to begin to answer the question of its uniqueness and, in most cases, the sources of its problems. In his or her report, a consultant will want to summarize that history to put the rest of the report in context and also because many in the organization will find it interesting.

Developing the history also begins to address the question of what behavior is characterological—that is, consistent and enduring—contrasted with behavior that is reactive—that is, in response to a specific event or force. Unfortunately, too many consultants try to change organizations with short-term techniques that cannot possibly affect the characterological problems they neither recognize nor know how to deal with. Characterological behavior, by definition a product of long-time cultural consistency (Levinson, 1994), is much more resistant to change. A contemporary example is the effort to make public utilities, historically composed of more dependent people, more competitively aggressive. Any effort to change characterological behavior necessarily is highly disruptive to the organization. One need only look at the years of difficulty AT&T has had as it has tried to undo the effects of its regulated past.

Once one has a sense of what one is dealing with, and therefore can decide whether one is capable of dealing with this problem in this organization at this point in time—or even whether one wants to do so—the next step is to develop the factual information. In short, this is the examination process. Here one describes the organization in detail, including the data that describe its functioning. This body of factual information then becomes the basis for the consultant's tentative judgments about what he or she has learned and the inferences he or she has made from the data. What does the consultant think about what was learned? How does the consultant understand the information as contrasted with how it is understood by the management of the organization itself or outside observers? For example, many hospitals attributed their problems to managed care when in many cases their problems were a product of poor management.

Next comes the ticklish part when the assessor must offer his or her understanding of the inferences. This is the point at which the consultant must offer his or her judgment about the "why" of the problems delineated. The consultant's judgment in this part of the assessment will depend on his or her own theoretical orientation. Consultants from different disciplines may make different inferences and draw different conclusions from the same data. Here the assessor stands on his or her own discipline, training, and experience.

Finally come the recommendations. Based on the consultant's grasp of the history, the factual data, and his or inferences and conclusions, what does the consultant suggest that the organization do about its problems? The consultant's recommendations then ideally become the basis for the organization to debate its options and make choices.

The consultant's presentation of his or her report follows a five-step process: What did the consultant do, what did he or she find, what did he or she learn, how does he or she understand what was learned, and what does he or she recommend doing about it? Sometimes the consultant will be confronted with quarrelsome disagreement as he or she reports these steps. In one instance a corporate board member disagreed vigorously with my recommendation that the executive offices and the chief executive be moved to a different location than the rest of the company (Levinson, Sabbath, & Connor, 1992). By the end of the assessment, I knew and understood a lot more about the organization and its problems than he did. I stood my ground firmly. He yielded. In another instance, a group of scientific vice presidents, disappointed with my recommendation that they move from their ivory tower location to offices closer to the people they were supervising, quarreled with my methodology. After they had vented their anger, they recognized that they knew nothing about my methods and that theirs would not apply.

One useful way to help the beginning consultant to develop confidence is to organize the training in groups. In my own case (Levinson, 1981), I limited my two-semester graduate class to 15 and divided the class into three groups of five each. I found the organizational sites for them and introduced them to the chief executives. They then had to present themselves all of the way down in the organization, explain why they were there, what they were going to do, the confidential nature of their work, and the feedback process. Then they had to develop a study plan—interviews, observations, analysis of factual data—and devote a day a week to their immersion in the organization. In the fall semester I introduced psychoanalytic theory (Levinson, 1987), issues of leadership, managing change, and similar topics essential to understanding organizations. In the spring semester we devoted class time to discussion of what they were learning in their organizations and to preparing for feedback and termination. Of course, various constraints may make this arrangement impractical for others, but the key issue is organized immersion to whatever extent possible.

It should be self-evident that the usefulness of any assessment technique varies with the competence of the user. A technician can take an X-ray picture; a skilled radiologist is required to interpret it. This caveat is critical because there are too many practitioners in all fields who equate knowledge about a given technique with professional competence. This is especially the case with behavioral science consultation to organizations. To make such an equation is to blind oneself to what one does not know and therefore to be irresponsible in practice. Humility is the keystone of wisdom. The individual assessor is heavily dependent on his or her own ethics and judgment. That is indeed a heavy responsibility.

2

ETHICAL PROBLEMS AND CONSULTING GUIDELINES

Any psychologist who consults with organizations should first become familiar with *The Ethical Practice of Psychology in Organizations*, edited by Rodney L. Lowman (1998) and APA *Principles of Psychologists and Code of Conduct* (1992). Consultation with individuals, families, and groups is fraught with ethical considerations. Consultation with organizations is even more complex. In addition to those sources of guidance, here are some ethical and professional issues that have arisen in the course of personal professional experience.

Although the person who uses this manual necessarily is concerned with what is going on in the organization with which he or she is working, the person must also be alert to external pitfalls that may make it impossible to help the organization understand, let alone resolve, its problems. For example, a school superintendent could not understand why his community twice had voted down a school bond issue. The local high school was badly in need of repairs. Rainwater leaked through the roof, requiring pails to be put in the halls during each storm. Assessment disclosed that community leaders recognized and supported the need for more money. Why, then, did the bond issue fail? Only some weeks after the assessment was completed did the consulting team learn that the principal of the parochial high school in the same community did not want more money to go to the public high school. His parishioners, a sizable proportion of the local taxpayers, did not vote for the bond issue. In another instance, unknown to the local management of one of its subsidiaries, a corporation headquarters had decided to let that subsidiary wither. The local manager, wishing to act on the consultation, could get no support for his prospective initiative.

OBSOLESCENCE

A major function of anyone who offers psychological help to another is to make him- or herself obsolete. By helping other people to get information about themselves that otherwise could not come into their purview or that they could not understand, or by supporting others toward taking certain actions necessary for the others' well-being, the psychologically oriented consultant offers a method that ideally clients will be able to carry on by themselves. This is valid whether the client is an individual, a couple, a group, or an organization. A psychoanalyst will teach his or her patient how to decipher dreams and to free-associate. A marriage counselor will teach a couple methods for tempering their anger and steps for resolving problems. A group-process consultant will help group members better understand their conflict and also how to help each other clarify their differences and effect compromises. An organizational assessor demonstrates not only how to go about getting information but, more important, how to feed back that information to the client system so that it can critically examine the findings and decide what to do about them. Ideally, although it is not always possible or practical, the whole organization should share in the problem-solving effort. The consultant's method should become part of the organization's processes.

The assessor should constantly remind the client system that the task of an assessor is to help the organization function optimally. That is the assessor's only reason for being there. While doing so, the assessor should remind those in the client system that, necessarily, the assessor will be exiting from that system when he or she has made this contribution.

One important way of making oneself obsolete is to teach or demonstrate various methods that members of the client system can then carry on by themselves. For example, a team of consultants, after assessment, helped the management of a large corporation undertake a significant change. The team carried its methods into the major divisions of the corporation. Not long after that process had been completed, radical change in the marketplace required the organization to change again. Once more, the consultants helped. Over a period of several years, the organization had to change parts of itself six times, but when those subsequent changes became necessary, members of the human resources staff, having learned from the consultants, could carry more of them out themselves. There was only one thing the internal staff could not do, for obvious political reasons: Talk confidentially with the chief executive officer (CEO) or other senior officers to whom they reported.

INTEGRITY

A critically important aspect of any helping relationship is the consultant's need to maintain absolute integrity. This is not only a matter of being honest, keeping one's word, observing the rules of the organization, and respecting the responsibility and authority of different people, but also avoiding misperceptions. It is easy when working in an organization to socialize with various individuals and groups when they normally socialize, such as at lunch, dinner, special parties, or celebrations. An assessor must be particularly careful to avoid being seen as more friendly with some people than others and especially as being a pipeline to higher management. Almost inevitably, given the universally widespread paranoid propensities among people, some will think an assessor is such a conduit, especially when he or she must meet regularly with higher management to keep them informed and to summarize general findings without violating confidences. When an assessor learns about such suspicions, he or she must speak immediately to the suspicious person or group to correct the misperception. Otherwise it is likely to spread, causing others to become guarded. The assessor may be able to anticipate this problem in the initial presentation to the organization by referring to other organizations with which he or she has worked and inviting present employees to consult anyone they may know there about their experience.

Obviously, the assessor must resist the pressure from some in the organization to give them information, such as the manager who pressed the assessor to tell him whether he was going to be fired. Perhaps less obviously, the assessor must keep silent about what he or she hears that is not directly relevant to the task at hand. For example, the division head of a major corporation confided to the assessor that he was having an affair with a woman outside of the company. Subsequently that vice president told his CEO about the affair and also told him that he had told the assessor. The CEO, when telling the assessor about it, said, "You knew about this all the time, didn't you?" The assessor admitted that he did but undertook no further discussion. That experience reinforced for the CEO the assessor's commitment to keep confidences.

Another aspect of integrity is the need to protect the client from him- or herself. Sometimes, in a rush to demonstrate the intention to be open, a client will want to share the assessment feedback not only with employees but also with others outside the organization. The client may not be sufficiently aware of the possible hostile use others could make of the findings that might undermine the client's position or that of the organization. For example, hearing about low morale in the client organization, dissident stockholders might want to launch a campaign to get rid of the CEO, or learning about sales decline, some who seek out troubled organizations to force them into premature sale might do so. The assessor should urge the client to be cautious, suggesting that the client think about the possible negatives of sharing information without considering what should be shared with whom. In addition, after my initial report to the CEO, when I report to the next lower level, I usually give them numbered copies of the report so that they can follow my presentation. As I recommend in chapter 11, I have them return the copies immediately after the presentation to ensure that there will be no copies that can be passed on to others, at least until the chief executive is ready to engage with his or her employees in dealing with the issues reported or, after adequate consideration, chooses to make the report available to others. I do not distribute copies to others until and unless the client is ready and willing to do so.

A more difficult aspect of protecting the client CEO from him- or herself occurs when the assessor must exercise some control over the client, a role reversal, to ensure that the consulting task is accomplished. For example, a school superintendent engaged a consulting team of graduate students who were enrolled in my Harvard seminar. They proceeded with their assessment effort but repeatedly he broke his appointments with them and often was nowhere to be found when they were on site. Frustrated because they could not complete their work without talking to him, they went to his office one day without an appointment, in effect trapping him there and forcing him to participate in the consultation about his problem. It should be no surprise that he later resigned.

In another situation, a student consulting team in a hospital had great difficulty getting the nun director to review their findings with them. She would stop them in the halls to ask questions but would not make an appointment for a formal meeting until they finally told her they could not give her information on the run, that there were serious problems to be dealt with and that she must take time to talk with them. Reluctantly, she finally did. Her method of dealing with the consultants replicated how she dealt with those who reported to her and was a major problem in the hospital.

WHO IS THE CLIENT?

The director of a social agency sought assessment because of staff inefficiencies. One of the major problems was the diffusion of authority. The director was diluting decision making with repetitive group process. As a result it was not clear who was in charge and rivalrous staff members vied for power. When it was time to report back, I insisted, as is my usual practice, on reporting first to the director. Even though my ultimate interest as an assessor was in the more effective functioning of the agency, he, not the agency as a whole, was my client. He had retained me; I was accountable to him. Other senior staff members, particularly those who were rivalrous for his power, protested. They insisted that the report should be presented to all of them as a group. I responded to their complaints by pointing out that no matter how much the director involved them in his decision making, he, and he alone, was accountable to his board. That board had put him in charge. I, the assessor, was obliged to recognize and work with the appropriate authority. In subsequent steps all of the members of the staff would be part of the feedback process. How he and they then would decide to work on the organization's problems was up to them, but they had to recognize and accept his authoritative position or they would be unable to resolve their internecine problems.

The assessor must always support the leadership in his or her relationship with an organization. This does not mean that the consultant must agree with the definition of the problem by the head of the organization, that the consultant must allow him- or herself to be used by that person, or that the consultant must accept at face value what he or she is being told. Nor does it mean that the consultant ought to allow him- or herself to be an instrument for the accomplishment of certain ends by various people in the organization. It does mean, however, that the consultant must recognize that the management of an organization has a responsibility for the organization that the consultant does not have. The consultant cannot undermine that management, nor does he or she have the right to operate in the organization without keeping the accountable management apprised. Of course, the consultant must not violate confidences in doing so. The consultant must be viewed as an ally of the organization toward the more effective adaptation of the organization. If the consultant competes for power, if he or she tries to use the organization to gratify his or her own needs, if the consultant seeks to manipulate the organization, then he or she is being both unethical and immoral.

When the president of a petroleum company subsidiary asked for consultation because he was having painfully repetitive conflicts with his subordinate officers, assessment interviews disclosed that the interpersonal friction was a result of a certain neurotic behavior on his part. I recommended that he get professional help. He did so. Subsequently, a conflict arose between him and the corporate president to whom he reported, who coincidentally had been in a week-long seminar on leadership I had conducted previously. Knowing from the subsidiary president that I had reported back in writing, the senior officer asked for a copy of the report. I refused, saying that the subsidiary president was my client and that my report to him was confidential and to him. The senior objected, saying that in effect he had paid for it inasmuch as the subsidiary reported to him. Besides, I knew him from our joint seminar experience. Once again I regretted. Their differences degenerated into a lawsuit. The senior executive died suddenly, but the lawyers for the parent firm deposed both the subsidiary president and me. Although there is no legal protection for confidential relationships when psychologists consult with organizations as there is for consulting with individual clients, I still refused to give them the report and would have continued to refuse had not the subsidiary president himself decided to release it.

The client may not be the person who made the initial contact with the assessor. Sometimes higher management wants to see the assessor in action in some minor part of the organization before engaging him more fully. Sometimes the ostensible client is accountable to someone else with greater authority or power. Sometimes the prospective client is making a gesture at the instance of a superior but has no intention of serious work. Whatever the case, the assessor must learn about these issues and act accordingly.

FORMULATING THE CONTRACT

In appendix B there is an example of a proposal letter. Although once signed, that constitutes a contract for the services specified, sometimes new or different services are requested. The contract therefore must be renegotiated. In some cases, new unforeseen demands are made on the assessor. For example, a corporate headquarters agreed to an assessment proposal, the assessment to be undertaken at a distant plant. On arrival at the plant, the local manager insisted on having the assessor meet others who were not included in the original proposal. The assessors obliged. The client, the chief executive, refused to pay for the extra time. When pressed by others to extend his or her efforts, it is up to the consultant to state the boundaries of the contract, even though the consultant would thereby disappoint the host who is not the client. Sometimes the client him- or herself asks to extend the work. That, too, calls for renegotiating the contract. The professional who offers service, whether attorney, accountant, or consultant, usually bills for time unless there is a contractual agreement for a fixed sum for the service.

Sometimes not clearly specifying the boundaries of the contract in the beginning creates difficulties. A vice president of human resources asked the consultant to meet with his CEO and an executive vice president. The consultant assumed he was meeting them so they could become acquainted with him before undertaking an assessment. Instead, they asked for advice about a managerial problem. The consultant did not explain to them that they were asking for consultation, and the consultant discussed their problem with them and helped them to arrive at a solution. When neither a diagnostic effort nor further consultation followed, the consultant billed for his consultation. The officers protested that they were only getting acquainted and refused to pay.

When the consultant is formally involved in managerial selection or when some individuals or groups in an organization are likely to view his or her recommendations as threatening, even though the consultant has discussed findings with them, to protect themselves against potential suit some consultants ask their corporate clients for a contract with legal protections. In that case, the consultant has his or her own attorney draft such a contract and submits it to the corporate client's attorney for final formulation. I have never done that nor have I been subject to suit. Yet, in a litigious environment, particularly in working with large corporations, some consultants feel the need for that protection in addition to their professional liability insurance.

Certain threatening events may arise from situations that are beyond the control of the consultant or about which he or she may be ignorant. For example, the top management of a major corporation was meeting to determine the fate of a vice president who had become inappropriately involved at an off-site company meeting with the wife of one of his subordinates. They asked that I attend to offer whatever psychological insights might be helpful. An assistant took notes of the meeting. Subsequently, that company sued a customer who had not paid his bill. (In any sort of lawsuit, paperwork might be subpoenaed, however irrelevant to the case it may be.) The customer counter-sued, after subpoenaing the defendant's records, alleging that the defendant systematically had manipulated its customers. The evidence for the allegation was the presence of a psychologist at that top management meeting. The first I knew about the counter-suit was a telephone message from my assistant that a federal marshal was trying to find me to serve a subpoena to testify at a forthcoming hearing two days later. The subpoena was valid only within a 100-mile radius of the federal courthouse where the hearing was to take place and I was beyond that range. I was concerned that I could not protect the confidentiality of my client, and I did not want to be fodder for a fight between attorneys. Fortunately for me, the conflict was resolved without my testimony.

When consulting in a large organization, other consultants, both psychological and otherwise, also may be in the organization. To avoid confusing the client personnel, it is important for the psychological assessor to maintain appropriate boundaries from other consultants or even to refrain from the engagement until the others have completed their work. For example, a prospective client wanted me to undertake an assessment in his factory while an industrial engineer was also doing a time and motion study. I demurred, saying that having both consultants on the same premises at the same time would confuse employees and distort the effort. The prospective client, not knowledgeable himself about psychology, disagreed. The engineer understood psychology, the client insisted. When I still declined to perform a simultaneous assessment, I lost the client. Of course, that very authoritarian manner told me what the problems were likely to be in that organization and how difficult it would be to help him change.

In another situation, while I was consulting in one division of a large company, the top management officer group was engaged with a different consultant who had them and their spouses confront each other in vigorous criticism. The other consultant, untrained in psychology, repetitively tried to intrude into the subsidiary. I supported the subsidiary president in his adamant refusal to allow that intrusion into our work.

AFTER THE FEEDBACK

When the initial phase of the assessment is completed and the organization has discussed the feedback, there are several possible options. The organization leadership may decide to work on the recommendations by itself, without the assessor. It may disagree with the recommendations and go off on its own. It may do nothing. It may seek one or more other consultants. It may choose the same consultant to help it work on the issues illuminated. In the last case, a new or amended contract is called for with specified time frame and costs.

Sometimes there are inadvertent postconsultation consequences. At the request of a vice president of human resources, I interviewed all of the top management of a large manufacturing corporation. There was universal criticism of the chief executive for his arbitrary, impulsive over control of the company and them. After I summarized their feelings for him in a written report, we agreed that I would return a month later to help him and them work out their concerns. Three weeks later he announced that he had sold the company to a large conglomerate. Those whom I had interviewed were delighted to be rid of him and attributed his decision to sell to my intervention for which they expressed their enthusiastic appreciation. Obviously, any such decision would have had to be months in the making, involving financial and legal consultants as well as the company board, so it could not have been a consequence of my consultation. Some years later, I was consulting with the chief executive of the corporation that had bought him out and had since fired him for that same behavior. That CEO commented that the report I had written was both accurate and useful. I was startled and worried. There were only two original copies of the report: I had one and the former client had the other. How could the present CEO have gotten a copy? Did someone in the subsidiary corporation leak it? Was I vulnerable to the accusation of violating professional confidence? The present CEO alleviated my concerns by telling me the report had been found in the former client's files.

From time to time, the assessor will encounter problems beyond his or her competence or knowledge. The assessor should make it clear to the client when another kind of competence is called for and refer the client to other consultants in that specialty. The assessor should always convey the attitude, "I want to do what's best for you." If there is something about the information that the assessor is gathering that he or she does not understand (for example, arcane financial data), the assessor may call on a specialist in that field for an explanation. In that case, the assessor ought to pay for the cost of that consultation.

Inevitably, all assessors run into psychological problems in their consultations that they do not understand. Sometimes that is a result of issues in the assessment that touch on the assessors' own deep-seated conflicts, of which they may be unaware. It is helpful to have one's own psychological consultant to help the consultant understand the bloc. For example, a consultant found herself angry at the CEO of the company she was working with and to whom she was about to report. She was aware of her anger but not its source, and she was fearful that it would show in her feedback session. She turned to her own consultant, who helped her see that the client awakened in her her long-standing hostility to her own father. When the consultant does not have his or her own consultant for such issues, it may help to talk over the problem with a professional colleague.

It is important to recognize that the client organization is dependent on the assessor. From time to time after an assessment, especially if the consultant follows the assessment helping the organization with implementing his or her recommendations, members of the client organization may seek out the consultant for guidance or referral or even to answer residual questions. Former clients have called as long as ten years after a consultation. The consultant has an obligation to respond. In fact, it can be helpful to the client if from time to time the consultant calls former clients to ask how things are going. Such calls are especially helpful if there are some residual paranoid feelings on the part of the client who, for example, might well feel that he or she is not as competent as the consultant thought to deal with the complexities of leadership. It is that continued concern of the consultant for his or her former client that differentiates good psychological consultation from run-of-the-mill consultants who dump their data on the client or merely run in and out.

ASSUMPTIONS AND CAUTIONS

System-oriented assessment requires (a) a perspective on an organization as an integrated set of subsystems continuously seeking to maintain an equilibrium while adapting to internal and external forces; (b) the assessor to stand outside the system even though at times he or she may be a member of it and to maintain a professional distance from it; (c) that the assessor view him- or herself in an active relationship with the system as a whole and that his or her attention be given to improving the effectiveness of the system even if key recommendations have to do with significant individuals and groups within the system.

There are a number of assumptions behind taking such a position. The first is that no intervention can be undertaken without affecting the system as a whole. One does not necessarily have to change the whole system in any given intervention, but every intervention has a rippling effect of varying intensity on the whole system. The second is that the assessor is indeed an elite person, just as any skilled person is an elite with respect to the layperson, and cannot presume to be egalitarian. The assessor brings to the consultation with an organization a certain frame of reference, a certain level of understanding, and a certain capacity to help. If the consultant does not bring these, he or she is of no use to the organization.

The fact that the assessor is an elite person with respect to his or her professional work means that psychologically the consultant is not the "equal" of those whom he or she is seeking to help. They are dependent on the consultant for that help. In that situation, in that relationship, for that purpose, the consultant has more power than they. The consultant must not gloss over the power differences. I make a special point of this because of the psychologically naïve position that some psychological consultants take that they are no better than their clients. They may not be "better," but they do bring knowledge and skill that the client seeks and is willing to pay for. In that sense, and in the context of work with the client, they are not equal. To assume that they are is pretension that denies powerful psychological issues that underlie the consulting relationship.

The very fact that a consultant brings specialized capacities inevitably means that the members of the organization develop certain attitudes toward the consultant that, in the technical sense, are referred to as *transference* (Racker, 1968). Transference refers to the fact that in a relationship where one party has greater psychological power than another, involuntarily and unwittingly, the person with less psychological power inevitably attributes to the other powers, talents, attitudes, and potential behaviors that the other may not in fact have or intend. Such implicit expectations are derived from their experiences and expectation with earlier figures in their lives on whom they have had some significant degree of dependence.

The second assumption, that the assessor is an elite person with respect to specific training and knowledge, means that the assessor has moral and ethical responsibilities to the client and client system. Therefore, the assessor must give due attention to the effects of his or her behavior on the system, because the assessor is perceived to have power whether he or she admits it or not.

The third assumption is that the assessor must make an assessment. One way or another, he or she must assess the system itself, the kinds of help it may need, what adaptive excellence it can attain, with what kinds of efforts, and what he or she expects as a reasonable outcome of the consultative efforts. Inevitably, the assessor will be making such judgments whether he or she is aware of them or not. It is important for the assessor to clarify them.

All assessment is tentative hypothesis and therefore is subject to continuous test. An assessment thesis cannot be tested if it has not been made conscious. To make an assessment, the assessor must have some grasp of the client system as a whole. That is, he or she must have some understanding of what the organization does, how it goes about doing it, with what effectiveness, with what energy, and with what degree of adaptive success. The assessor must know something about the history of the organization and the effect of the past on the present, something about the developmental history of the organization and the crises it has experienced as a result of which it operates in certain ways as contrasted with many possible other ways. The assessor must know something about the values and aspirations of people in the organization and particularly what they expect of themselves. The assessor should know also what the strength, resources, and limits of the organization are. Taking these together, the assessor may then be able to formulate a way of helping the organization.

In the process of arriving at an assessment, of course, the assessor will be talking to people at all levels of the organization. The assessor will be reading reports and examining experiences, hearing how people feel about themselves and their organization, and what their respective competitors are doing. The assessor will be forming a judgment about where the organization stands with respect to where it would like to stand and how well the organization copes with the task of perpetuating itself while simultaneously managing current realities.

WHERE IS THE PAIN?

The assessor first must determine where the pain is in the system. Obviously, no consultant is going to be called into an organization unless somebody has a problem.

Most frequently, the problem for which an organization seeks help is the problem that must be dealt with first. For example, a school superintendent asks the consultant to assess how decisions are made in the community with respect to educational matters. Rejection of his recommendations may be the manifest content of his pain. The real problem may well be that he has been discounted by the community, does not understand why, and does not know what to do about it. The assessor, therefore, is always in the position of having to try to understand what lies behind the presenting complaint, what underlies the pain being expressed. The professional task, then, is to try to discern the system disequilibrium that lies beneath the pain that in turn is manifested in the form of frustration, exasperation, misplaced energies, maladaptive behavior, or even failure to cope effectively with the realities the organization faces.

To do this, the assessor may introduce him- or herself throughout the organization, to get the whole picture, as it were. As the assessor moves among individuals and groups, simultaneously he or she is helping to discharge tension by bringing them together to help formulate what the issues and pains are. The assessor is already serving as a model for them to help resolve some of the difficulties they face in the process of doing that. Of course, some people become frightened, some are threatened, some read more into what the assessor says than he or she intends, and others will test the assessor to see whether he or she is trustworthy.

While retaining his relationship to the organization, the assessor must clearly keep him- or herself outside the client system in a role that is amenable to continuous testing so that people can trust the assessor's independence and integrity. Furthermore, if the assessor remains outside the system, then he or she does not get caught up in the emotional issues that go on in the system and thus is able to retain a position of independence and integrity that any organization coping with confusing problems desperately needs. If the assessor becomes involved in the organization's emotional struggles, he or she cannot help becoming part of the organization. The organization cannot afford to have the assessor competing for power within the structure or using the structure to serve his or her own needs, because in neither case can the assessor be helpful as an assessor or consultant.

The assessor must define the limits of his or her function, what he or she can and cannot do. For example, if a chief executive says to the assessor that he or she is expected to develop management for the organization, the assessor must make it very clear that that is a management function with which he or she can assist but not one for which he or she can be responsible.

The assessor must clarify for him- or herself why the client organization is calling on him or her rather than somebody else and why now rather than some other time. Clear answers to these questions will help the assessor define realistically with the client what is reasonable to expect of the assessment. In one situation, after an unenthusiastic experience with a previous psychologist, a chief executive, who had been in a seminar with me, asked me to take over. What soon became apparent in my continuing interaction with him was that I was the psychological substitute for his sons, neither of whom wanted to be in the business or close to him, and he wanted me to lecture his subordinates (as he must have his sons) into being effective rather than engaging with them around resolving the company's problems.

ORDERING INFORMATION

The assessor's initial task is to hear people and to put together the multiple kinds of information the assessor gets. The assessor may be overloaded with information. It may be difficult for the assessor to sort it out, and the situation may continue to be ambiguous for some time. Nevertheless, the assessor must trust his or her own capacity for obtaining and organizing information and ordering it into some kind of a system to arrive at an assessment.

The assessor must conceptualize the pain. Then he or she must put a name on the pain. The assessor must touch people where they hurt and make it possible for them to recognize that hurt by whatever means of identification possible. Some recognize their own pain when their feelings and reports are fed back to them. Others see it through examples of third persons, still others by parable, metaphor, or interpretation. Finally, working together with them, the assessor has to help open avenues through which they can begin to take action to relieve the pain. In doing so, the assessor has established him- or herself as an outsider who is a stable identification figure, someone who is allied with the organization and the people in it toward the perpetuation of the organization.

Nevertheless, the assessor must be prepared to cope with transference feelings. Some people will try to incorporate the assessor onto their side of a given problem. Others will reject the assessor with considerable hostility. Still others will assert that the assessor brings them nothing new and that his or her point of view can only create more difficulty. Some will not want to talk with the assessor. Many people in the organization will want to keep repeating old ways no matter how ineffective they may have been. And many will want to see the future as mere extrapolation of the past, which the assessor now threatens. All of these perceptions of the assessor, in turn, will result in testing behaviors that the assessor must manage. In making his or her assessment, the assessor will have to judge whether the organization's problem is one that he or she has the competence to work with.

There are a number of difficult psychological problems for assessors when they begin to get involved with organizations for the first time or when they move from other roles in the organization to internal assessment. Ordinarily, people who are involved in organizational change or human resources activity operate with a tacit assumption that they are there to give, to do, to help others. Whatever their personal concerns, these tend to be masked by the helping activity they undertake. However, when they are asked, as in an assessment process, to step back and examine the subject of their intervention, as well as their own feelings about what they are doing, a number of powerful feelings begin to come to the fore.

The first problem is a feeling of guilt. There is often great concern about the assessor's "right" to look into the client's system and then to make assessment inferences about that system and presumably to discover that system's "secrets." Frequently, the beginning assessor feels that he or she is a voyeur who has no right to be examining the client's "innards." Such guilt sometimes translates itself into asking one of the client system's officials to arrange one's schedule or putting one's appointment schedule in the hands of a single contact person in the organization. Doing so, in effect, abandons one's assessment to the organizational representative. Sometimes such feelings make for problems in asking penetrating questions or digging out information. Sometimes they result in an apologetic, helpless relationship to the client organization.

Such feelings seem to be quite natural and relatively universal. It becomes necessary for assessors to understand what is happening to them and why. The "why" has to do with vicarious guilt for seeing forbidden sights and experiences that stem from early childhood, particularly from taboos about sexuality. Thus, unconscious reactions are stirred up that seem to have little relevance to the situation at hand, except that the assessor becomes quite uneasy. These feelings, and others to be mentioned subsequently, should be talked through with someone else, perhaps professional colleagues, instructors, or, if they are too troublesome and interfere with the work, a psychotherapist.

The second problem that the new assessor experiences is that of being overwhelmed by the data. There is just too much information and the new assessor does not know how to go about organizing the data. Even with a detailed outline as in this manual, the new assessor often feels that it will be impossible to put all of the information together and make sense of it. The assessor does not allow for immersing him- or herself in the data, and, by osmosis, sensing its coherence, which takes time. Only after the assessor has been immersed in the organization for some time and has pondered the information does it begin to organize itself into systematic relationships.

A third problem is the assessor's discovery of the inadequacies of many of the key figures in the client system. The new assessor discovers for the first time that there are many people who are not as good as ideally they should be. This frightens the assessor, who feels that he or she may be forced into recommending that such people be fired. The new assessor has yet to recognize that none of us is perfect and that all of us have inadequacies.

In addition, the new assessor does not yet recognize that, as an organizational assessor, he or she will be making recommendations about ways of doing things rather than about individual people. When these ways and means are specified, various people may or may not be able to carry them through. For example, one company chief executive, told that his role now required much more interaction with the public as well as with his employees, said, "I can't do that." He isolated himself in his office until his board fired him. Whether executives, managers, abbots, medical directors, and others can do what has to be done is another question—and the observation about that issue will be made not by the assessor but by themselves or their superiors in the organization.

A fourth issue has to do with the stickiness of some problems. Many are very complex and involve subtle and difficult considerations. Some are unsolvable. Some must continue for some time before amelioration, let alone solution, is possible. In their wish to do good, some consultants are unwilling to accept the limitations of the situation or of their knowledge and experience. However, every assessor must learn to understand that some problems are going to continue. This may be because the organization does not have the resources to resolve them, or because there is insufficient pain for anyone to act on them, or because other forces at this point in time do not allow solution—for example, the bank will not extend its loan repayment schedule. The assessor's recommendations may only help to palliate some of the pain, and, in other circumstances, he or she simply may have to decide that there is nothing the assessor or the organization can do, however unfortunate, sometimes tragic, sometimes unhappy, the situation may be. To illustrate, one young executive was saddled by his parents with the responsibility for the family business but unable to get his father to give him sufficient financial control to run it. His father, rapidly becoming senile, was being manipulated by an outsider who was trying to take it over. The son could not desert his parents but had to stand by helplessly, and at great risk to himself, until his father died. Assessment was of no help; counseling was.

Such experiences naturally leave the assessor feeling inadequate. He does not know what answers to offer or what to do. Anyone who is at the frontier of knowledge or who must cope with ambiguity and complexity inevitably has such feelings. Those who would consult with organizations simply have to learn to live with ambiguity, with their feelings of inadequacy, and to take one step at a time toward assessment and intervention. An assessor need not respond to a request for immediate answers or feel compelled to give them any more than a counselor is expected to resolve a client's problems overnight. Sometimes it is impossible to know what to do until one has sized up the situation comprehensively, taken time to become immersed, while at the same time maintaining appropriate distance from it and thinking it over until he or she develops a comprehensive statement of assessment and the steps that follow it. The assessor who cannot tolerate ambiguity and must jump into action is likely to be responding to his or her own anxiety with recommendations that are more intended to appease that anxiety than to be useful to the organization.

Frequently, the assessor risks becoming overidentified with the last person he has interviewed, especially before he or she has interviewed a wide range of people. If the assessor tends to see the world too much through the eyes of the people just interviewed, the assessor is likely to find him- or herself taking sides, becoming angry and frustrated. The assessor may unwittingly see his or her role as that of punishing whoever is managing incorrectly or disruptively. The assessor may be critical of organizational processes that have not adequately developed for many complex reasons. Whatever the case, when an assessor finds him- or herself angry, the assessor should step back and ask why. Sometimes it will be necessary for the assessor to talk to a consultant to try to understand what is happening to him or her in the situation and why his or her anger arises. Otherwise, the assessor is more likely to use the consultative relationship as a device for appeasing his or her own anger. In that case, the consultant can only be destructive to the organization.

This, then, raises the question of psychological distance. Assessors must maintain a relationship with the client system such that they can observe the whole system and act on behalf of the effectiveness of the system *as system* rather than on behalf of any of the groups or persons within it. Frequently, people will try to entice assessors into taking their side after they have said something. They might ask, Don't you agree? or What other solutions do you think there are to these problems? If the assessors feel uncomfortable about not having answers to these questions and jump in with a response that leads to further discussion, they become inappropriately engaged. Such questions are partially a testing device and partially an effort to gain an alliance. The task of assessors is to indicate that they are allies of the whole organization and that they do not know whether to agree or disagree because they have not yet seen the whole organization. In any case, assessors will make their own point of view known when they make their assessment recommendations. By that time, the consultants will have given sufficient consideration to the issues to offer the organization some thoughts in the direction of solutions. If, however, assessors feel they must appease people out of guilt, fear, inadequacy, anger, or what have you, they lose their neutral role. Then there is no stable external orienting point for the organization as a system.

Frequently, assessors feel that they are indicting people by being critical. This results from a combination of all of the previously mentioned factors. However, their task is to feed back observation and judgment about how things are done in the organization and to suggest, at least as a basis for discussion, in what other ways they might be done. The decision about how any recommendations might be implemented, if at all, or whatever other methods might be involved, are those of the people in the organization. They are not necessarily the assessors'. They may be engaged with the employees in an alliance to help them cope with their organizational problems, but, in the last analysis, the right of the people involved to choose what they will become engaged in remains inviolate.

It is easy when being critical to address oneself to weaknesses and limits without thinking at the same time that these same people have strengths. Frequently, observing that others are human, one sees their weaknesses without recognizing their strengths. All too often, we are astonished to discover how people about whom we have made negative judgments have been able to cope with and surmount many extremely difficult problems. Only after continued experience with such a phenomenon do assessors become aware of the many hidden strengths in an organization that rise to the surface only as people are forced to mobilize themselves to tackle whatever problems they are facing.

The task of assessors is to write what they see and hear, to organize their data and ponder them, to immerse themselves in the data and the organization. As one does so, one is much like a person who is swimming in a sheltered pool of fresh water in a brook whose otherwise strong currents are flowing by vigorously. One feels the rocks and shoals as one steps into the water and when one stops swimming. One becomes aware, without fully being able to see, where the holes and sharp points are and where there is clear space to swim. One senses the eddies and currents, those one can see and those that are hidden beneath the surface. In the end, as one becomes accustomed to the swimming hole and as one revels in the experience of being in it, one has mapped out for oneself a three-dimensional structure that guides one in the way one makes use of that newfound resource. The same is true for assessors in an organization. There is no substitute for immersion or sensing, feeling, or coming to know the complexity with which they are dealing at both a cognitive and an emotional level. At the same time, they must always deal with themselves as they slip on the psychological rocks or bruise themselves in uncertain encounters, or, for a few moments, are caught up in the current and feel helpless.

During all this, assessors do three things: (a) They begin to make senior people in the organization feel comfortable with upward appraisal, which frequently is going to come through in such assessments. With assessors at their side, employees are less likely to be injured by feedback, and, with the help of their allies, better able to cope with it. (b) They offer themselves as models for how one goes about getting information, relating to people, withholding judgment, organizing experience, presenting it for discussion, and opening themselves to constructive criticism. (c) They demonstrate that, despite their necessarily transitory relationship with the organization, a condition they are likely to share with many employees, managers, and executives, they maintain the integrity of that relationship. However brief their time may be, they use that time in a manner that is constructive for all of the people involved so that they can further their own effectiveness and that of the organization. They can derive gratification from doing so on the basis of their relationship with the assessors, rather than out of the often unduly competitive mutually destructive ways of doing things that go on in organizations.

Consultants and students of consultation often make the egregious assumption that their task is to study a problem, formulate a report, even with the help of the client system or sometimes in spite of it, and then leave the client system to effect change or help it in the process. The major focus therefore is on the product or outcome. Little is to be gained by that kind of conception. In fact, much of the time consultants will find themselves rejected and their consultation come to naught.

The central thrust of an assessment is the development of relationships between the assessor and the organization. Only when such a trust relationship has been established and the organization experiences assessors as allies against the pain it is experiencing or the problem it is unable to solve can assessors and their client proceed to the next step in ameliorating the situation. Only out of such a relationship can the organization accept the assessors' finding of painful or difficult barriers to its adaptive efforts. Otherwise the organization will experience such feedback as indictment or unwarranted criticism. Misguided attempts at open confrontation under the rationale of "being honest with the client" usually result in rejection for this reason.

The question of integrity and honesty lies in the relationship and not in what is said in a report. It is one thing for the assessor to be open but another for the organization to be open enough to receive and digest what is being reported. Timing in the context of a relationship is of the essence.

WHERE TO INTERVENE

After carrying through their introduction and orienting the organization to their undertaking, having defined the nature of the organization's problem, managed the transference attitudes, and mastered their own anxieties, assessors must now determine with which of the various points of entry they will seek to work. In part, this will depend on where the pain is and what kind it is. In part, it will depend on the skill and competence of assessors and, in part, on what area of the organization is most amenable to their entry. For example, it is not unusual for the top management of an organization to want to observe how assessors manage their relationship to a component of the organization before inviting them to its level.

Assessors may have various points of entry available to them and a range of foci, depending on their interest and training, for bringing about change. Which they choose will depend on their assessment of the problem, the point at which they have the best opportunity for beginning to deal with it. For example, an assessor's orientation and skill may have to do with bringing about structural change in the organization that may relieve some of its problems. This is akin to a physician who works with the skeletal–muscular system of a person. The assessor's interest may be in the processes of the organization, its various information systems, control systems, communications systems, and modes of handling human resources problems. This would be akin to the physician who deals with the digestive system, the nervous system, the cardiovascular system, and other subsystems in the human being. Or the assessor may be concerned with effecting a re-establishment of the internal equilibrium of the organization, particularly when there has been considerable internal conflict. This may be viewed as being akin to the re-establishment of an internal biochemical physiological balance in the individual. The assessor may deal with failure or disruption of one or another component of the organization through merger, or loss of market, or loss of people. This attention to insult and injury would be the equivalent of dealing with an accident on the part of an individual. Finally, the assessor may be concerned with developmental crises such as shift from an entrepreneurial family management to a professional management. Organizations go through such crises as they move from one growth stage to another, requiring different modes of structure and different ways of coping with changing environments, more complex management, and higher levels of conceptual capacity to grasp complexity. Such crises are the managerial equivalent of the specific crises of normal development among individuals, such as adolescence and middle-age, as well as the specific problems of men and women who go through physical changes during these periods.

The assessor therefore must understand the operation of the whole and the fact that any change effected in any one part of an organization has an effect on the whole. This is not to say that one should not recommend changes in one or another part of the organization, but rather that in doing so one should understand the consequences for the whole. It may well be that there are no significant consequences but there also may be. A simple example is the recommendation to change promotional practices in one unit that may then reverberate in other units. The assessor who does not understand this can be of only very limited help and sometimes may even be destructive to the organization.

This concern is especially important when the assessor is using members of the organization to help with the assessment. An analogy is the practice of teaching a Navy corpsman to do appendectomies so that he might deal with such emergencies on a submarine cruise if he is guided by a physician by radio or television. However, unless there is an understanding of the whole body and the various systems involved, one would never trust the corpsman to handle such a complex problem by himself. If he did not know how to control internal bleeding or stitch a surgical wound and take other steps to restore the physiological equilibrium, a patient might die. Similarly, a physician may offer an aspirin to a person with a headache, something a layperson could do, but the physician would be alert to other possible symptoms that would indicate that the headache would require something more than an aspirin. So it is with assessors. Sometimes they may recommend a simple change, but they are always aware of the complexity of the system.

In fact, continuing with the medical analogy, frequently there has been considerable criticism of physicians who have specialized in treating one or another aspect of an individual without fully appreciating the implications for the whole. As a result, they have treated symptoms with no reference to the possible basic causes that precipitated the symptoms. This is all too often the case with organizational consultation.

Assessors may focus on any level. They may recommend significant change in the organization as a whole, as for example in long-term organizational change. They may recommend changes at the task level, as for example leadership. They may recommend changes at the group level toward building effective management teams. They may be concerned with one or more individual executives who may need coaching for better managing their subordinates or grasping the psychological currents in the organization as a whole.

In whatever way they choose to focus, the assessor has a responsibility for knowing what they do not know. An important part of making an assessment is to assess whether the assessors themselves can do something about the problem that they discern. If they cannot, which might be the case if the issue were a marketing or financial problem, ethical and moral considerations require that they refer the client to someone else who has the skill or competence in that area. Not to do so is being irresponsible.

Assessors must always support the leadership in their relationship with an organization. This does not mean that they must agree with the definition of the problem by the head of the organization or that they must allow themselves to be used by such leaders, or that they must accept at face value what they are being told. Nor does it mean that they allow themselves to be an instrument for the accomplishment of certain ends by various people in the organization. But it does mean that they recognize that the management of an organization has a responsibility for the organization that they do not have. They cannot undermine that management, nor do they have the right to operate in the organization without keeping the accountable management apprised of where they are. Of course, they must not violate confidences in doing so. They must be viewed as allies of the organization toward the more effective adaptation of the organization. If they compete for power, if they try to use the organization to gratify their own needs, if they seek to manipulate the organization, then they are being both unethical and immoral.

In addition, there is the major problem having to do with the management. Frequently, assessors generate information that is fed back to management, resulting in no change. Assessors or other consultants then often interpret this inaction as management's resistance to change, unwillingness to change, hostility, evasion, or sheer laziness. Sometimes such judgments are correct. However, most of the time when such information is fed back, managements simply do not know what to do with it or about it. Despite the fact that they are mature adults, they frequently feel utterly helpless about how to cope with the problems at hand. I think of the CEO of a savings and loan firm, criticized for not doing more to house the poor, who did not know how or where to begin to do so. This helplessness usually is not recognized by consultants, especially organizational development consultants and those who see their task as facilitating communication but not making recommendations. Such a nondirective orientation frequently leaves management in a desperate position, which they deal with simply by withdrawing and indicating that they do not think much of the consultant's work. Sometimes, as a consequence, consultants will ally themselves with one or another faction in the organization that seeks to fight top management to get results. By doing so, consultants lose their professional position and their strength.

Sometimes poorly trained or insensitive consultants make it impossible for the client to change. They may do so by holding up norms of behavior to which they expect the client system to adhere and whipping them with criticism when they do not attain them. They also may do so by indicting them or attacking them for their inadequacies, which increases their resistance and defensiveness, making it impossible for them to change. When such consultants deflate their self-image, they automatically increase their depression, their anger with the consultants, their sense of inadequacy, and their feeling of futility. Such consultant behavior has arisen in the past from a group dynamics orientation with a heavy emphasis on openness and confrontation. Unfortunately, it also has resulted in public criticism of the client system for its inadequacies, thus unfairly blaming the client system for the shortcomings of the consultant, and, in the process, setting back organizational consultation in the eyes of its prospective clients.

Another failure on the part of consultants is failing to understand the personalities of the individuals at hand, the manner in which they receive information, and the specific kind of help they need to be able to use the information. It is astonishing to see how highly literate people distort what they read, let alone what they hear, and how often assessors must repeat and clarify what they have put on paper. Assessors frequently evolve great programs with managements that ultimately fail because of such misunderstanding. Unfortunately, some assessors need to defend themselves publicly for the failure that is largely their failure to understand the personalities of the managements and to effect a solid continuing relationship in a step-by-step fashion so that the outcome is not going to be the failure that then becomes a public scandal.

Sometimes assessors or some of their constituents become impatient with the inability of top management to move as quickly as they think it should. Therefore they are prone to jump into action. My old mentor, Karl A. Menninger, spoke of two kinds of phenomena that undermined efforts to help others: *furor therapeuticus* and *furor inandes*. By *furor therapeuticus* Menninger referred to the urge on the part of the helper to get quickly into the heart of the curative process with a patient. He pointed out that this rush to cure often serves the needs of the therapist more than those of the patient. *Furor inandes* refers to the therapist's need to get the patient well. That is, the clinician unconsciously views the patient's progress as testimony to his or her own skill and competence. One way or another, come hell or high water, the therapist is going to make the patient get well. Psychologically, the patient may have all kinds of reasons for not getting well, but by concentrating on the curative process without understanding the patient's struggles and helping the patient become aware of them, the therapist serves his or her own needs rather than those of the patient. So it is with organizational consultation. The impatience of the consultant reflects his or her underlying *furor inandes* and can only be distrusted.

These behaviors are not unusual in organizational consultation. Many consultants, particularly those in the organizational development field, impulsively jump into changing organizations whether the organization needs what they have to offer or not. Then there is the intensive need to fix the organization whether that is possible or not from their vantage point. Frequently, the needs of the consultants, psychological or financial, are being served by such behavior while they rationalize it as being totally in the interest of the organization. Being an organizational consultant, therefore, requires continuing introspection and careful re-examination of what one is doing and why.

Assessors are often in a position to help people think through and weigh their options. Both the assessors and they must tolerate the tension of ambiguity. If the assessors themselves cannot tolerate such tension, if they have the answers already developed and cannot wait until the client system gets ready to find such answers themselves or work through those the assessors recommend, then the assessors cannot help that organization.

One can help people as individuals, groups, and organizations to perceive the kinds of problems they have to deal with, but then one must also understand that people must be able to mobilize their resources, cope with their doubts and anxieties, and feel themselves adequately supported to take the necessary actions. Sometimes people have to acquire the skills necessary to be able to take such actions, skills in communication, evaluation, appraisal, and technical proficiency. Without them they can only fumble and blunder.

TERMINATION

Working with anybody long enough to establish ties to that person, group, or locale always incurs the problem of separation: fear, depression, anger, and the awakening of some of the anxieties that appeared early on in the assessment. It is fair to assume that the initial concerns and attitudes that were expressed by the client and the client system in the early part of the assessment will now recapitulate themselves as the client system reacts to the prospective imminent departure of assessors (unless they are to continue working with the organization). These include regressive behavior (acting in ways that presumably were once abandoned) and the temporary reappearance of some of the earlier symptoms of hostility. These are not uncommon as the client system regroups itself to move on without assessors.

Ideally, the client system has passed through a series of positions ranging from heavy dependence on the assessors to being able to operate freely without them. Ideally, the consultants have also managed the dependency in such a way that they have not made the client system overly dependent on them, that at all times they have allowed the client system to free itself of them, and that they themselves have facilitated that freeing activity when the problems to be dealt with have been adequately resolved.

The freeing process can be facilitated if the assessors make it clear from the beginning that the client system is the property of the client, that it is not theirs. It is assessors' responsibility to check with the person in the organization to whom they are accountable about where they are in the assessment and how the process is going. The more demoralized the organization, the less it is able to organize and follow through on its own, the more assessors will have to take a directive hand in structuring the assessment process, as illustrated in the Kansas Power and Light Company example given later. However, they must be careful not to maintain this directive hand in the decisions to be made. Assessors should encourage people in the organization to make their own decisions when such opportunities arise as the assessment proceeds. The assessor who unwisely keeps his or her heavy hand too long on the organization will make it more dependent and he or she will be cast in the role of a Rasputin or Machiavelli.

KEEPING TRACK, AVOIDING HARM

Assessor owe it to themselves and their clients to keep a continuous diary of their experiences in and with the organization. They must be able to retrace their relationships with the key people in the organization and the various transference phenomena that occur, as well as the various ways people use them as a model for assessing and solving problems. By being able to reflect on what has gone on in the organization as a result of these relationships, especially the effect of their behavior has on it and the effect theirs has on them, assessors can better understand those dynamics and what has gone on within themselves. For example, early on in the Kansas Power and Light study, two of the three of us, having worked in different parts of the organization in the same community, got into a heated argument while we were driving home. My sociologist colleague criticized me for taking over from the local manager when we started that morning. I had asked him to designate his best and worst crews, which he was unable to do. When he could not, I simply assigned each of us to different areas. I pointed out in response that the elderly manager, burdened with a sick wife, could not handle his managerial responsibilities, so we had to move on without his help. Our third colleague, listening to this discussion, observed that the conflicts we were observing among the employees in that community were reflected in our own argument. When they could not get adequate guidance from their manager, some took the initiative to do what they thought they should. Others complained that by doing so they usurped the responsibilities of an overwhelmed boss.

Assessors must be especially careful to avoid doing harm. In medicine there is the concept of iatrogenic illness, meaning illness caused by the physician or the treatment method. If assessors cannot help, at least they should do no harm. The assessor will have no way of knowing what effect they having unless they keep track of their behavior and people's reactions to them. With this concern in mind, they can give careful thought after each contact in the company to what has gone on.

FUMBLES AND BUMBLES

In their alliance with the organization, in the process of arriving at an assessment and helping the organization to mobilize its resources toward more effective adaptation, assessors must get and interpret data from outside the organization (sometimes with the help of organization members). I lay heavy emphasis on interpreting the data because I feel too much attention is given to morale studies, attitude surveys, opinion polls, and other kinds of survey feedback where raw information is fed back to the organization without adequate psychological understanding of what the information means. As a consequence, often people work from raw data to little avail.

For example, typically an attitude survey or morale study may show that people feel that they are not getting sufficient communication from higher level management. Based on such information, higher level management may intensify its memos, newsletters, and published reports when what people want is greater interaction with their management. The real problem may well be that people are afraid of or angry about prospective changes, real or imagined. They may be dealing with that fear and anger by displacing their own feelings inward, onto the organization, just as during the Vietnam War angry college students attacked their own university buildings and in some communities enraged Blacks trashed their own neighborhoods. Frequently, the multiple complaints that appear in such surveys in organizations reflect underlying feelings of not being held in high esteem by higher management. When management responds to such surveys by changing physical aspects of the environment and responding directly to specific requests, then frequently the complaints shift to other phenomena, indicating that no real problems have been solved. Therefore, the assessor must bring to assessment and intervention a capacity for understanding and interpreting what goes on at a level beyond manifest feedback.

THE INTERNAL CONSULTANT

It is difficult for internal consultants to operate in these ways. Usually, they cannot separate themselves sufficiently to take an objective view. Frequently, they are caught up in the competition for power or resources within the organization and tend to be depreciated by power figures within the organization who are paid more or who have higher positions.

However, this does not mean that internal consultants are helpless. Often internal consultants can or have established trusting relationships with many people within the organization. When they are seen as knowledgeable and trustworthy and as persons whose interest is in organizational effectiveness, at least they can be helpful to those at a peer level or below that in the organizational hierarchy. When also they are fortunate enough to be viewed as a professional, additionally they can help higher management. If the organization has divisions or components and internal consultants are in a corporate role, they more easily can be called on for help by any one of those units. Many internal consultants have developed unique programs.

A number of years ago, when various behavioral science consultations at the U.S. Department of State failed, I was called on to help. It would have been foolhardy and futile, let alone extraordinarily expensive, to undertake an assessment in such a complex organization in a highly politicized context whose people were scattered literally all over the world. I suggested instead that a group of department heads lead task forces to study a list of problems they themselves had specified. They were hesitant to do so until I assured them that I would guide their efforts. When they completed their work, they wanted me to report on it to their superiors. I declined, compelling them to do so. They did their work so well that they published an internal document of their findings. As a group, they would have been an important continuing internal body, but their administrative superior, fearing their potential competition with his role, disbanded them. The important lesson is that internal consultants, sometimes requiring the help and support of an external consultant, can do a creditable job.

Internal consultants recognize their own limitations in much the same way that physicians know that they cannot remain objective in treating members of their own family and therefore refer them to others. Also, internal consultants may be unable to confront people with issues and problems as readily as external consultants can. Often internal consultants do not have the power or status and therefore will not be heeded. In addition, they cannot be party to many of the confidences among higher management or maintain some of those within the system. Usually, then, when significant changes are to take place, they can operate collaboratively more usefully with an external assessor.

When internal assessors collaborate with an external assessor, internal consultants usually have the advantage of knowing their way around the organization and some of its crucial history. Therefore, they can be valued informants. They can help acquire and organize the kind of information that will facilitate the assessment and the corrective effort. They also have available on a continuing basis information about cross-currents, feelings, opinions, thinking, problems, conflicts, and other aspects of the organization. That information may make for a fruitful collaboration. In such a relationship, the external assessor must be careful not to interfere with the internal relationships of the internal consultant. Concomitantly, the internal consultant must not bear the self-perception that he or she is not adequate and that the assessor is the authority. Such feelings will make for a rocky relationship. They need a close, mutually collaborative, mutually supportive relationship for the effectiveness of their joint and individual tasks as well as for the success of any organizational change.

Internal consultants would be wise to build up an organizational assessment as outlined in this manual, both as a basis for their grasp and understanding of the organization and for evolving hypotheses to be tested in organizational change processes. There is no substitute for systematic comprehensive understanding of the organization, for step-by-step notation of the activities that have been undertaken to bring about change or to ameliorate problems, and for keeping track of successes and failures as well as errors and achievements.

3

THE POWELL-KOLE COMPANY: EXAMPLE OF AN ASSESSMENT

We have established some guidelines for consulting with organizations. The next step is to illustrate what a completed case write-up looks like.

In this instance of a small company, deliberately chosen so that the reader is not overwhelmed with information, the write-up follows the outline in appendix D, but not all topics in the outline are touched on. For some, there are insufficient data. Others are omitted for space reasons. A complete write-up of even a small company could well approximate 200 typewritten pages. Usually an assessor will complete as much of the outline as is necessary for his or her needs. For example, in this case there was no need to dig more deeply into financial data or the specifics of the contracts with clients or personal information about the employees below the top management.

This example of a case write-up is offered to help the assessor organize his or her thinking as he or she goes along. Ordinarily, the assessor prepares it for his or her own information preliminary to constructing the report, illustrated in appendix B, which is to be presented to the organization in the final feedback process. *This is not that report.* Examples from the Powell-Kole case also are offered at various points in the assessment process.

I. GENETIC DATA: HOW THE ORGANIZATION BECAME WHAT IT IS

The Powell-Kole Company, located in Waltham, Massachusetts, is a firm of marketing specialists that uses a group of computer-oriented tech-

---

This case summary is considerably more condensed than a full case write-up to keep the manual short. It is intended to illustrate how the assessor might organize his or her data. The identifying details of this company have been disguised. The relatively small size of the company and the condensation into a summary, although limiting the information to complete the outline fully, nevertheless serve to guide the beginner in organizing data. This summary is the assessor's integration. It is not the report he or she will feed back to the organization. For that model, see appendix B.

niques to analyze specific markets, and based on those analyses, to develop new products intended to achieve a specific share of their respective markets. The request for assessment from the chief executive, Victor Stinson, followed the unexpected conflict that arose after an initial restructuring effort three years before, which it has been in the process of implementing, and the rapid increase in the company's work since its inception.

First Impressions

Victor (everyone calls him by his first name) came to the reception room to greet the assessor and ushered him into his office. Victor is just past middle-age, graying, dark brown eyes, well-dressed and well-groomed, with a very correct and slightly nervous manner. His large office is dominated by a desk, but quite simply furnished. Obviously, he does not lavish money on himself or the work environment.

The initial interview with Victor revealed a pattern that was to characterize the assessment. The first part of the hour, when the assessor asked about the business issues of the company, was very formal and uncomfortable. At one point, when the assessor asked Victor if he, the assessor, had understood Victor's concerns, Victor stiffened noticeably and replied that he had no concerns, only areas of interest. When the conversation shifted to Powell-Kole's projects, Victor produced a scrapbook of pictures of products that the company had helped develop and the tenor of the meeting became much more relaxed. One sensed that it was far easier in this company to talk about products and projects than business or organizational issues.

Initially, Victor mentioned four key issues for Powell-Kole. The first involved the problems of obtaining and servicing new business, particularly in the absence of a corporate marketing and sales function. Second was the development of computer programs to simulate the range of customer responses, now a bottleneck for the company. Third was the need to capitalize on the company's research and development to produce a product that could be manufactured, and fourth, to hire qualified people to keep pace with prospective growth and sales. Also, despite his initial denial that he had no concerns, Victor was concerned about what employees perceived to be the company's goals and strategies, how well they understood them and agreed with them, and how well the goals and strategies filtered down from top management. Finally, he was concerned about whether the organization perceives a drain on his time as a result of the growth that leaves him less time for them.

In a later interview, Victor changed his tone again. The issues that he mentioned were not problems or even concerns, but as he had said initially just areas of interest. In that interview he also discussed the strength and weaknesses of his top management. He seemed to complain about his brother, Richard, and Stephen E. Johnsson, director of production. He said that he was disappointed in his brother's performance, his lack of forcefulness as a supervisor, and he considered the administrative area, for which Richard was responsible, the weakest area in the company. Stephen was the strongest performer in the company, but he worked so hard that he did not know when to quit, and, occasionally, toward the end of the week, he had become irrational and totally committed to one way of doing things. Victor portrayed his own role as one of delicately managing the weaknesses of these two executives as well as dealing with the many other issues he faces.

Background of the Organization

In 1985, Nathan Powell and Vernon Kole shared an office at MIT and did analytical consumer marketing studies for private firms. They had a batch of stationery printed with Powell-Kole Associates as the letterhead. A year later Nathan felt that the business had grown enough to consider going into it full-time. He approached two of his graduate students, Victor Stinson and Bertram Honig, and invited them to consider joining the venture. They decided to get into the business slowly. Bertram had just finished his master's degree and was single. As such, he volunteered to be the first employee. The firm operated out of Victor's Cambridge apartment, with everyone working on the studies, and accounts being kept on the back of an envelope. Nathan indicated that he wished to be named in the firm's title, and, after weighing the options, the new partners agreed to the name Powell-Kole. Vernon Kole did not wish to continue with the new firm but his name was already on the stationery, so to avoid the cost of new stationery, they kept the name. Kole went off to a major corporation. Victor completed his doctorate and joined the firm full-time several months after its founding. After a year, Nathan felt secure enough to resign his MIT teaching post and work full-time as the CEO of Powell-Kole. By 1987, there were seven employees, Victor was head of analytical studies, and Bertram was spending half his time on computer engineering and the other half on finance. There was a small amount of special computer work for clients.

The firm was still quite small in 1988 when Bertram came to work full-time. Victor had become executive vice president by that time. Bertram had been one of the outstanding students of an MIT professor who was a close associate of the founders and a part-time consultant to the firm. Originally, it was planned that Bertram would work on developing contracts with clients, but when Victor landed a large contract with a major manufacturer, Bertram headed this contract that became the firm's first significant commercial success. This project was not only the stimulus to Powell-Kole's economic growth, but also established its reputation.

Major Crises Experienced by the Organization

In 1989, the firm witnessed another dramatic event: the departure of its founder and CEO, Nathan. Nathan explained that his decision was the result of a long series of arguments with Victor, then the number two person in the firm. Nathan felt that the pursuit of a manufactured product was chasing pie-in-the-sky and that the firm should devote all of its energies to the consulting business. Victor, backed by Bertram, favored trying to capitalize on its research and development activities and then market one of its computer products, which it is now doing. The company has had a history of trying to develop a patentable manufacturing product without significant success.

There is another aspect to the Nathan-Victor conflict. Nathan was perceived by employees as an easy-going man, a believer in decentralization, a person ready to listen to employee problems. Victor, in contrast, appears to be more driven, a believer in top-down management and eager to push the company to greater success. Nathan had said that this conflict had reached a level where it affected the company and him personally. When he received an offer of a good government job, he resigned. Victor bought out his share, incorporated the company, and floated its first stock offering. Later, Nathan decided to start his own consulting firm.

Victor and Richard incorporated the company in 1990. Victor, 50 at the time of the assessment, continues to be its chief executive officer, chair, and president. Richard, then 43, is executive vice president. Victor's leadership has been the crucial factor in its development, both in the ultimate design of its products and in its relationship with its clients.

Despite the fact that the firm's expertise rested on analysis, manufacturing was always, in fantasy, an element of the Powell-Kole business. It was always a logical component of their marketing orientation, but more important, it represented a way to capitalize on technical know-how and an opportunity to make it big. If they could develop proprietary computer technology with a large market appeal, then manufacture by subcontracting as well as selling the programs, the rewards would be substantial. This, in essence, was what Edwin Land had done with Polaroid, and this dream seems to haunt all of those who followed figuratively in his hallowed footsteps at MIT. Said Victor, "We incorporated this firm in 1990 with the dream of discovering a product we could manufacture and make a million."

II. DESCRIPTION AND ANALYSIS OF THE ORGANIZATION AS A WHOLE

A systems view of the organization suggests that there are four systems at work in Powell-Kole: one concerned with marketing, searching for clients

Figure 3-1

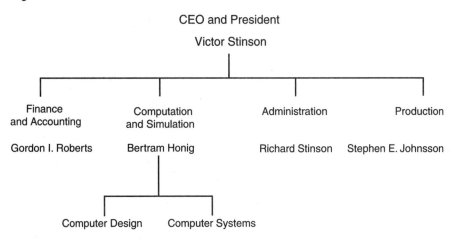

The Powell-Kole Company Organization Chart

and preparing proposals; a second concerned with project management, completing the project as specified in the proposal; a third focusing on customer relations, meeting the client to deliver the completed project and follow-up; and a fourth centering around personnel management, the assignment of projects to one of the different groups, the assignment of personnel to work on the project, including evaluation, promotion, and reward of individual performance. (See Figure 3-1.)

Plant and Equipment

The company is located off the fabled entrepreneurial Route 128, in an area of buildings that house technical and industrial firms, such as Sylvania and Raytheon. Its offices are in a fairly modern and quite clean building. The grounds are simply landscaped and well-kept. On entering the front door, one encounters not an office but a concrete and metal staircase. Reaching the second floor and opening the heavy metal door, one enters the main office. The receptionist is on the immediate left. To the right is a small reception area, with modern but inexpensive furniture, and advertising, computer, and news magazines on the coffee table. The receptionist offered the assessor coffee.

The building reflects an air of impermanence. Few improvements have been made to the original rental space. The walls are actually partitions of plywood paneling, open at the top and bottom. Outside of the reception area, there were few pictures on the walls.

The organization occupies four different work areas. One houses the corporate offices and staff functions as well as one of the project groups. In the second area is another of the project groups and the third houses the technical staff and their array of computers. The fourth area is more often used for consultant's offices and work spaces for the more temporary personnel who are not immediately involved in client projects.

Most of the employees were dressed more casually than Victor. Shirt sleeves were the rule. Only two or three of the men wore ties. There seemed to be a lot of bustle as people seemed to go back and forth quite frequently. Most of the employees were in one-, two-, or three-person offices. There was also a large conference room with straight-backed chairs, a television, an overhead screen, and a mobile whiteboard.

Most of the company's assets, largely equipment, are leased rather than owned. Although this has some positive financial implications and makes it possible in a declining economy for the company to reduce its risk considerably, it also contributes greatly to feelings of impermanence. The underlying theme seems to be, "We're working on a day-to-day basis here" despite the extended time on some of the projects.

Financial Structure

When Victor bought the company in 1990, he and his wife Ursula signed promissory notes, guaranteeing the company's initial financing. After 4,500,294 shares of stock were issued in 1997 at $50 a share, the officers and directors owned 44%. Present stockholders, including officers and directors, own approximately 52% of the shares, thereby controlling the company. It has not paid any dividends since its incorporation nor does it intend to in the near future.

The company reserved 118,000 shares of stock to be issued under its qualified stock option plan and 227,000 shares for its nonqualified plan. The option price under the qualified plan is 100% of the fair-market value of the stock on the date of the grant. Under the nonqualified plan the price is 85% of the fair-market value. Options to purchase may be granted to employees, directors, advisors, and consultants. Options under qualified plans expire five years after they are granted, and under the nonqualified plan 10 years. But options cannot be granted to employees who own more than 10% of the company's stock. The holders of options have the opportunity to profit from a rise in the market value of the stock.

In 1997, its gross revenues were $11,235,246 and, in 1998, $11,087,489. Its net income in 1997 was $882,850, and in 1998, $684,610. At the end of 1998, it had a working capital deficit of $1,170,449. Unfavorable economic conditions and delays in payment by one or more of the company's clients following the economic downturn in 1997 were blamed. In addition, heavy nonrecurring losses followed efforts to lay the groundwork for foreign, especially European, business. Sales in 1998 were lower than those in 1997 because of the time and effort devoted to developing international sales and diversification of sources of income. (More detailed financial data are in the company's 10-K report.) Victor originates approximately half of the company's contracts. The rest come from other officers, stockholders, and consultants.

From its incorporation in 1990 until the end of 1998, the company derived approximately 43% of its revenues from its largest client, Scott Paper Company, before it was acquired by Kimberly-Clark Company. During that same period it derived 99% of its business from its four largest clients, Scott Paper Company, General Foods Company, the Quaker Oats Company, and Philip Morris, Inc.

The company has five-year employment contracts with Victor ($430,000), Richard ($221,600; both are directors), and two-year contracts with three other key executives: Bertram Honig, vice president, computation and simulation ($240,000); Stephen E. Johnsson, vice president, production ($180,000); and Gordon L. Roberts, vice president, treasurer and director ($190,000). Nolan Davidson, secretary (who has a separate legal office), also a director, is compensated $150,000 for legal advice plus added compensation for attending each board meeting and board committee meeting as may be necessary totalling $190,000. Two of the company's key business and marketing consultants are William B. Lawrence and Dr. Jerald K. Stern, each of whom receives 14% of the contracts he initiates and services and 7% of those initiated but not serviced.

Human Resources

Four vice presidents report to Victor: Richard, Bertram, Stephen, and Gordon. The company has 12 administrative, accounting, and clerical personnel, and 22 full-time and 22 part-time staff members. Of the staff, 32 are executive, technical, professional, and creative staff members, four of whom have PhDs or equivalent advanced degrees, and an additional six currently are completing their PhD requirements. Two hold MA's, and eight others hold BA's. Many of the staff members and consultants were Victor's students or academic colleagues. Some of these staff members are salaried, others work on a per diem or per project or other bases as the company needs them.

The human resources functions are handled by an outside consultant. The company also uses, as needed, various expert consultants in such fields as systems analysis, psychology, sociology, anthropology, econometric techniques, and finance. The company does not employ any permanent sales staff nor does it advertise or otherwise publicize its services, but it intends to develop a marketing and sales arm.

Despite the number of people with professional degrees, there are no MBAs. Neither Victor nor any of his top management colleagues have had any management training. None has ever worked as a manager in any other firm.

There is little in the way of orientation and training. Staff are expected to learn the ropes by themselves. The sophisticated nature of Powell-Kole's business requires that they hire already technically qualified, highly skilled people, and the nature of the company's work means that there is very little work for people who are not so qualified. This also implies that there are no career ladders at Powell-Kole, and therefore no formal plan for career development. There is a definite professional hierarchy, but it is not clear how one moves from one level to another. Because most of the work is on a project basis, members of the staff have a lot of flexibility about deciding with whom and on what kinds of tasks they will work. Job titles vary considerably and sometimes apparently without logic. Many people seem unsure of what their titles are, partly because titles "slide around" and often are project-specific, and partly because many of the people do not care. There are no distinctions, such as junior or senior assistant within clerical jobs, and no consideration is given to growth or upward mobility for the assistants. Except for assistants and low-level technicians, working hours are flexible.

There is no formal system for promoting employees, nor even a consensus on what promotion is. Is it a change in title, a change in pay, or both? A promotion might be bargained for; it might also be the result of outstanding piece of work, or it might be a response to the need of a project. Promotions and other personnel matters tend to be handled at the group level, so practices will vary according to the group leader, with very little attempt at internal compatibility.

Most of the people at Powell-Kole, professional and nonprofessional, seem not to know how their performance is assessed at all. The company also has few fringe benefits: Most employees report that they prefer the equivalent in cash. This partly accounts for the mobility of professional persons around the Route 128 high tech firms.

There are seasonal cycles to the work load with the peak early in the winter for those products that prospectively might be introduced in fall advertising or in the following spring. Planning tends to be done on a day-to-day basis.

Consultant Reports

In the summer of 1996, Bob Harvey, president of his own management consulting firm, which had been advising Victor, designed an organizational structure that would better handle the company's increased work force. The results of this study were published and formally adopted, but the company has not adhered to the proposed timetable for its implementation. The most important recommendations in the Harvey plan were the increased responsibilities of the group directors and the decentralization of short-term marketing efforts to the project group level.

Product Service History

The company serves its clients with a series of data collection and proprietary computer programs simulating human responses to various stimuli, which the company uses in some of its services. The business is highly competitive. In certain aspects of its business the company is in competition with either or both the new products divisions or departments of large consumer products manufacturing companies, some of whom may be its clients, and with standard market research organizations, individual consultants, and market research divisions of major research organizations. Most of these are larger, better known, and possess greater resources than Powell-Kole. Computer software companies that specialize in systems analysis are also competitors.

Among its major clients at the time of the assessment were Scott Paper Company, Quaker Oats Company, General Foods Corporation, Bristol-Myers Squibb Company, Coca-Cola Company, Philip Morris Company, and General Mills. Approximately 97% of its revenues at the same time were derived from these, its largest clients.

The company's business consists primarily of work related to the development of new products for these large consumer manufacturers, but it intends also to develop its own proprietary products. Initially, the company's work centered on the study and analysis of particular consumer markets, following on Victor's interest in the response of population groups to new objects and events, a topic in which he had done research as a graduate student and college professor. More recently, the company has concentrated on the development and evaluation of new product prototypes following the analyses of particular markets and participating in the test marketing and national introduction of new products. It has become increasingly involved in the active development of new products, including their packaging and advertising.

The company's activities for its clients comprise three distinct phases. Phase I consists of studying the structure of a particular market (e.g., the market for a new brand of coffee in the Western United States) to determine the features of the products that underlie the patterns of substitution and competition between existing products found in consumer behavior. Based on this analysis, the company develops a variety of concepts for new products and tests these to determine (a) what proportion of consumers in national or regional samples prefer each new concept to all the currently available products and (b) with which current products each new concept competes. In this way, through field observations, interviews, and other techniques, the company collects and analyzes data to arrive at a description of the various qualities that the new product, package, and advertising should possess to attain the market share that the client and the company have arrived at as the agreed goal. The last stage of a Phase I project typically comprises a 1,500-person evaluation of several different descriptions of the new product as well as of existing products in that market.

As of the end of 1998, the company had completed 21 Phase I studies for seven clients and had nine more in progress. The company charges between $400,000 and $600,000 for a Phase I study, providing pretax margins of approximately 25%.

In Phase II, the company generates the prototype of a new product by evaluating the responses of groups of representative consumers to various qualities and components of the product being developed, such as color, shape, texture, and so forth. For example, in designing a new carbonated beverage for a client who specified a certain percentage of a particular market for carbonated beverages as the goal, the company tested consumer responses to many different shapes, colors, textures, tastes, fragrances, and so on for product and container, and advertising themes and motifs to arrive at a prototype whose various qualities conformed to the description evolved and tested in Phase I and that the company believed would perform in the market to the stated specifications. To test the prototype, the company or the client tests the product by introducing it in a test market (usually a city or portions of one or more states).

As of the end of 1998, the company had completed eight Phase II projects, all of which were accepted by the respective clients as meeting the agreed-on goals. At that date, the company had also completed the major portion of two further Phase II projects, and had begun work on three additional Phase II projects. These 10 Phase II projects have been or are being performed for a total of four clients. The company charges between $2,000,000 and $3,000,000 for a Phase II project. Some Phase II contracts provide for basic plus contingent incentive payments to the company and give the company the right to terminate the contract in the event of serious disagreement with the client and to receive a termination payment. The company's pretax margin on Phase II projects approximates 8%, excluding incentive payments or other bonuses.

Phase III involves assisting the client in the design and implementation of a marketing and advertising plan for the new product, first for its test market and then on its introduction nationally. As of the end of 1998, the company had not completed any Phase III projects but had three in progress. The fees for a Phase III project range from $1,500,000 to $3,000,000, with expected pretax profit margins of between 10% and 15%.

In the past, the company has declined to undertake projects for organizations that are unwilling or unable to delegate broad authority for the development of the proposed new product to the company. The company believes that without such concentrated authority, the new product may be distorted because of the injection of subjective elements by various persons and groups in the client's organization. The company believes that, in such event, the new product could tend to depart from the description evolved in Phase I and might contain inconsistent and self-contradictory elements.

Some of the company's services are performed under written agreements or exchanges of correspondence with its clients that sometimes are of an informal character and that may not constitute legally enforceable contracts; other projects are performed under oral agreements or understandings. The company believes that, because of the nature of its work and because the work is performed for only a small number of clients, this informal approach is both workable and desirable.

As of the end of 1998, work in progress and backlog amounted to approximately $8,837,500. A substantial portion of the work in process and backlog consists of Phase II and Phase III projects. Such work is customarily terminable by the client or the company at any time on short notice. A Phase I study requires approximately six months; the Phase II development and evaluation of a prototype requires from one to one-and-one-half years; and Phase III work will depend on the client's own timetable.

The company is exploring the possibility of developing two computer products on its own. It will perform Phase I and Phase II work to develop those products in the same manner that it does such work for clients. The company intends to select those types of products for which it believes the best potential market opportunities exist. Probably one of those products will be for the analysis of a snack food or dessert. Another might be for foreign travel. It has already done complete or partial Phase I projects in both of these food product areas, and intends to explore with its clients whether either or both of these areas would be of interest to them. If so, the company may select one or both of these areas for the first of its proprietary products; if not, the company will seek to develop other product areas that will interest its clients or prospective clients. If either or both of these food products is successful, it intends to develop other proprietary products and services as, for example, foreign travel.

The company intends to carry at least one of the proprietary products through evaluation in a full-scale test market before offering the product for sale or licensing. It would bear the costs itself, anticipating that it could recover them from future sales or licensing or possibly by selling an interest in the project.

In selecting particular products or service areas within which to undertake proprietary development, the company intends to work in consultation with its major clients and to select, if possible, new products or services that would be of interest to one or more major clients. The company also intends, as a general rule, to offer newly developed proprietary products or services first to one or more of its major clients for purchase, license, or joint venture before offering them to nonclients. However, it recognizes that moving in a proprietary direction, despite the promise of increased profitability, could create conflicts with present clients.

Thus far, the company has spent approximately $400,000 in performing for its own account partial Phase I studies of the national market for snack foods, the national dessert market, and the national travel market with special reference to foreign vacation travel. Of these costs, a net amount of approximately $290,000 after deducting sales expenses has been recouped by its sale of the dessert study, on a nonexclusive basis, to four separate manufacturers (among them clients of the company) for their own respective use and the similar nonexclusive sale of the right to use the snack food study to one client.

In addition to its contracting service for business clients, the company has also undertaken several projects in the field of public policy research and planning. These have included a project for the Peace Corps and a study for the Office of Economic Opportunity, which sought to apply some of the company's computer-based marketing and financial techniques to the development of small businesses. The company also advised a gubernatorial candidate in the 1996 elections with respect to certain elements of his and his opponents' campaigns.

The company has so far invested approximately $1,188,719 in developing a series of computer programs used in its new product development work for clients. It has licensed to one of its major clients, at a one-time fee of $300,000, the nonexclusive right to use certain of its data collection procedures and proprietary computer programs for that client's own in-house new product development work. It may also do the same for others.

In addition, the company has thus far expended approximately $1,148,057 in the development of a series of data collection procedures and computer programs designed to simulate the responses of different population groups to many of the variable characteristics that, in various combinations, generally make up the differentiating elements of packaged consumer products. Of that amount, approximately $993,901 represents costs of developing a model that is now being used routinely in the company's work. The company intends to develop other computer simulation programs designed to take the place of field interviews and thus they will be usable in Phase I work.

Human Resources

All 22 full-time professionals, eight of the part-time professionals, and all of the office staff were interviewed during the assessment. Some of the concerns expressed in the interviews related to the dramatic growth of the company over the past several years. That made the earlier organizational structure inappropriate, and the new one is still in the experimental stage. In addition, although gratified with the current size of the firm and its likely continued growth, testimony to its success, top management was uncomfortable with their greater distance from their employees. They do not like having to supervise rather than rolling up their sleeves and attacking technical problems, and they are experiencing the loss of a feeling of a family firm. The firm now has a need for more business skills and a more sophisticated managerial orientation.

Virtually all of the staff interviewed described their work as both demanding and challenging. The work itself was the most frequently mentioned reward in the firm, after salary. Several said that their work is more important than their salary.

Seasonal Cycles

There are seasonal cycles to the work load, with the peak early in the winter for those products that prospectively might be introduced in fall advertising or in the following spring. Planning tends to be done on a day-to-day basis, depending on when the contracts come in. Long-range activities, such as development of new markets, tend to be assigned to Bertram on an ad hoc basis, with little consideration given to integrating those tasks with the rest of the organization's work.

With regard to planning, Powell-Kole basically is a reactive organization. There are no contingency plans in the organization that people seem to be aware of. Although employees are aware of the ups and downs of project funding, management has not indicated how full employment could be sustained if clients cut back on their project needs. Of course, there will always be a need for new products, and that means necessary package design and testing, but given the intensity of competition and the growing variety of investigative methods, it is difficult to imagine employment stability despite the backlog. Aside from the current projects and the continuing operations related to them, there are no specific plans for optional directions or efforts. No specialist in manufacturing has ever been brought into the company to further that concept. Nor has any thought been given to how such an effort would be integrated with the on-going projects of the company. The main theme in the company with respect to the future seems to be, "We'll get by."

III. INTERPRETATIVE DATA:
INFERENCES DRAWN FROM THE ANALYTIC DATA

Current Organizational Function

The company is constantly scanning the environment for consulting opportunities. As a service business, it is highly dependent on the market and the need to respond to it competitively. Most of the professional staff recognize the need to keep the flow of projects coming and Victor's significance in doing so. Although a few other senior staff bring in some business, the ethos is that everyone is expected to keep his or her antennae out for anything that even slightly suggests a project that Powell-Kole could do.

The most critical aspect of the outside world for Powell-Kole is, of course, the rapidly changing business environment in which they operate. Until recently, most of the marketing stimuli from this environment came through Victor and the two consultants. Now the company has stated its intention to expand that effort to the group level as well. Part of the reason is the adverse reaction of the group leaders to the heavy dependency of the company on Victor and the two consultants who are not part of the organization. Another reason is the need to decentralize the marketing effort as the organization grows larger. Unfortunately, there is not enough structure among the project groups to differentiate what group would pursue business in what industry or area. As a result, attention to the outside market has been dispersed throughout the organization. The already organized project groups differ in whose domain prospective clients might be involved, and personal dislikes seem to play a role as well. This situation has the net effect of reducing the effective awareness of the company of the outside information available to it.

One problem that the new reorganization plan tried to address has to do with the performance management of the group directors. The criteria for measuring the performance of the group directors recently have been changed and therefore are still not firm. Victor seems to be highly ambivalent about the role of the group directors. On the one hand, he does not want to give up his contacts with the client companies nor does he want to act on either of his vice presidents who are problems for him. He wants the groups to solve their own problems, especially because the vice presidents they report to have neither managerial training nor managerial experience. On the other hand, his constant fear of mistakes by the project staff leads him to keep the group directors on a short leash, to involve himself in daily problems, and to maintain their dependency on him. Victor's inability to let go of the group directors' day-to-day efforts makes it difficult for him to direct his attention to the long-term goals of the company. This has resulted in the projected reorganization that was intended to give the group directors more authority. Actually, the reorganization has been perceived as having no real impact or change on the company.

One result of this style of management has been the departure over the years of many aggressive performers, who were unwilling to tolerate the dependency and interference. Another result has been the encouragement of passivity in the employees who remain. Victor is essential to this passivity. As a "parent" who is able to solve lower level problems by quick intervention, he encourages the notion that employees are dependent children, not ready to venture forth on their own.

Victor remains active in his role as a trouble-shooter for project difficulties. The weakest link at Powell-Kole is not marketing but project management. Victor is thus placed in the dual role of finding the promised land of the manufacturing operation and maintaining the flow of projects whose failure could threaten the survival of the business. This leaves top management with a high degree of flexibility, but many employees are confused. Although technical marketing decisions get a broad range of inputs, the critical business problems—customer relations, marketing, strategy, and so forth—seem to be decided by very few people and passed down through the organization for implementation.

Emotional Atmosphere of the Organization

Executive actions at Powell-Kole are designed to maintain the status quo. The status quo is that of a small, entrepreneurial high tech firm that produces a variety of consumer marketing projects and turns a modest profit. Growth actions are not integrated into the top management's or employees' conceptions of the purpose of the firm, other than those aspects related to immediate profit-making. Technical activity is likewise related to maintaining or perhaps improving the status quo, rather than making radical changes at the frontier of technology. At a personal level, employees' actions are designed to keep out of trouble with the bosses, and the bosses react only when the pressure becomes great enough—and then only to restore the previous equilibrium.

Attitudes and Relationships

Relations with employees generally can be described as paternalistic to varying degrees. Group managers are included in certain key decisions, but invariably are excluded from the decision making of the executive committee made up of the officers. Professionals are relatively free in their choice of working hours and project scheduling within the required time boundaries, but they do not influence the company's choice of clients or projects. Management rarely tells them anything about how the firm is doing or where it is going. Lower level technicians and assistants are treated as second-class citizens. They are not given much consideration with respect to personnel policies. Although Richard tries to represent their concerns in executive committee discussions, he is given short shrift as a "bleeding heart." The business of the business is business, not personnel policies for people who are there to assist but otherwise do not "count" for much. Of course, salaries have to be competitive with those of other companies in the area, but no one sees an advantage in retaining assistants with forward-looking sick leave, parental, seniority, or similar progressive policies. Essentially, the assistants are expendable and replaceable.

The customer, by way of contrast, is treated as the most important individual in Powell-Kole's business. Management is careful not to challenge the client's definition of a problem, and reprimands professionals who do for fear of losing a project. The reluctance of management to loosen control of managing client relations keeps the groups from acquiring their own areas of independent expertise. Top management holds tightly to itself information about successes or failures with clients.

The company belongs to several trade associations, but the trade associations seem important to top management primarily as a way of reinforcing their self-image of marketing professionals who have demonstrated their success to the outside world.

Masculine–Feminine Orientation

Assistants, the only women and the least educated/skilled members of the organization, are expected to serve coffee to the executives and cater to the otherwise male employees. They receive very little consideration in return.

Powell-Kole is a masculine organization. Housed in an industrial park, its surroundings are functional and rarely adorned with artifacts not related to work. The CEO keeps a ceramic piece on his credenza, but the ceramic piece is a model of one of the consumer packages that the company had a hand in developing. Colors are essentially brown and green, the colors that came with the building. In the conference room is a convention-quality display of the products that the firm has had a significant hand in developing, together with a chart showing the increase in sales of one of the products from the time of the redesign of its packaging. The focus of the company is on showing the superior quality of its projects when compared with those of its competitors.

Feminine is regarded as second class. At one point, Richard, the executive vice president, the person most nearly regarded as a mother figure in the company, was looked down on by the rest of management as weak. He is handled gingerly by his brother Victor, and carries little weight in decision making. He has also suffered in the eyes of the senior professionals for having represented the assistants' position about problems they are having working for top managers. Of course, because they report to him, that is exactly what he ought to be doing.

Powell-Kole is able to achieve a stable masculine atmosphere by denying or distancing itself from its feminine element. To refer to teamwork is acceptable, but when someone refers to his involvement as participatory, the project managers are quick to deny it. Concern with people rather than concern with tasks is viewed as a feminine orientation, and the project managers and top management keep those two issues separate.

Psychological Contract

The psychological contract, the unconscious expectations employees have of management and management has of employees, relate heavily to dependency (Levinson et al., 1962). Management gets the contracts, assigns and pays the employees, and, however inadequately, manages them. It assumes the employees' dependency. Basically employees assume and expect that management will provide them with interesting work but will not include them in, or warn them about, its major decisions. Management expects employees to channel their aggression into attacking technical problems, performing quality work on schedule, and taxing themselves with high personal and professional standards. Without being aware of having such an attitude, it assumes that employees will satisfy their need for affection by the gratification they get from their work, their relationships with each other, by serving the interests of the company, and by high regard for their professional standards as well as from their interaction with colleagues while working effectively on teams toward common achievements.

Management is disturbed that, as the company grows larger, employees may show less loyalty, perhaps by fewer late hours or other forms of voluntary commitment. It seems that the project organization, with its emphasis on control of the work groups, is a way of trying to preserve the business character of the past.

Many employees seem content with this limited psychological contract. The psychological contract is complemented at a conscious level by a social contract. For example, at a conscious level, the professionals particularly feel that management should provide them with better evaluation of their performance. They want to know more definitively how they stand with management and how good their work is. However, inasmuch as these are self-motivated people with demanding consciences, at an unconscious level it would relieve their necessary built-in propensity for the severe self-criticism that characterizes professionals with high standards. Also, as part of the social contract, they want more information about the pace of the business, the better to counteract rumors about layoffs. They also want to know where the company is going, and what role they can play in helping it reach its objectives and meeting their aspirations.

Authority, Power, and Responsibility

Employees feel that management is unsure of itself and poorly qualified to lead an ever-growing company. The executive constellation of the organization centers around Victor and Bertram, with Bertram being Victor's alter ego. As the organization grows, the ability of these two people to wield power is slowly being eroded. Victor grows increasingly remote, and Bertram's forays into the project groups seem increasingly illegitimate. The power of the project managers is growing, and they are learning more about managing and relationships with clients. Top management still does not trust the project managers, and, as a result, the directors, who are eager to assume greater responsibility, grope to acquire expertise and engage in a running battle with ambivalent leaders for more power. If the company is to have adequate management to cope with a changing, more competitive environment, it will have to face up to these responsibilities: the need for better management skills, the need for clearer and more formal reporting relationships, and the need for better communication throughout the company.

Key People

At the first meeting, Victor appeared nervous, almost timid, and concerned about his success. He is extremely formal in his manner, and dresses neatly. He engendered a feeling of distrust in the consultant, as though beneath that polite exterior there was a ruthless and cunning jungle fighter. His self-image is success-oriented and macho male. His behavior toward his employees is extremely withdrawn. He is less visible than any other member of top management. He is visibly worried about letting subordinates learn from their mistakes, yet he hopes they will assume more responsibility. When he speaks of the future of the company, he hopes that its growth will place less of a burden on him. One senses that the current needs of the organization are beyond his ability to meet, and that he will unleash all of his defenses rather than face this fact.

Bertram is a boyish-looking man in his late thirties, with a slightly stooped posture and glinting eyes. He has an unsettling, macabre laugh. His lack of self-awareness and his view of himself as primarily a problem-solver rather than a power broker probably leads Victor to find him unthreatening. Bertram's energy seems boundless. He is not ruthless; rather he is insensitive to how his interventions affect others.

IV. ANALYSES AND CONCLUSIONS

This assessment suggests the implication that any set of recommendations must first get past Victor's resistance to criticisms of his style of management and help Bertram better control his impulsive intrusions. The recommendations must address Victor's concerns, leave him in control, and must be realistic in their expectations of his leadership capabilities. As the firm grows larger and reporting relationships more formalized, Bertram's lack of interpersonal skills may make it more difficult for him to move around the consulting projects he now advises.

Explanatory Formulations

Powell-Kole was formed to enable a group of MIT professors and their graduate students to work together on computer-based marketing projects that would be both interesting and remunerative. The first five years of the company was one of difficult struggle as it sought to establish itself in a highly competitive environment and to demonstrate its competence. Its success was consistent as the scope and sophistication of its analytical work grew. With the departure of its founder and its incorporation as a vehicle worthy of investment, together with continuing alliances with major consumer manufacturing customers, it demonstrated its ability both to diversify and innovate. This diversification gave impetus to its underlying fantasy that one day it would also be able to invent a product it could manufacture that would make its founders and stockholders rich. From 1985 until 1988, the company grew from three people to 45 and its volume from practically nothing to $11,087,489.

As it approached the end of the 1990s, the company began to show its strains as its top management became more keenly aware of the pressures on itself, simultaneously concerned with getting business and managing the processes of the services it was selling. It also experienced the continuing frustration that it could not seem to develop its cherished fantasy of developing and manufacturing a product that would ease its dependency on services and increase its profitability. Its marketing purview is limited to a handful of major consumer manufacturing organizations with which its CEO has the predominant relationships. It has no formal marketing activity, despite its recognition of the need for one. Nor does it have particular management skills or talents. The combination of these features of the organization makes for a certain tenuousness among employees about the organization's future. The increasing size of the company has led to a reorganization that has not been fully realized, largely because the CEO is reluctant to decentralize marketing and management activities to project managers. The company continues to operate like an extended family under an authoritarian, distant father.

One reason for this pattern of behavior lies in the company's origin. It was founded by a professor and his students. The mentor–student relationship was simply transferred to a real world situation. Although such an arrangement, capitalizing on the students' creativity and productivity, has been fruitful for the many entrepreneurial companies that have spun off from the universities in the Boston area, most seem to struggle with the same problems attendant on success and growth. They have difficulty moving to the next stage—namely that requiring professional management.

This pattern of managerial behavior was perhaps more difficult for Victor to cope with because he started as a student, not a mentor, and propelled himself into the senior role when his mentor left. He is not the kind of person who is comfortable in his relationships with subordinates or in being other than in full control. The company is his vehicle for masculine identity. He likes to think of himself as a leader and decision maker, builder of the business. He exerted his needs for mastery through developing his technical competence and then the business. As a developer and generator, he moved from academic abstractions and the comparatively more easily controlled methods of analysis to the less predictable and controllable arena of people. His success now brings him to the edge of possible failure.

Prognostic Conclusions

The prognosis for organizational change depends on several key variables: the rate of growth, especially growth in the number of employees; the stability of the business, especially given the contraction of consumer manufacturing into larger conglomerates and the increasing variety of analytic techniques; and the ability of the company to recruit and hold talented people. If the marketing business remains stable with minimal growth, Powell-Kole stands a good chance of continuing to manage its current level of conflict and dissatisfaction without changing the problem areas described previously. In short, the company seems to be coping with first-order adaptive activities (see appendix C). If the business falls off, Victor's self-image will suffer. Although a more rational approach to business planning would be called for, probably he would revert to the behavior pattern he knows best and emotionally is most comfortable with: rolling up his sleeves, making all the decisions himself, and not telling anything to anyone he does not trust.

Conclusions and Recommendations

In the report to Victor and then to the top management group, followed by the rest of the employees, three conclusions may be presented. First, the rapid growth of the first few years has placed a strain on managerial resources. This has caused a decline in cohesion and a need for better coordination among the different parts of the organization. Second, again resulting from the growth in size, Powell-Kole needs quickly to address several areas, such as communicating company goals, better appraisal of individual performance, bridging the separation among the various functions, developing a mediation or conflict-solving mechanism, and strengthening its ability to implement plans more forcefully. It is also important for top management to agree on and develop a long-term strategic direction for the company. Third, management training for all of the current executives, managers, and directors will be necessary to enable them to deal with these issues.

To help implement these conclusions, Powell-Kole needs the temporary assistance, over a two- to five-year period, of a chief operating officer, a seasoned business manager who can help the company address all of these areas and provide managerial guidance. Such a person should have been identified with the successful management of a large organization of the scale Powell-Kole hopes to reach in the future. Such a chief operating officer should be neither a computer professional nor an entrepreneur but a manager who can help the current management team develop policies and procedures, clarify job roles and group functions, and plan for the future. This person should be qualified to fill three important functions: preparing a management development program; being responsible for policy formulation; and helping with strategy formulation. The chief operating officer should understand what the problems will be like in the next stage of the organization's development, the long-term nature of organizational change, and be able to facilitate the company's transition to a more professional style of management. This person should be, by nature, a person who does not seek power and one who will coordinate the goal-setting process rather than impose his own goals. Such a person should be able to make sure that plans are carried out but not set in concrete.

Because of the level of experience necessary to fill this role because Victor's previous acceptance of a mentor and also because of the short-term nature of the needed managerial assistance, probably it will be wiser to recruit an older man (Victor will not tolerate a woman), perhaps someone in his mid- to late-50s with demonstrated experience in the management of large organizations. Perhaps, because of contraction and consolidation among large companies, such a person could be found among the company's client corporations whose consumer product manufacturing experience could be advantageous.

Obviously these recommendations will immediately run afoul of Victor's fears and anxieties. He has already told the assessor of his concerns about two troublesome subordinates and about his worry because of the growing distance from his employees. These issues manifest his pain and are where the consultant must begin to help him. Before making them in the form of a public statement, the consultant should review these recommendations repetitively with Victor, talk over the problems they pose for him and how he might take short steps in their implementation. His previous experience with a consultant gave him answers but no help with his fear of loss of control nor any perspective on the new, higher levels he might achieve. Continuing consultation with him that would help him to experience the consultant as a helpful ally could enable him to learn to manage his troublesome subordinates better, to give up some of the more trivial aspects of control in favor of controlling better the larger picture, and imagining the greater executive he could be as he turned over the activities he is not good at to someone who could carry them out for him without threatening his control. He could regret and mourn his losses while being freed up to pursue the wealth and prestige he has always sought. This consultative effort might be slow going but there is enough pain in Victor and the organization to make it feasible.

4

INTRODUCING THE ASSESSMENT

As we have seen in the Powell-Kole case study, the consultation was precipitated by Victor's "concerns." Essentially he was worried about his growing distance from his organizational family and his possible loss of control as the organization grew and he would have to rely on his subordinates for contact with his clients. He could not undertake the recommendations of his previous consultant, paralyzed by his fear that he would lose his contacts and thereby his control of his organization. This issue, the anguish of the client, is fundamental to all consultation: No pain, no problem; no problem, no need for a consultant. Despite what anyone may say, no organization undertakes consultation "to make things better" unless someone hurts. Therefore, the basic question for every consultant regardless of the reason for a consultation request is, Where is the pain?

THE INITIAL CONTACT

If a person seeks out a consultant on behalf of an organization, or if someone in an organization is asked to assess an organization problem, the process of entry into the organization is a relatively simple one. If a person is assigned to the task, he or she has official permission to seek information. If a consultant is engaged, perhaps on the acceptance of a proposal, perhaps for preliminary exploration before a proposal or perhaps to deal with a crisis, whatever the case, the consultant should obtain a clear picture of the nature of the problem for which help is being sought; how both its causes and manifestations are viewed by the person who seeks help, who are the other influential persons involved whose cooperation must be obtained, and why he or she was chosen. The consultant should establish what expectations are being held of the consultant, how realistic they are, and to what extent they are possible to fulfill. This is especially important because the client may have implicit expectations of which the client is not clearly aware and on which the consulting relationship ultimately will flounder.

In one instance, when a CEO was not able to move his organization after a year of trying, on the recommendation of the in-house psychologist,

I was invited to consult. As a preliminary exploration, I suggested interviews with the eleven vice presidents. In two days of interviewing, it became apparent to me that they were in a depressed rage. Rather than wait for a comprehensive assessment of the organization, I suggested to the CEO that there be a three-day meeting of the executive group of the organization to decompress the rage, attenuate the depression, and organize that group behind his leadership. Long-term consultation followed, the formulation of the assessment being compiled as the consultation progressed.

Having clarified the expectations, the consultant, now about to propose an assessment, should convey to the client the steps he or she is likely to take, the probable time to do so, and the cost. In most cases, the assessor will want to propose a formal contract with a definite beginning and end. In other situations, particularly when the first step is preliminary exploration, it will be preferable to propose a limited contract followed by the option to renegotiate. Some consultants prefer to have a trial relationship with an organization based on time (three months, six months) or a successful conclusion of the assessment process followed by helping the organization implement the recommendations.

When a member of an organization is assigned to study a problem in the organization, this individual is confronted with the skepticism of the organization's other members. Frequently, they have been visited by external consultants whose findings they have ignored because the consultants "really didn't know the organization (the work, the technology, the people, etc.)." Therefore, the internal consultant must be seen as authoritative and knowledgeable.

If the assessment is to review a whole organization or a component of significant size, the consultant will want to organize a team to do the work. One useful way to select a credible team is to identify those in the organization who are respected for their ability to get things done. Those respected persons are likely to be the most trusted organization members. When such people report their findings, they are unlikely to be viewed skeptically, let alone be subject to argument or criticism. Moreover, they are more likely to influence others to implement the recommendations that result from their assessment.

The team leader or an external consultant will have to train the team members how to interview (see the suggested questions in appendix A), how to record a summary of each interview and of their observations, and teach them the content of this manual before they start to work. Frequent regular meetings of the team will enable them to share experiences and problems, to check their inferences and their effect on the interviewees, and to build their confidence in both their skills and their findings.

The initial contact with the key figure in the problem area or with the client is the most important one of the whole relationship. In a thousand subtle ways both the assessor and the client communicate with each other. If the client cannot like and trust the assessor in this initial period, their relationship will be a rocky one, if it continues at all. A consulting relationship should be an alliance of both parties to discover and resolve problems. This means that the relationship must be examined continuously by the assessor, and the assessor must be particularly alert to the effect of his or her own behavior on the client and the client system. (See Checklist 1.)

It is wise for the assessor and the client to review their relationship periodically and to renegotiate their goals and expectations. Unless this is done, both will struggle with outdated agreements or unresolved disappointments that will intrude on their work together. If both parties do not feel equally free to change the relationship or resolve the problem, the client

---

CHECKLIST 1: THE INITIAL ASSESSMENT CONTACT

- Who asked for the assessment?
- What is the power, status, or position of that person in the client organization?
- How did that person learn about you?
- What does that person state to be the reason for seeking assessment?
- Is the request directly for assessment or for a proposal from which an assessor will be chosen?
- If for a proposal, will the decision be based on fee, professional orientation, or references?
- Who makes the decision?
- Is there a time boundary within which the assessment is to take place?
- Is the problem a crisis or emergency? If so, what precipitated it?
- What did the contact person ask about you? What references did you offer?
- What are your feelings about the contact?
- About the contact person's attitude toward you?
- About the person's authority to seek assessment? About possibly taking on this problem in this organization?
- What kind of information, if any, do they want about you? References?

---

will feel increasingly dependent on the consultant and become angry for being in that position. Of course, in an internal assessment, the client may have no choice.

In addition, the assessor should arrange regular contact meetings with the client contact person to bring the client up to date in a general way on what is being learned and what issues are arising. If the assessment is an extended one, this meeting should be scheduled weekly. Appropriate spacing should be arranged for shorter assessments. The reasons are, first, to ease the client's uneasiness about strangers in the organization, and, second, to start the client thinking in the directions that are likely to appear in the subsequent final report. Ideally, there should be no surprises in the report as far as the chief executive is concerned. The CEO should have come step by step with the assessor. Without betraying confidences or making premature commitments, the assessor must sustain the relationship in such a way that he or she maintains trust, keeps the client informed, and helps prepare the client for the steps that will be necessary based on the outcome of the report. If the assessor does not do this, a long gap ensues between the initial contact and the report. Not only does this gap stimulate self-critical fantasies on the part of the client, but also, when the report comes, it is likely to be experienced as overwhelming even though the findings themselves are relatively modest. Unless this process is followed regularly and carefully, it is almost a foregone conclusion that nothing will come of the report, and the assessor will end the relationship with the organization with that presentation.

It should be already apparent that the distinction between assessment and intervention is an arbitrary one. The assessor is affecting the organization from the very moment he or she enters it. Therefore the assessment process frequently refers to the early stages of a relationship between the assessor and the organization, a series of interactions and transactions that ideally will lead to constructive organizational change. From the beginning during fact finding, by the questions he or she asks and the fact that they are asked, the assessor may bring into sharper focus the problems being experienced by organization members. The assessor may cause them to think more critically about their leadership and to question its effectiveness. The assessor's report, rather than being a private document for the assessor's own technical use, becomes an instrument of confrontation for the client organization that compels them to decide what they want to do and what further use they want to make of the assessor.

In the initial assessment period, both assessor and organization gain a clearer picture of the condition of the organization. They begin to think about possible modes of change and decide whether they wish to commit themselves to a longer term effort to understand and change major aspects of the organization.

EARLY NEGOTIATION

The kind of preparation preceding an assessment can profoundly affect its process and outcome. Any assessment necessarily is an intrusion into the daily and weekly work flow. In addition, there are often fantasies that the arrival of the assessor means that the assessor, particularly if he or she is a psychologist, will diagnose people and prescribe treatment for them. The entire tone of the assessment is affected by these fantasies and how they are resolved. Here are some steps the assessor must task to deal with peoples' feelings and expectations to function effectively in the organization.

At the outset, the assessor is in touch with a representative of the organization, preferably the top executive or administrator. The major task of the assessor is to establish a realistic picture of the assessment and an open, positive relationship with this person. The organizational representative must have the opportunity to raise questions at length about the assessment. If the first contact is with the CEO of an organization in which a branch or other kind of subunit is to be assessed, further comparable contact with the division leader or local manager will be necessary. (See Checklist 2.)

Assessors should indicate not only what they want to do, but also why, what risks the host organization runs, and how much time, cost, and effort will be required of the organization. Free give-and-take conversation should lead to a common recognition of the complexity and nebulousness of relevant issues and the realization that completely detailed definition of the steps in the assessment is not possible in the beginning. Discussion of such issues conveys acceptance of this ambiguity and confidence in the likely effectiveness of the assessor's consultation with the organization.

Three points must be made during this initial contact: (a) information about the organization will be held in confidence; (b) confidentiality will be maintained so far as specifics about any individual organization member or group is concerned; (c) the general results of the assessment will be reported to all members of the organization who are part of the assessment, although the exact way of reporting those results is yet to be determined. It becomes the responsibility of the assessor to recognize and deal with the meaning of the consultation to the people involved. An assessment is often seen as a means for headquarters to "spy," and realistic clarification must be made. (See Checklist 3.)

Except in those rare cases where the assessor has agreed to report only to a specific person or group and tells all others that that is the case, it is irresponsible not to provide feedback to people who have allowed themselves to be questioned, observed, or interviewed, because inevitably assessors create expectations on the part of those from whom they seek information. The feedback should be carried to the lowest level employees interviewed

CHECKLIST 2: THE INITIAL PROCESS CONTACT

- With whom did you meet?
- What is his or her power, status, or role in the organization?
- Who else was there? What were their roles?
- What questions did they ask you? How do you understand the meaning of the questions?
- Was this a pro forma interview (to show they were checking out several possible assessors) or a serious evaluation of what you could do?
- How respectful of you and your professional status were they?
- What is the time urgency?
- Are there significant others who were not part of the initial interview?
- Are there differences among the interviewers about the nature of the problem? About seeking assessment? About what kind of consultation?
- Are there sensitive areas, groups, persons, or situations in or associated with the organization that must be treated circumspectly?
- Are there senior executives or board members whose permission must be sought?
- Are there external problems—for example, labor strife, government investigation?
- Have there been other consultants? What kind? When? With what results?
- What did you propose as a first exploration step if you were to get the assignment? For how long? At what fee? With what feedback?
- How did they check your references?
- How did you feel about the interview? About the interviewers?
- What problems did you hypothesize might arise? With whom? Under what circumstances?
- How valid were your initial hypotheses about leadership style?

or questioned, and assessors should have the concurrence of the client that this will be done.

After the preliminary negotiations, it becomes important to familiarize the organizational executive and key associates with the assessor's associates, if any. A face-to-face meeting between such persons and the consulting

```
┌─────────────────────────────────────────────────────────────┐
│  CHECKLIST 3: UNDERTAKING THE ASSESSMENT                      │
│                                                               │
│   ▪ How do you understand the initial contact, as reflected   │
│     in your summary?                                          │
│   ▪ What factual information did you find?                    │
│   ▪ What inferences do you make about the influence of this    │
│     information on the organization? On employees? On          │
│     customers, suppliers, environment?                        │
│   ▪ What is the form of policies and guidelines? In notebooks?  │
│     Bound volumes? Which are posted?                          │
│   ▪ What assumptions about motivation do you infer from these? │
│   ▪ What programs (Zero Defects, TQM, reengineering, 360° feed-│
│     back) were once popular? What happened to them?            │
│   ▪ How contemporary is the organization chart?               │
│   ▪ According to your contact person, how does it jibe with reality? │
│   ▪ Is there a statement of organizational purpose? Vision? Mission? │
│     Strategy? Goals? Objectives?                              │
│   ▪ Are these adequately differentiated or confused? Are they tied │
│     to production, financial, service, or other goals to give them │
│     meaning?                                                  │
└─────────────────────────────────────────────────────────────┘
```

team overcomes the often unrealistic fantasies that the organizational representatives have about the team.

When the concept of the assessment has been accepted, the organizational executive and the assessor should plan how and when the assessment will be introduced to the organization. At this point it is very important to set some limits. The consultant should prepare a letter for the executive to be sent to all organization members, or review a letter that the executive prepares (see appendix B for an example). Failure to do either likely will result in a distorted presentation. The assessor would do well to (a) specify that all persons in the organization who are to be involved in the assessment must have knowledge about the assessment and its aims before the formal work begins; and (b) require that time be allotted for answering questions about the consultation and ensuring all members of the organization about confidentiality. That means oral presentation by the assessor to all organizational units. If interviews are to be tape-recorded, it is important to indicate that fact to prospective interviewees at the outset and also to indicate how confidentiality with respect to the tapes and transcriptions will be maintained. If a written questionnaire like the example in appendix A or some other formal survey instrument is to be used in which those who complete it are identified, explain how the responses will be kept confidential. Usually, employees have little reason to trust the assessor, but it might help to report in which organizations the assessor has worked previously so that anyone who wishes may call someone in that organization. (See Checklists 4 and 5.)

OBTAINING CONSENT

The manager of the unit to be assessed may, in given circumstances, find it difficult to assemble directly all members of the organization who are to be involved to be told about the assessment. In this case, in addition to the written statement, a method should be devised with the help of the client's staff to obtain feedback and questions from managers and supervisors of reactions to the assessment. Where people are scattered widely as in overseas assignments or work at home, specific plans must be worked out with the organization representative for announcements and both interviewing and questionnaires. However, preparation for the assessment is most effective when the assessor has been able to talk to all of the people who are to be involved. This is the ideal situation for which one should strive.

After holding management and supervisory (or their equivalent in nonbusiness organizations) meetings at successively lower echelons, it is useful to make a short presentation of the purpose of the assessment to groups of employees. In large companies, production groups should be seen separately from sales groups, for example, and similarly, different groupings where there are other kinds of distinctive functions unless the organization is too small for such differentiation. Such groupings facilitate questions and discussion. The presentation should include the following elements:

1. There should be a statement that the assessment is being done to learn about organizational processes and problems, not to assess individuals, and that the interviews, conversations, and observations are confidential.
2. It should indicate that management has given approval for the assessment as evidenced by their presence and the confirmatory statement they made in their introduction of the assessor.
3. There should be an explanation of the activities that the assessors will be undertaking. If there is a team, all members should be introduced with short explanations of their professions followed by an explanation of how the team will operate. For example, "Some people will be interviewed, some people will be seen on the job, some will be seen in a group."
4. Emphasis should be placed on the important statement that some people will not be seen (if that is the case), that there

CHECKLIST 4: BEFORE INTRODUCING THE ASSESSMENT

- Did you prepare a letter to all unit participants, or help the accountable executive prepare one, that described the reasons for the assessment, what you (and your associates) will do (the sampling process), what the feedback process will be, and promise confidentiality?
- Did you agree with the accountable executive when to distribute the letter and how (if by computer, closed-circuit TV, written memorandum)? Did you establish a process for presenting the analysis in successive accountable levels to everyone in the unit?
- Did you prepare a formal orientation in your announcement presentation?
- Did you indicate who would or would not be interviewed (not by name but by sampling)?
- Did you reemphasize confidentiality? What the assessment is not?
- Did you indicate that you would clear with supervisors and managers so as not to interfere with work and that you had worked out the sampling procedure with the human resources department?
- Did you indicate how interviews would be recorded? From notes? By tape?
- Did you establish a contact person in the organization who would distribute and collect questionnaires (if they are to be used) or will you do so?
- Did you indicate that those who did not want to be interviewed, if any, need not be?
- Did you inform or get support of any outside persons—for example, labor leaders, political, or regulatory authorities?
- Did you clear with the legal department? The public relations department?

are time limits, and choices will be made on the basis of the assessor's judgment about how he or she might best learn about how this organization functions and how people within it work together.

5. Information should be given about exactly when the assessor or the assessment team will arrive and how long they will stay. After this presentation, time should be allowed for questions, which usually take about 15 minutes.

CHECKLIST 5: INTRODUCING THE ASSESSMENT

- Did you (in conjunction with the appropriate human resources person) develop an order of presentation (steps)?
- Did you (in conjunction with the appropriate human resources person) develop a sampling plan and schedule of presentation?
- Did you inform and explain to the editor of the in-house newspaper or magazine? And set up a question-and-answer in it?
- Who from management accompanied you? To all shifts?
- Did you complete the personal announcement process in a timely manner?
- What kind of reception from whom? How? At different levels? In different units, functions, activities?
- What worries did they express (confidentiality, downsizing)?
- What questions did they ask (feedback, when, how, to whom)?
- How did you feel about the introduction process?
- What kinds of countertransference (one's feelings about the client may figure in the way one assesses things) attitudes arose?
- What physical differences were there in the various locations?
- What sociological differences were evident?

If the person through whom one enters an organization is responsible to a board or higher level management, it is important to be certain that those levels understand what is being done in the organization and have authorized it. This protects both the assessor and the contact. This means that the assessor must obtain clearance from union officials (if there are any). Work group meetings, particularly, must have time for questions and discussion, especially to make clear the limits of the assessment. The assessor must explain that this assessment does not involve their family or home life. (If one were to wish to examine those aspects of living, one would be unlikely to do so through the place of employment.)

If the problem is limited (e.g., conflict among members of top management), this procedure need not be followed in such detail. However, where practical and possible, to forestall rumors, it is good practice to inform lower level supervisors what the assessor is doing in the organization. Far better to allay unnecessary concern. Even if one is not in a position to offer more than generalities about what one is doing, such a statement, plus the opportunity to meet the assessor, relieves much concern.

If, in the assessment, a person may have no choice about whether he or she is designated to be interviewed, that should be made clear, but the degree to which the informant is willing to cooperate is something the informant can control. It is important for the assessor to understand that informants can dry up in subtle ways if they do not trust the assessor. People easily can answer questionnaires falsely or otherwise make them useless.

One of the major advantages of carrying the introductory and permission-seeking processes down through the organization is that it gives the assessor an opportunity to evaluate the kind of reception he or she is likely to get at different places in the organization. It is particularly important for the assessor to understand resistances or negative feelings toward the assessment and why they occur. The assessor then can bring the feelings to the surface, discuss the reasons for them, and, ideally, dispel them. No matter how warm the welcome, there are always negative feelings in a consulting relationship. No one likes to be scrutinized. Many people are likely to feel threatened. Such feelings cannot be wished away or ignored.

Some of the resistances or negative feelings can be sensed once the presentation is made to a group. Some, fearful and threatened, might wonder how the assessor could begin to understand what working in this organization is like without working there. Others, recalling previous unfavorable experiences with consultants, would like to escape from the possible questions and examination. Skeptics might question whether the findings might lead to significant action. Still others, caring less about the organization itself, might be more concerned about their own problem-solving efforts.

The assessor can infer from the questions asked, and the metaphors used in the asking, what kinds of difficulties he or she is likely to have when, where, and with whom. From the beginning, the assessor also will have some clues to the kinds of organizational problems he or she is likely to discover.

In the name of scientific objectivity, some consultants prefer to ignore such matters. Pure objectivity or detachment is impossible in the behavioral sciences. There is a significant literature on the impact of the consultant on the results. Better to recognize this problem and take it into account than to ignore it or pretend that it does not exist. A measure of objectivity can be obtained by having interviews coded by judges or using other similar efforts if that is necessary. However, I think it wiser for the assessor to evaluate continuously the effects of his or her own behavior and to respond to people as human beings.

THE INITIAL TOUR

Sometime during the entering process, and in a large organization many times during the contacts with various work groups, the assessor (and the team) will be taken on a tour of the physical facilities. In this way, the guides can show their organization, asking and answering questions of the team members, and in the process, get to know them better as the assessors demonstrate interest and understanding and provide a sample of how they will behave in the organization. If the assessor is not invited to tour (and that is a datum, too), the assessor should ask to be shown about. This is done not only to become familiar with the various work areas and to obtain a general idea of the work processes and work flow, but also to form some initial psychological impressions of the organization. These will include impressions of the building and work sites, attitudes of the guides and others the consultant meets, the way he or she is received, what things he or she is shown, what is omitted, and similar issues. (See Checklist 6.)

The assessor's impressions are critical ones. Assessors must attune themselves to their own subtle feelings as they go along because these reflect the impact of various environmental stimuli. Others are likely to be affected in the same way, but because the stimuli may be fleeting or sensed subliminally, their impact may not be understood.

It is important that the assessor note even hazy impressions immediately as they occur or the assessor will lose considerable data. Inasmuch as the assessor is his or her own most important instrument, the assessor should begin on tour to use his or her own antennae for sensing subtleties.

CHECKLIST 6: APPROACHING THE ORGANIZATION

- What did you see on tour?
- What were your first feelings about the organization, the setting?
- What occurred on the tour that made you feel good, bad, indifferent?
- What public information is available about the organization? Its history? Its executives?
- What is its track record or reputation?
- How rapidly does it pay its bills?
- If it is not publicly held, what sources of information are there?
- What was your immediate feeling about the plant, office, store, other facility?
- What impact did the physical structure have on you? The location? Furnishings?
- What impact might the physical structure have on the people who work there?
- What hypotheses did you form about the management or leadership style?
- What were the attitudes of the receptionist or other persons who received you?
- How promptly was your appointment kept?

For example, in one factory a worker deliberately flicked a small glob of grease at the assessor who was being conducted on an initial tour. Because the tour was being conducted by a member of management, one might hypothesize feelings of hostility between the workers and management.

On tour, the assessor should keep a careful eye out for slogans, bulletin boards, display cases, and other forms of communication, all of which are indicative of what the organization is emphasizing and how it does so. The assessor should also note how the buildings and grounds are kept, where different groups eat, coffee break locations and facilities, points of informal gathering, modes of receiving visitors, parking, transportation, kinds of magazines in reception rooms and offices, and similar cues about the organization. These cues offer the assessor the opportunity to formulate hypotheses about some of the issues he or she is likely to encounter in the organization. The assessor then can follow them up in the formal assessment. (See Checklist 7.)

Assessors will find it helpful to keep a diary of their experiences in the organization, to record events and observations that likely will not be reported in interviews or questionnaires. If assessors keep such a record of the process of their relationship to the organization, they will be able to trace the consulting relationship from beginning to end. The diary should include notes of the tour.

The guided tour is one way to be introduced to a number of the settings. If the person in charge of these settings conducts the tour, that individual can introduce the assessor to his or her key subordinates at various levels, and probably will give a version of current problems in each area along the way. The person conducting the tour is likely to know the reasons why general procedures are what they are. The individual can describe relationships with other settings in the organization and is likely to communicate which setting functions are of greater or lesser importance to him or her and to the organization, trouble spots, new ventures and so on. While hearing about these matters, the assessor already should be asking him- or herself how this person's view may fit with others in the setting.

The orientation of the manager- or supervisor-guide to the people in the setting merits special attention inasmuch as that person is in such a strategic position to affect their experiences. Does the guide focus on people primarily, or does the guide give his or her attention to the functions and processes they carry out? Are people, when referred to, described primarily as problems or resources in the setting? If one observes a crisis—a workplace injury or software breakdown—or someone approaching the supervisor with a special question, how does the supervisor react and what are its implications? One may find considerable consistency in the supervisor's reactions. Perhaps he or she takes a teaching position in all such interactions. Perhaps the supervisor expresses disgust by manner, facial expression, or what he or

CHECKLIST 7: THE INITIAL TOUR

- Who took you where? How well did your guide explain organizational details, as well as what you were looking at? How enthusiastic was he or she? What did he or she emphasize? Ignore?
- Who reacted to your guide? Where?
- Who reacted to you? Where?
- What aroused your feelings (positive or negative)? Where?
- What stimulated new hypotheses about the organization's problems? Strengths?
- What messages did you see on the bulletin boards? The hallways? The walls? Showcases?
- What were the restrooms like? Food services? Lockers?
- Who wore what kinds of uniforms? What did you observe about cleanliness, sanitation?
- What equipment did people use in their various settings? How does work flow?
- What about safety, lighting, environmental pollution, parking, transportation to and from work, condition of buildings and grounds?
- What services and facilities are there for babysitting, child care, elder support?
- What training facilities are there? Shopping facilities? Service facilities (check cashing, barber and beauty shop, post office)?
- How much privacy is there for which people (e.g., offices, work stations)?

she says, feeling that people should not bother him or her with these things or that such occurrences reflect their excessive dependence on the supervisor. All such observations must be correlated because they aid the assessor in understanding the nature of experiences that people probably have as they interact with this person in authority.

Several types of phenomena to which the assessor should be alert are possible during the tour:

1. How interested is the manager–guide in showing the assessor around? Is the manager–guide actually bored with what he or she shows the visitor or is he or she involved in helping the assessor understand these important elements of the organization?

2. What particular facets of the setting does the guide emphasize: the people, the product, the processes, the services performed, the history of the organization?

3. How do people appear to the assessor? Are they tense or relaxed, hurried or casual? Do they seem confident in what they are doing or harassed and uncertain, "running to catch up"? What is the quality of interactions between the manager–guide and his or her subordinates? Does the manager seem to see people as resources or problems? Does he or she have a differentiated view of them or are they merely a mass that populate the area? How does the guide approach them as they are introduced (or are they)? How do they react to the manager and the assessor? Do they put on a good show of working hard? Do they ignore both the manager and the assessor? Do they look fearful? Do they seem to welcome the contact?

4. What crises occur during the tour? Does something go wrong? How is it handled? Do people bring problems to the manager? How does he or she respond? What kinds of situations arise that require people to divert attention from orienting the assessor to taking care of regular work?

5. During the guided tour, the assessor pays attention to the uses of space within the total territory inhabited by the organization. The territory includes office, factory and warehouse buildings, the space between and around them, and the floor area within them, or similar facilities in nonbusiness organizations. It is also important on the guided tour to learn about the distribution of people and equipment or other physical facilities over the various areas and the activities taking place in various sectors of each area. This will lead to the preliminary catalogue of settings and work roles that subsequently might be sampled.

II

ORGANIZATIONAL ASSESSMENT PROCESS

5

THE ASSESSMENT PROCEDURE

The formal assessment procedure usually involves several steps: (a) a breakdown of the organization or unit to be studied into its component parts; (b) the planning of a sample of interviewees to be representative of those parts or of the organization as a whole, including careful attention to leadership; (c) if the number of employees is large enough, a supplementary sample of people to be questioned by printed form; (d) observations of people at work; (e) an examination of already available records and relevant data; (f) and interviews with persons important outside the organization. The last may include former employees, others in the community who know the organization, competitors, suppliers, and other similarly informed people, or external staff of the parent if a unit or an organization is being assessed. The assessor may not know who the relevant others are until the assessment is under way. The six steps outlined may not always be taken in sequential order because much will depend on geographical proximity, seasonal pressures, and the results of periods of observation that the assessor undertakes.

RELATING TO THE ORGANIZATION

As already indicated, an assessment study involves relating to an "organization." But what does that mean? One does not relate to an organization except as one relates to people in it, and particularly to the management. These people may be representative of a group or class of employees. In many of his or her interactions in an organization, an assessor speaks with more than one person at a time. The organization has subdivisions that are psychologically distinct for the members of the organization. For instance, an assessor may be working with a member of the sales department. The sales department setting is the dominant reality for those who work in that area. The assessor is not at that moment relating to the organization as a whole and thus must recognize the sectors of the organization that are most significant psychologically to each person and group seen. Such awareness minimizes disruption of the boundaries of the organization and permits respect for the feelings of people about such issues as who should be talked to, who first, and why.

In some cases, teams of people cut across functional boundaries. Yet individual team members are accountable to their functional superiors. The assessor should learn how accountabilities are defined and what issues of integration they pose.

The assessor will be treated in many different ways. Sometimes assessors are perceived as evaluators who judge instantaneously the innermost competencies of people. They may be the "unwelcome guests," or may be sought as heroes, allies that are needed to give "management" or "the workers" the right point of view, or as punishers, or as rewarders. (These perceptions often suggest the kinds of relationships people experience with one another in the organization.) The assessors' approach must be one of reassurance and support. Yet they may have to move into sensitive areas that are important for understanding the feelings and behavior of people.

An organization is composed of persons in authority and peers or "siblings" who are accountable to these authorities. Each setting within the organization has some favored or disfavored position with respect to key figures. Personnel in each setting have a message to send to the CEO. This will include some words of affection and some of hostility. Each member of a setting tries to obtain some reaction from the assessor that will indicate the assessor's views or stance and how the setting stands in the assessor's eyes—for example, "New product development is having it very hard," or "This is one of the best sales divisions." It is tempting for assessors to begin a conversation by mentioning what they have observed in their earlier contacts. The content of assessors' remarks and the tone conveyed can very easily influence what is then learned. For example, if an assessor says, "New product people are really having a difficult time," to a member of sales who feels that they are not, or to other teachers, "The special ed teachers don't get enough resources," the assessor communicates that he or she has already taken a stand in the organization. This may, in fact, prevent the person in sales from talking about some of the difficulties sales personnel have in dealing with those same new product staff. The same is true of the teachers. Furthermore, such evaluative statements have considerable potentially destructive impact on people. Employees (even if they are called associates) read a great deal into such statements and often project their fears in their interpretations of what they hear. Assessors must exert care to avoid encouraging such distortions, however tempting it may be to show that they are "in the know." This temptation is extremely hard to resist, but failure to resist will be costly.

Assessors do not have the comfort of their own offices during fieldwork. Assessors may be given a space, but it is "borrowed." Sometimes, for long periods of times, assessors will be moving from relationship to relationship and imbedded in the organizational process. They cannot withdraw for an extended period and examine what has taken place. They are learning not only about the feelings, thoughts, and behaviors of other people but also altering their own behavior in response to others. In the uncertain situation of assessment, in which next steps are not always clear, some adaptive resolution of an assessor's anxiety may take place without recognition of just what he or she has done to adapt until reviewing diary notes.

Assessors also need inclusion in the organizational life. In a sense, they wish to "belong." Assessors need some affectional interchange; they want to be liked, accepted, recognized. But they need to have control over the situation insofar as they are seeking information from people, and they need to have this information before leaving the setting. Too often, the assessor, trying to "be a nice person," may not ask questions to which he or she needs to know the answers and leaves the field without the information necessary to evaluate the situation.

Assessors must remember that the members of the organization have some idea of what assessors need to know to understand their work situation. The members of the organization will respect assessors more if they can maintain some distance and sustain interest in more and valid information, rather than giving all their energy to winning them over. Assessors must recognize and control their own behavior and preoccupations. If assessors adopt the favored style of an organization without being aware of it (e.g., passive compliance, interpersonal bantering), they may forget that this style is a quality of the organization.

One other consideration: Every organization must have a "back room." There are some secrets that are part of organizational life but not readily accessible. To understand what is happening in an organization often involves a problem of judging, for example, whether one should gather the personal history of a key executive who had a major personality disturbance or whether to permit a confession about a shady company transaction at a given time. The goals of the assessment must be kept in mind. One certainly should not go into exploration ventures aimed at getting intimate, sexy, or dramatic information, except as these bear on and contribute to assessment goals. And sometimes these must be avoided, even if they would contribute substantially, if the assessor will not have the time or opportunity to deal constructively with the anxiety that revealing such information provokes in people. For example, suppose the assessor learns in the course of interviewing an employee that the employee's boss is embezzling funds. What is the assessor's responsibility to the organization? To the employee? If he or she encourages the employee to talk, the assessor must be prepared to help the employee deal with both the reality and his or her feelings about telling or not telling.

Because all organizations increasingly have become technical, assessors should ask themselves, What do I *really* know about the technology in use here and, particularly its potential to affect positive changes in the organization? Can I comfortably ask the necessary technology-related questions? Is there a reliable source in the organization who will provide me with technology-related assistance when needed? If not, assessors may have to seek such a source outside of the organization.

FACTUAL DATA

Every organization has at least some of its policies and procedures on paper. Too many formal policies suggest rigidity and overcontrol; too few may give rise to inconsistent, conflictual, or chaotic behavior. Some have historical data on file. All have financial reports or records. (See Checklist 8.) Most have annual reports. Many have job descriptions, personnel statistics, and assessors' reports. They should become acquainted with what is on paper and develop a perspective on how it all fits together. In some instances the assessor will be the only person who has ever thought of these data as being interrelated. Usually the assessor will be the first to think of their collective import for the organization. The assessor must therefore be particularly alert to the language of these materials. Implicit in both the kind of written materials and the language used in them are attitudes toward the people who are to be governed by them and assumptions about what motivates people.

Every policy and every practice implicitly carries some assumptions about motivation because each intends people to behave in certain ways. Much of the time these hidden assumptions have dubious validity. An example is a safety program that includes publishing on the bulletin boards or in a company newsletter people who had on-the-job accidents on the assumption that people will not want their names published and therefore will avoid having accidents. Performance appraisal systems, Management by Objectives, Zero Defects, and similar programs implicitly assume that pressure and judgment by superior or subordinate are important devices for motivation and may imply a carrot-and-stick philosophy. Incentive compensation systems put heavy weight on money as motivator. Paternalistic orientations count on people to be motivated out of loyalty and guilt. Management rarely examines their psychological assumptions. More often they become angry when their practices do not work well and attribute the failure to the negativism of their employees.

> ### CHECKLIST 8: HOW IS THE ORGANIZATION FINANCED?
>
> - If nonprofit, is it registered with state authorities for public examination?
> - Is it dependent on campaigns or big givers?
> - If campaigns, are they conducted by the organization or by paid consultants?
> - If by paid consultants, what percentage of the take do they get?
> - If big givers, who are they and what is their influence?
> - If educational organizations, how influential are alumni and what are their emphases—for example, how the alumni focuses on the organization (football vs. scholarships)?
> - If churches or religious organizations, how are new membership campaigns conducted?
> - With what success and what trends?
> - How does it compare with similar organizations?
> - If a business organization, publicly held, what is its MVA record?
> - How much stock? Which kinds, bonds, reserved for employees?
> - What do stock brokerage flyers say about this company? Business journals?
> - How rapidly does it pay its bills?

OUTSIDE INFORMATION

All organizations have relationships outside themselves—with competitors, suppliers, cooperating organizations, agents, professional associations, and so on. The assessor will find it useful to understand how the organization looks to these respective publics and should arrange interviews with their representatives, with the permission of the client. In these interviews assessors should indicate that they are trying to help the client and would like to understand how the outsiders view the organization and its operations. These perspectives will enable assessors to understand how the client organization operates and what impact it has on others. Again, they may be the only ones who have ever thought of these issues not in narrowing marketing terms but in terms of the way the organization adapts to its competitive environment.

There are a number of ways, in addition to interviewing, to get such information. Many newspapers have morgues or files by subject. Historical societies often have much information on file. Large organizations frequently will be the subject of articles in trade or professional magazines that may be located through libraries. Some will be available on the Internet or other online databases. Organizations, of course, vary in the amount of information available about them. The sheer availability of various kinds of information is a datum of diagnostic value.

PATTERN OF ORGANIZATION

Assessors should remember that they are undertaking a holistic approach to the organization, interested in understanding the whole system rather than the interaction of one or two forces. I raise this caution because, as discussed in the next steps, it will be easy for assessors to become preoccupied with parts of an organization.

Almost all organizations have some form of organization chart or plan that defines accountabilities. (See Jaques, 1996, 2001, for problems in accountability.) Assessors should obtain an organization chart from the person who is the major contact. However, they should not take the organization chart to represent the way the organization actually operates. Frequently the organization chart is not up to date. Sometimes it has not been distributed. It is not unusual for working relationships to grow up informally that may vary from what the organizational leadership intends, particularly if an organizational chart has not been published. Then, too, the informal organization, or the way the business of the organization actually gets done, may vary considerably from the way it is *supposed* to be done.

The assessor will find it informative to ask different people in the organization to draw an organization chart and to compare these with what the assessor has been given. The assessor will also find it helpful to know from each informant to whom the informant feels responsible, for what, whether on the chart or not, and how this individual is evaluated by whom. This will help the assessor round out the pattern of organization. If the organization chart is secret information, or if no chart exists, problems of leadership may be of special significance. Members of the organization may struggle with questions of legitimate and illegitimate authority, as given in the example in appendix B.

An early overall description of the organization must include enough detail about its internal structure and activities to guide the direction and depth of later stages of the assessment. The principal methods for accomplishing this early objective are the guided tour, already discussed, and interviews with informants. With respect to the latter, most organizations have workers, often in insignificant roles, who have been around a long time and have much to report on the history and evolution of the organization during their tenure. The assessor should seek out such informants.

PLAN OF THE ASSESSMENT

From the initial mapping of the organization and early impressions, the general plan of the assessment is developed, to be modified on the basis of later observations. If more than one assessor is involved, this will require later coordination of results. A balance will have to be established between overlap of coverage for cross-checks and independent observations and activities for purposes of broad coverage. Enough flexibility should be built into the general plan so that the information to be forthcoming can be implemented in planning successive steps.

Some settings and subsettings will receive more intensive attention. These should include all settings with large populations or having central functions that are particularly indispensable to the accomplishment of the organization's basic activities. (For contrasting discussion of boundaries, see Hirschorn, 1990; Sherman, 1998.)

Although every setting is in some sense indispensable to accomplish organizational goals, there are clear priorities. In a production organization it would be essential to analyze intensively the various manufacturing settings, the management function, and probably some of the office settings. If the organization is engaged in the sale of its products, the sales settings would also be selected for intensive analysis. And those particular production, sales, and office settings that had most members and were mentioned most frequently in the descriptions heard during the guided tour should get most intensive analysis. Cues such as these make it easier to decide which settings are indispensable to accomplish organizational purposes and which are heavily dependent on sources outside of the organization or on corporate employees or on customers or suppliers.

Assessors will then have to arrange interviewing and administering questionnaires so that they can be certain to have a representative sample of the organization. Assessors should interview all of the top management group, however that is defined; the heads of each of the major functional groups to be covered; and randomly selected members of each of those functional groups. I prefer a 10% sample of middle-management and a 5% sample of line employees, and I am sure to interview specialists such as the single chemist in an electric power plant, and representative people on all shifts. The senior human relations person usually is helpful in mapping the larger organizational terrain. The immediate manager of a unit must be consulted to avoid disrupting the work of that unit by arbitrarily choosing interviewees.

The remaining members of each of the groups may be sampled by questionnaire. Questionnaires should be administered in groups as soon as possible after entering the organization, ideally before the formal interviewing, and they should be collected immediately on completion. This prevents contamination of the replies and provides data to be pursued in interviews and observations. Samples of an interview schedule and questionnaires are in the appendixes. However, the assessor may use whatever forms he or she chooses.

The number of people to be interviewed will depend on how much time the assessor has and the cost. The assessor should allow between and hour and a half and two hours with people at the senior executive level and informants outside the organization (sometimes more time may be necessary), and at least an hour with those below that level. I find it easier to make notes during the interview and to dictate a comprehensive summary after each than to tape-record the interviews. Transcription from tape recordings takes at least four times as much time as the interview itself. There is considerable repetition in a series of interviews in the same organization, and often much of it is incidental to the purposes at hand.

The assessor will have to make appropriate adaptations in organizations that do not follow the usual organization chart pattern. A school will involve students and teachers, as well as administrators. A hospital may have visiting staff who are not employed by it and are not part of its managerial accountability hierarchy. Healthcare organizations are involved in complex networks of relationships with insurance companies, HMOs, group practices, and affiliate networks, as well as government bodies. (See Checklist 9.)

APPROACH TO THE SETTING AND ITS INCUMBENTS

For administrative reasons and effective functioning, the assessor should move into a setting in steps suggested by the persons with formal authority: successive introductions from top executives through intermediate management and supervisory personnel to the line personnel. Unless this is done, people at each level are uncertain about the legitimacy of their spending time with the assessor.

The assessor may find it easy or difficult to enter a setting for general contacts or detailed observations and interviews. The assessor may find that the detailed observation he or she wishes to make is strenuously resisted either by all the persons in the setting or those in the setting with formal authority who must be seen in any case so that the request to enter the setting be honored. Whether a setting is difficult or easy to enter is an important datum in itself, because this often tells the assessor something about the way in which people in the setting see themselves or are seen by other parts of the organization. It will also tell something about the personality and favored working style of the key figure in the setting. The assessor may find, for example, that outsiders are barred from a certain setting because

> ## CHECKLIST 9: THE PRELIMINARY INVESTIGATION
>
> - Who did you choose to interview? Why? With what results?
> - What feelings did you encounter? What resistances?
> - What initial hypotheses did you confirm or reject?
> - Did you feel ready to prepare a formal proposal or should you get more data?
> - Did you develop a formal proposal? For the whole assessment? In what steps? With what budget? Time boundaries? Introduction and feedback steps?
> - What did you report to the contact person or group?
> - What did you recommend?
> - How many people (all) in top management are to be interviewed?
> - How many people (10%) in middle management are to be interviewed?
> - How many people (5%) among line workers are to be interviewed?
> - How many people were individual contributors or unique specialists?
> - How many board members, outside influentials (labor leaders, politicians?) are to be interviewed?
> - How much transportation time will be required?
> - How much scoring time, cost, integration time for questionnaires?
> - How much time for studying corporate documents?
> - How much time for visiting plants, offices, outposts? Team meetings?
> - How much is to be allocated for travel and subsistence costs?
> - Is there to be a cushion for unexpected costs (like additional interviews for political reasons)?

it is a "secret" area in the organization. There may be objective reasons for this: Activities there may involve confidential relationships to customers or classified military information. Or people in the setting may be preoccupied with a serious organizational problem that cannot be revealed to the assessor until greater trust has been established.

The analogy to other forms of interpersonal relationships is obvious: Even among friends, when one friend asks another about issues that are sensitive to the other, the latter may avoid or deny what he or she is sensitive about, or even may become angry and hostile. Similar psychological processes may be operating in the organizational situation when the assessor is denied access to certain settings or activities for reasons that may not be apparent.

The practical question is, What is to be done when access to a setting is difficult or denied? Usually this will occur in the initial contact with the person or people in formal authority in that setting. It is helpful at this point for the assessor to communicate that he or she accepts the fact that there is no time to cater to him or her at the moment. But the assessor should also communicate that he or she would like to understand this lack of time if not at the moment, then when it is more convenient, because it helps him or her understand work in this setting.

The general tone of this approach by the assessor is to invite those in the setting to work with him or her on understanding this problem, even if it is appropriate for the assessor to leave the setting temporarily and come back at a more convenient time. In any case, the assessor should attempt to establish a collaborative relationship rather than an exploitative one. Often resistance is mobilized because the assessor is seen as allied with top management against lower levels. The assessor can grant that he or she has been able to penetrate this far into the organization only because management has allowed it. However, the assessor can demonstrate that his or her orientation is not to get answers that will be used against people by management but as an independent professional functioning with the agreement of management to learn and to understand for constructive purposes.

To allay such anxiety, I have found it helpful to invite skeptics to call anyone they might know in any of several organizations with which I have previously consulted. They might not know anyone in any of those organizations but the fact that I have invited them to do so often assuages their worry. If the assessor has extended such an invitation early in the assessment when questionnaires are distributed, repetition of the invitation now in a face-to-face circumstance reinforces the assessor's position.

In undertaking interviews, the assessor should remember that the interview has much more psychological meaning to the interviewee than is likely to be apparent. Both parties to the interview have to consider not only their relationship with each other but also their different relationships to the organizations in which they work. The interviewee will want to state what he or she has to say in his own way and at the same time to avoid being shown up. The interviewee needs to maintain his position in the organization and his self-esteem after the assessor is gone. The assessor needs to satisfy his or her own organization (whether a consulting firm or a group of colleagues), the client, and him- or herself. But the assessor cannot let the pressure to satisfy his or her needs result in exploiting the interviewee. Thus, the assessor must listen and observe, letting the interviewee generate and give information that helps the assessor understand how the interviewee experiences the organization and his or her work life.

Assessors should precede each interview by introducing themselves to the interviewee, asking the interviewee how he or she understands the purpose of the interview, restating the purposes of the assessment, emphasizing its confidential nature, and if that is the case, indicating to the respondent that he or she need not be interviewed if he or she does not wish to be. Before asking groups of employees to complete the organizational and job attitude inventory (appendix A), after introducing him- or herself, restating the purposes of the assessment and its confidentiality, the assessor should invite questions and extend the same invitation to call people in other organizations to check on the assessor. Even if a clear description has been given in the letter to all employees and in the public presentation, most people will remain hazy about the intent and purpose. Some will have heard rumors that need to be corrected. The assessor should not take for granted the respondent's understanding, no matter how often the assessor has indicated publicly the nature of his or her work in the organization. When the interview is completed, the assessor should permit the respondent to ask any questions to further clarify the assessor's function. Often individual interviewees will ask if their answers are like the replies of other respondents. This usually is a question to test the interviewer. The assessor should repeat that inasmuch as the interviews are confidential, the interviewer cannot disclose what other individuals have said, but sometimes the assessor can offer a general response that satisfies the questioner but does not reject the questioner or his or her questions.

The assessor should indicate to the interviewee that each interview will be examined along with others and that a summary of the assessment will be reported to the organization as a whole, if that is the case. The assessor should indicate the same to groups to whom he or she is administering questionnaires.

OBSERVATION AND ON-THE-JOB CONTACTS

One of the major problems with organization assessors is that they depend too much on interview and questionnaire data. Too few observe the actual processes of work, workflow, communications, and work relationships (Kotter, 1998; Mintzberg, 1973). The on-the-job contact is a way of ascertaining how a person feels about the work situation while the employee is in the work setting.

I prefer to spend as much time as I can observing these events by being on site, asking people to explain to me what they do, how they do it, and the problems inherent in getting their work done. This may involve sitting in executive offices or keeping notes on the events of the day or walking from machine to machine or attending various kinds of meetings (including those for distributors, salespeople, outside visitors, boards of directors) or sitting in on training and orientation programs. On the plant floor, if that is the work site, I prefer to bring my lunch bucket to be able to take coffee breaks and lunch with the employees.

On both the plant floor and out in the field, such as riding in the trucks of a public utility company, the assessor should wear clothes appropriate to the setting. On the floor, a gray work smock is sufficient; he or she need not wear overalls. Nor need he or she pretend to be "one of the guys." Employees will know that the assessor is not one of them, so pretense will only offend them. The assessor's interest in their work and the problems related to it will generate confidence and the assessor will learn much informally. The assessor will find it helpful for later analysis to sketch the layout of the work site and the points at which people congregate for coffee or lunch and to note who goes with whom and what the various topics of conversation are.

When and where possible, if I am interviewing in a work setting or observing the work process, I ask the interviewee to show me what he or she does if that requires some form of equipment. If safe and convenient, sometimes I ask for permission to try doing the work. That gives me a sense of how it feels to the person who must do so repetitively and also demonstrates further my interest in his or her work.

In one plant of a company that made farm implements, a group of workers, most of whom also farmed nearby, gathered around a radio at lunch to listen to the conservative commentator Paul Harvey. It did not take great sophistication for the assessor to grasp the political bent of these workers. Later, in the context of the rest of the assessment, as outlined in chapters 8 and 9, the assessor could infer the relevance of this orientation to his or her understanding of the organization.

The assessor's sketches and accompanying notes will give a picture of the organization as a combination of interdependent behavioral settings. Also the assessor will observe readily the required role performances, the work to be done, and the nonrole performances. In addition, the assessor will also observe how authority figures function and how people relate to them.

Often assessors will be asked about themselves and their work, which will give assessors an opportunity for further explanation. And they need not be afraid of entering the conversation on noncompany topics like baseball or cultural events. In smaller organizations I have found it helpful to visit the plant floor regularly. In some instances I also have found it helpful to explain to visiting guests, such as distributors or executive candidates, what the assessment is all about if I am asked to do so by the management.

There are no simple rules for initiating contact and conversation on the job. "How long have you worked here?" can provide an easy start for someone because the answer is simple and it refers to the past, which is generally less threatening than the present. Such a question leads naturally into such things as, What led you to work here in particular? or, What had you expected this place to be like? Such questions often will stimulate expression of attitudes about the setting. What do you do? or, How do you spend your time? often is an incisive way to enter into the area of the person's functions and skills. Variations of this are necessary when one is in the work setting with the person. Even though the functions seem clear, it is best to hear the other's description. If nothing is mentioned about other people, it is important to note this and to ask, "How does your work fit in with the others around here?" or "I noticed that somebody comes by every once in a while. Why does he do that?" If the assessor notices a look of chagrin or pleasure following such an incident, he or she should ask the person, "What happened then?" The most important principle is that of digging deeper, particularly in finding out about sources of feelings that are observable. "What's wrong?" or "That seemed to come out well," are comments usually worth more than those that provoke merely factual information.

Observe different levels of comfort in dealing with the assessor. Perhaps, for example, only a small proportion of people in a setting may look the assessor in the eye when speaking. The assessor then must ask him- or herself why the others do not and learn more about this phenomenon. Are those people in this setting ashamed? Angry? Fearful? Of what?

Note how work is initiated and terminated. There may be a rush from the job at break time and heavy sighs of relief. As a supervisor passes, one may see a subordinate gritting teeth or turning to a coworker and saying something that leads the other to laugh. The assessor must keep his or her attention sufficiently dispersed to understand interpersonal relations that occur "naturally." (See Checklist 10.)

An assessor should look for experiences that appear stressful to people. What kinds of occurrences disrupt or disorganize people and lead them to seek help? What situations stimulate worry? Although one can and should ask about these, there are many opportunities to observe them in everyday life on the job. For example, when something dramatic occurs that is visible to all of the people in a setting, the assessor should scan the setting to assess reactions. If, for instance, an assembly line is shut down or breaks down frequently, that may not be as disruptive as it might seem. People might welcome the respite. Do people help get it started or do they evidence relief

CHECKLIST 10: ON-SITE CONTACT

- What processes did you observe? For how long?
- Did you try to operate any of the equipment? Which?
- What influence did the task requirements have on the feelings of the employees?
- What influence did the task requirements have on your feelings? The setting as a whole?
- Are there special clothing and required equipment? What effect do they have?
- Are there informal groups at breaks and meals? Who goes where? What do they talk about?
- How does the supervisor or manager manage? How do the employees respond to that style of management?
- Are there problems of resources? Maintenance? Supplies? Material? Equipment? What effect do these problems have on people? On efficiency? Quality? Profitability?
- What did the setting participants ask you?
- What do they think about themselves for doing this function? (Appendages? Servants? Prime movers? Innovators? Rescuers?)
- Are there time clocks? Buzzers for breaks and meals?
- What happens when these signal breaks in the work process?
- What do they worry about? Quantity? Quality? Pay? Danger?
- How much control do they have about what goes on in the setting?
- How are new people oriented? Trained? Integrated?
- How do others outside of the setting look on it?
- Who are the informal leaders?
- What is the prevailing tone or mood?
- What happens to people who do not conform?
- Were there significant episodes? About what?
- What processes have been introduced (Total Quality Management? Zero Defects? Leaderless groups? Sociotechnical systems? Scanlon Plan? Gainsharing? 360° Feedback? Others?) With what success? What problems?
- What training has been provided for which of these processes?
- How do which people feel about what innovations?
- What kinds of resistances did you encounter? Where?

and wait for others to solve the problem? Do supervisors move in smoothly and calmly or do they become peremptory with the person(s) involved? In the office situation, what occurs when a new person comes into the setting on business? Who handles him or her? What do the others do while such a transaction occurs? What do persons in and out of a setting say about those who work in that setting? Is background information necessary to a fuller comprehension of usual or characteristic setting experiences? Which are the persons most talked about? Which are favored and disfavored? What kinds of personal characteristics and work characteristics tend to be the focus of conversation?

How can conditions of observation be sufficiently standardized to permit later comparisons? Work roles differ enormously in the activities they require and the time spans necessary to accomplish any given activity. Continuous observation over an indefinitely long time span would be the only way to be assured of getting "the whole story" of work role requirements confronting a given person, and that obviously is impossible. On the other hand, brief time spans for observation probably will yield an unrepresentative sample of activities in a given role, because behaviors conforming to some role requirements may occur too infrequently to fall within the observation period. A minimum of two hours of work activity should be observed to provide a reasonable opportunity for a satisfactory sample. (See Checklist 11.)

DISPERSED SETTINGS

In these days of sometimes widely distributed work groups, especially among managers who may be reporting to superiors halfway around the world, it may be too expensive or time-consuming to interview all the members of such groups face to face. In that case, the assessor would have to do so in an expedient manner, interviewing when they meet as a group or by telephone or even e-mail discussion. In those instances, the assessor would have to ask the interviewees to describe where they work and how they go about maintaining contact with their peers and superiors, as well as the special problems created by distance. (See Black & Gregersen, 1999; Maruca, 1988; Townsend, DeMarie, & Hendrickson, 1998.) There may be particular problems of work in foreign countries, feelings about supervising foreign nationals or being managed by them, being "forgotten" by higher management (especially if there are no plans for integrated return to the United States). There are also likely to be problems of creating and sustaining a team of dispersed members and communicating in the absence of face-to-face contact. Because the heavy emphasis is likely to be on telephone contacts or e-mail, superiors must be particularly sensitive to the tone of

> **CHECKLIST 11: ASSESSING THE SETTING**
>
> - Did people enjoy leaving the job to talk with the assessor? How did they break off the interview when or if they were called by their supervisor?
> - Did people go into some detail in explaining their jobs or did they brush over what they do? Did they feel their work is a sufficiently important aspect of what goes on in the setting and organization that they feel the assessor should know it well?
> - What are difficult, frustrating, or trying aspects of the job? Which are most gratifying?
> - Can and do people resolve many of these difficulties themselves? From whom do they get support or technical help?
> - Do they feel comfortable calling on others for help?
> - What other people are mentioned during the conversation? Which are viewed positively and negatively and why?
> - In the total contact, does the person focus primarily on his or her job, the setting, or the organization as a whole?
> - How much focus is there on the purposes served by his or her activities?
> - Does he or she see him- or herself as a specialist with considerable skill or as doing something that anyone can do?

voice and to the nuances of feelings in the voices of their reports and the tone and style of e-mails. Because they cannot communicate readily face to face, nor can their managers observe them in their managerial practice, there is greater pressure on distant employees to demonstrate their effectiveness by results, numbers without any information on the style of behavior used in attaining them. Comprehensive performance appraisal, especially if it requires feedback from the distant manager's subordinates, may be culturally inappropriate or otherwise futile.

WORK EXPERIENCE: RATIONALE

As the assessor interviews a person at his or her job, in describing the situation the employee can demonstrate what he or she means. This is apparent enough in the factory–machine situation in which a person shows the machine part being made or a process he or she could not describe adequately in an office. Such a demonstration also can be equally useful for understanding a desk job. An executive may have an interaction during the interview with someone he or she had mentioned earlier. Discussion can then clarify what this shared interaction meant.

The fact that the assessor interviews someone at the work site ensures the interviewee of the assessor's interest in his or her work. The assessor demonstrates that he or she is interested enough in what can be learned to come "all the way" to the interviewee and that part of the company that the latter knows best. Whether the interviewee be working on a machine or computer, at the warehouse dock, or an executive desk, the assessor is meeting the employee on that person's own home ground.

On-the-Job Interview

An on-the-job interview can make a unique contribution to the understanding of how a person's work influences his or her total psychological experience. The setting of the interview enables the assessor to see and sense what goes on in a person's life at work, and the assessor may talk over these observations with the individual.

The on-the-job context of the interview ensures a heavier focus on work than is likely if the assessor sees someone in another place. Obviously, if the same employees interviewed on the job were seen in the assessor's office, the interviews would change drastically. The same principle holds true as the assessor moves any distance from someone's work situation, even to a special office within the company.

The assessor must approach the setting and its personnel as an empathic learner and must communicate to every person interest in their view of the setting. They know best how aspects of the setting, superiors, tasks, and peers are important to *them*. Their assessment of others and their reactions to the setting have some validity. The individuals themselves are the best informants about how they themselves feel about their job and its many facets.

The assessor should communicate in feeling and words: "I want to learn about your work and what it means to you and people around you. You are really the only one who can assess your inner experience. I want to learn about what you see, feel, and think. I need and will appreciate your help. I do not want to interfere with your work too much, but I cannot learn from you without visiting with you. I hope you will be willing to help me at this time. If not, I will understand." As rapport is established, the interviewee may give a rather general description of what he or she does and how he or she feels about doing it. The assessor always seeks further understanding of the person and the situation. The assessor frequently must ask the person to "show me what you mean" or "tell me more about that so that I can understand better." At times, the assessor may even ask the person to teach him or her some part of the job, because this will make it easier to share experiences that the person is having or has had in the past.

Such an endeavor can communicate to the individual not so much the assessor's prying but a reflection of sincere interest in understanding what the person feels about what he or she does and the clarity with which the person sees his or her work. Even after more inquiry, usually some conscious or unconscious avoidance or omission of work life is evident. The person may begin to fear what the observer might do with the information to be gained or may feel that certain areas about which he or she is keenly concerned or preoccupied are "inappropriate." People often need help from the assessor to enable them to communicate freely.

The assessor may have to reassure the interviewee that an interview is not intended to be judgmental. When the emphasis on the person and *his or her* views seem too threatening, the assessor can turn to talk of less anxiety-laden areas, perhaps other people. From the outset the assessor indicates that what is learned from an interviewee and others is confidential. If an assessor is asked what "others" say, he or she can reassure the interviewee that his or her own view is most important. What specific "others" say is, of course, confidential. This is not a reprimand but a reminder and a way to tell the person that the assessor means what he or she says about confidentiality. As indicated earlier, however, if appropriate, the assessor might make some general statement that satisfies the interviewee but does not distort the assessor's effort.

Negative feelings are often difficult to communicate. Often we all experience deep feelings of which we are unaware. If they are feelings of anger, these psychologically can magnify to them the effects of their conscious hostile feelings toward the company, their supervisor, their colleagues, or their task. In short, they may become disproportionately angry when they talk about their work experience. In fact, they may even feel that they should not be so angry without knowing why they are, and sometimes apologetic for expressing their anger. The assessor can help the interviewee by demonstrating the acceptability of these consciously experienced negative feelings. "No one has a perfect job," "Everyone finds some parts of his or her job less satisfactory than others," or similar statements communicate that the assessor is not him- or herself afraid of anger or hostility. Such communication asserts that the assessor is sincerely interested in all facets of the person's experience at work.

The on-the-job interview permits the assessor to observe a person reacting to his or her job situation—its demands, its uniqueness—a small sample of the total work life experience. The assessor sees what the individual's task demands in thought and motor skills; the number and quality of interpersonal transactions; sources of gratification and frustration. Such observations alone help the assessor to learn much about those experiences that have particular psychological and emotional impact on the person.

Interviewing on the job extends what the assessor can learn. What an individual says about what the assessor observes provides a check on what the assessor thinks the person's experiences mean to him or her. Or when he or she has been told about an experience, the assessor can stay alert to observe it in the person's work life. Sometimes, the individual is unaware of those facets of the work experience that the assessor's observations tell him (the assessor) are important to the individual. The interviewee may tighten up, flush, or betray some other sign of stress when his or her supervisor approaches. One might infer the stress whatever the individual may say about the reporting relationship. But its significance differs if the interviewee describes this relationship as stressful or pleasant or lacking in conflict. Thus, the assessor's presence in the situation helps him or her to judge and differentiate what an individual wants to be true, believes to be true, and what *is* true about the individual's psychological reactions to his or her work situation.

The on-the-job interview contrasts in form and goals with other consulting contacts with people at work, such as those occurring during tours or incidental visits. In those contacts, the assessor is getting acquainted with people and giving them the opportunity to perceive his or her purposes accurately. Chance strongly determines what sample of their work the assessor observes. Sampling across the organization rarely is representative. The assessor is seeking general themes shared by numbers of individuals.

The assessor may learn from one person about her reaction to some union problems; from another, certain characteristics of his supervisor whom he likes; from another, her reaction to a recent change in job functions or product. If the assessor happens to have many contacts with one person, the assessor may come to know that person well and know his or her reactions to these many conditions. But what is learned from one individual cannot be compared systematically to what is learned from each of the others because the depth and extent of contact is not equalized for all people seen.

Sampling errors in visits and tours around an organization are bound to occur. Sections vary in their visibility and accessibility. Some people are rarely seen because they work at "the other end" of a plant. The assessor spends more time in the "favorite" settings of the person who conducts a tour. These are some of the natural conditions of fieldwork in assessment that make it exceedingly difficult to acquire equivalent data from all parts of the organization. The on-the-job interview procedures compensate for such sources of error by sampling job roles and settings and standardizing the duration and form of the interview and the representativeness of the job sample as much as possible.

Selection of Interviewees

The assessor should base the selection of individuals for on-the-job interviews on the number of major settings and job roles in the organization. The early mapping of the organization and general impressions provide this information.

Ideally, for purposes of understanding influential factors throughout an organization, the assessor should see two individuals in each of the major job roles existing in each setting. If one setting becomes the focus of special interest, increase of this sample is necessary to provide more comprehensive understanding. Similarly, if time restricts the number of people whom the assessor can see, sampling should be decreased in those settings or job roles that appear less likely to contribute knowledge being sought by the assessor. Such decisions often must be arbitrary.

The sampling for the on-the-job interview or other methods is a function of the assessor's goals. In an exploratory assessment that seeks to understand a total organization, weight must be given to broad coverage in as many settings and job roles as time permits. However, if an assessment seeks to understand the work problems of a given group of individuals (perhaps at a particular level in the hierarchy of an organization) or the impact of some particular organizational problems or events, the assessor must sample heavily those individuals most directly concerned. Such sampling decisions are never of the "either-or" type, because one setting or group is never isolated from others and all settings are not equally critical for understanding the experiences of people in an organization.

The assessor should be fully aware of his or her areas of heavy and light sampling so that he or she can qualify appropriately or assert findings. For example, if the assessor has seen no one in the local sales setting of a company, he or she cannot know that general themes discovered in contacts with other people in other settings are relevant to local salespersons. Similarly, if the assessor has seen 12 of the 15 people in the data-processing setting, the assessor can feel confident of the generality of findings for the setting as a whole.

Structure of Interview

The on-the-job interview should be conducted in a reasonably standard way. However, this does not mean that exactly the same things should be done and said with each individual. The standardization sought is that each interviewee is given maximum opportunity to disclose those aspects of the work experience that are psychologically significant to him or her. This requires that the assessor compensate for individual differences in anxiety and its expression, talkativeness, clarity of description, and investment in the analytic process. The assessor may have to guide one person away from being repetitive, and in another instance he or she may have to prod for more depth in a specific area that the person is skipping over.

Despite such differences as these, there are ways the form of the interview can be standardized to achieve equal opportunity of expression for each person. One way is to control the *duration of the interview*. An interview of 50 minutes provides a balance between the assessor's need to cover large numbers of people and the time it takes to enable a person to reveal his or her major involvements in and reactions to various facets of work life. Clearly, if one person is interviewed for 15 minutes and another for two hours, the latter is likely to discuss a wider range of topics.

Specific behavior in the interview (standing, sitting, shouting, whispering) will vary considerably depending on the actual work situation, but some standardization is possible and necessary. The assessor should structure the interviews so that he or she can *converse with the interviewee at least one-half of the scheduled time* (whether this is distributed over the interview period or in blocks of time). The assessor may spend some of his or her time doing the interviewee's job. Special attention must be given to loud noise or lack of privacy without so distorting the interview situation that the on-the-job conditions no longer prevail. The variety of situations defies simple rules. The assessor may talk with the interviewee during periodic breaks in work rhythm or away from the job site for 5- or 10-minute intervals during the hour or discuss confidential topics when others are out of earshot.

Representativeness of the work sample during which the interview is held should be controlled whenever possible. The attempt consistently should be to find a representative hour of a person's work experience. Planning the occasion of the interview with either the interviewee or someone else familiar with the interviewee's job role is helpful. Observing a human resources interviewer during one of his interviews or a machine adjuster while she is setting up a machine is highly desirable. When this is not possible or it turns out during an interview that another time would have been more representative, the assessor seeks to understand the other situation as well as possible from the person's description.

Conducting the Interview

In conducting interviews on the job, the assessor, as he or she has with others, must first meet the individual's need for a rational, reasonably unconflicted understanding of the assessment and the assessor. The assessor should introduce and identify him- or herself at the outset of the interview and must clarify or reclarify as necessary the purposes and structure of the interview. The assessor must recognize what threat and discomfort may be experienced by the individual and allay or control these so that they do not become dominant or accentuated. The assessor must make the experience as constructive as possible for the interviewee within the limits of the relationship and its purposes so that the interview be fruitful for both.

The purpose of the interview should be described as a means of "learning from you, because you know your job and reactions to it better than anyone else." This rationale for the interview and its goal, learning what his or her work means to the interviewee, often must be reasserted in one form or another during the interview. Some individuals will persist in trying to give "right" answers. The assessor continually must reemphasize that the assessor is interested in this person's individual reactions to work and its components.

The assessor can encourage a frank, individual reaction by stating from time to time that all people respond differently. He or she should be careful not to convey judgment about the person's statements or answers to questions, because this would communicate that there are right and wrong or acceptable and unacceptable answers.

At times, to more fully understand something the person has said, it may be helpful to ask the individual to show the assessor what he or she means. Beyond this, it is sometimes appropriate, depending on the assessor's predilection and the type of task, to ask the person to show the assessor how to do something. This not only can convey the interest in the person's unique situation, but also can provide insights into areas of experience that cannot be described. This further asserts the person's expertise in the job compared to that of the assessor.

Hence, the tone throughout the interview is one of the assessor and interviewee working together during their time so that the assessor will know as well as possible what this person's work experiences are and what they mean to him or her. Asking in one form or another what the individual does in the job or how he or she spends time provides an opening for conversation if the individual has been unable spontaneously to describe his or her reactions to the work situation. Asking the individual about something the assessor sees him or her do serves a similar purpose. As the person talks about the work and its requirements, the assessor questions the individual more about those areas that the assessor does not understand so well and particularly those areas that seem of special affective significance. "What happened then?" asked after a person grimaces or smiles can yield important insights.

After 15 to 30 minutes, the interviewer should deliberately assess what he or she has and has not learned about the person, separating those areas that the interviewer feels he or she knows well, those in which he or she wants further information, and those in which he or she knows little, if anything. This assessment should guide the assessor in the remainder of the interview.

CHECKLIST 12: CHECKING THE INTERVIEW

- What are this person's sources of involvement and lack of involvement, satisfaction, and dissatisfaction?
- How does this person's work contribute to his or her knowledge and judgment about him- or herself?
- How does this person perceive and respond to others at work?
- What meaning does this person's activity and productivity have for him or her?
- What are normative stresses for this person and what coping techniques (see appendix C) does he or she use in dealing with them?

The general questions to be kept in mind to ensure coverage of key areas during the interview are included in Checklist 12.

At the end of the interview, as in every contact, the assessor should take time to thank the person and to demonstrate the help the interviewee has given by illustrating something learned from him or her. It is important to leave the interviewee with an experience of having contributed. This is not meant to be an insincere gimmick. There is no interview in which the assessor does not learn *something*. For example, saying to an individual at the end of an interview that there are many more facets to his or her work than appeared evident before the interview, and exemplifying one of those, conveys to the interviewee that the assessor has learned something of how the interviewee sees his or her tasks. The particular statement and example will vary for each person. The statements that are most successful are those in which the assessor incorporates awareness of positive or negative feelings the person has revealed about his or her work. By this the assessor conveys that he or she has sought to understand this person as an individual and that the person has been successful in contributing to this goal.

Recording the Interview

The interview should be recorded as soon as possible from the assessor's notes. The particular form and exhaustiveness of these notes must vary depending on the bent, skills, and memory of the assessor and the particular situation, including the response of the interviewee to note taking. But every effort should be made to record sufficient data during and after the interview to permit an adequate analysis.

The assessor should record, in order of their occurrences throughout the interview, what the interviewee says, does, and feels; the interviewee's reactions to others including the assessor; and the assessor's reaction to the interviewee. The record of the interview should highlight specific occurrences during the interview period such as interactions with others, specific job activities, the interviewee's emotional reactions, and references to him- or herself. Any topics concerning nonwork, tasks, coworkers, or the person's setting should be included, as well as questions that the interviewer asked that might have led to these, because spontaneous and requested statements often differ in their significance.

As already indicated, the assessor will have a significant impact on the information he or she gets and the feelings of those with whom he or she works. The assessor must gauge that impact continuously.

THE PERSON WHO SEEKS HELP

Sometimes, if the assessor is a mental health professional, people may ask him or her about personal or family problems. When the clinician sees a nonpatient, the "contract" is a different one but just as binding an arrangement as the one made with a patient or client. In the case of assessment, the nonpatient or nonclient is an employee who is approached by the clinician and is asked to give information about him- or herself and his or her work for organizational purposes. Thus, the "contract" involves an agreement between two parties to work toward a goal that does not assume that the clinician and the employee will become therapist and patient. If they do, that constitutes a breach of the "contract."

Because of the nature of this contractual agreement, the clinician as an organizational analyst with nonpatients explains clearly at the beginning of each interview in what role the clinician is placing him- or herself and what he or she expects of the other.

A breach of the contract may occur when either (a) the interviewee expects and wants the assessor to treat him or her as a patient—that is, to assume the role of a clinical diagnostician and therapist or coach, and the assessor complies, or (b) the assessor interprets the interviewee's references to psychological difficulties—for example, the statement that he or she has been a psychiatric patient, as a request that the assessor act as a therapist, and the assessor complies.

In some cases, the interviewee may refer to the assessor as a person skilled in treating patients and ask for help and advice spontaneously. It would be callous and inhumane to refuse to respond to this plea, but the assessor must be absolutely certain of the interviewee's motive and purpose in introducing such a request in the interview. This will avoid such unfortunate and destructive situations as an interviewee claiming that despite the assessor's claims about the purpose of the assessment, he or she is in fact trying to find out who the crazy people are in the plant.

To deal with the situation where a person asks for advice the assessor should (a) ascertain clearly the nature of the employee's request by repeating the individual's statement, to confirm how correct the assessor's impression has been; (b) tell the employee that his or her request has been understood; (c) call to the employee's attention, by a brief review of the opening statements made at the beginning of the interview, that the purpose of the interview is not to have the assessor act as a psychological assessor; (d) give appropriate advice about ways of getting professional help; (e) tell the person that he or she must assume the responsibility for future contacts with the assessor if he or she wishes to discuss the matter further (it must be made very clear in the person's mind that the assessor is willing to be of help, but that this is the person's choice).

TERMINATION

Whatever the length of his or her work in the field, the assessor is faced with the task of anticipating and dealing constructively with the termination of his or her relationship there. Unrealistic expectations, inaccurate perception of motivations, and concerns about the consequences of what they have revealed occur frequently and understandably in the people the assessor has interviewed. Administrators and others often will ask for information about specific findings and impressions about sections of their organization. These requests will occur even though the assessor had said consistently during the assessment that he or she would take considerable time to analyze the data and that, in any case, he or she would not divulge confidences.

People will have asked the assessor to carry their messages to others even though the assessor had pointed out that what he or she learned would go no further in any identifiable way. People will demonstrate guilt for unloading information and reactions they had held back earlier, feeling that they had behaved unfairly by not being frank enough. Such reactions are a small sample of the many ways in which people demonstrate the importance of the assessor's relationship to them, the power that they perceive in the assessor and the assessment, and their fears and hopes about what the assessor might accomplish. The difficulty people have in taking the assessor at his or her word—their sometimes inaccurate and irrational perception of the assessor's power and motives—cannot be attributed to a few peculiar individuals. For each person who blatantly evidences these reactions, there are many who reveal them subtly and others whose reactions have been too insensitive to recognize.

It is important not only to clarify the "contract" of the assessment through the field work but again at the last stages of the field relationship. Particularly at this time, it is important to help people recognize their concerns and inappropriate hopes along with showing them appreciation for their investment and faith in the assessor.

Is it needless for the assessor to demonstrate that he or she is not omnipotent and omniscient? Not at all. Such unrealistic perception of the assessor is characteristic. It is important to confront people with the reality of the assessor's limitations, not out of simple scientific objectivity or modesty but as a means to aid them to recognize their strength and independence. Those who doubt the potential of an assessor to trip off such dependence and the varied attitudes that follow even later should reflect on what followed other situations in which they have taken part and even on speeches they have given. Are not the people who linger, question, and later phone often expressing a view of the researcher, clinician, or professor as powerful? Why else would people ask, "What should I do if . . . ?" when the assessor so often tells them that there is no simple formula for handling human behavior constructively?

The general procedure for the assessor to follow includes such actions as mentioning to people his or her imminent departure and, ultimately, a walk through the settings, saying goodbye and thanks individually. The assessor should give people a chance to ask additional questions and express any last-minute opinions and ideas they had not taken the opportunity to do earlier. The assessor should reassure them in whatever ways are appropriate that they have been helpful. The assessor should refer (privately) to particular shared conversations with individuals, conveying that he or she had in fact come to know them to some degree. The assessor must tell all that he or she will be coming back at a later date with a report on the assessment, if that is the case.

The last contacts usually are with the organizational representative who allowed entry and with whom the assessor planned the overall assessment. They should review where things stand, the general reactions of people to the assessment, and the assessor's own reactions. This review is usually carried on with considerable give and take in the conversation. The assessor usually picks up whatever loose ends, uncertainties, questions, and future plans need attention.

The feedback report is itself a critical part of the termination process, even if delayed several months. (See appendix B and chapter 11.) Resolution of the fantasies about what the assessor might do with the information cannot occur with any completeness or finality until the assessor has returned and reported. Only the report, a face-to-face experience, permits such resolution. After the feedback and discussion of it with people in an organization, termination of the assessment can be seen as reasonably complete.

6

GENETIC DATA

The momentum of an organization begins at its founding. It develops a way of going about its business, employs certain people who shape its activities, and evolves a mode of competing in the marketplace. This momentum often persists through generations of growth and management. All too often, consultants pay little attention to the significance of that momentum. Here it will be assumed to be fundamental to understanding the organization.

I. HOW THE ORGANIZATION GOT TO BE THE WAY IT IS

A. Identifying Information

The data listed in this section are used primarily for administrative and classification purposes. As in the lead of a newspaper article, this section contains the who, what, where, why, and how of the assessment. Except for the section on circumstances of the assessment and the one on special conditions affecting the validity of the assessment, the items discussed should be recorded immediately after the initial visit to the organization. The first five items can be stated in paragraph form.

1. Organization Name

Simply state the name of the organization.

2. Location

Location is also simply stated. Although the name and characteristics of a given location may have a significant influence on the nature and functioning of an organization, the purpose at this point is merely to identify the organization and to anchor it geographically. The question of possible significance of both factors is treated in chapter 10.

3. Type of Organization

All types of organizations may be assessed with this manual. In this case exactly what this one is specified—in other words, a plant that manufactures electronic equipment, an elementary school, a law firm, a church, a life insurance firm, and so on.

4. Organizational Affiliation

Is the whole organization being studied or one part of it? What is the relationship of this unit to the larger system of which it is a part, if this is the case?

5. Size

The organization is ranked relative to other organizations of the same type (No. 3), within the organizational whole (No. 4), and within the same geographic location, with respect to assets, employees, membership, stockholders, plant size, volume of business, and other comparative characteristics. Such data frequently are available from the organization's annual report. For business organizations data may be obtained from such sources as Dun and Bradstreet publications, investment firm analyses, Chambers of Commerce, and *Forbes* magazine. Similar compendia provide statistics for churches, hospitals, law firms, educational institutions, and other specialized organizations.

a. Financial Condition

Indicate relative strength in terms of financial resources and condition. A fundamental criterion of a business organization's success is market value added (MVA). This is reflected in the increase in its sales and stock price over a target period, and companies are compared with each other in the business press on this criterion. Another metric is economic value added (ERA), which is a measure of the company's true economic profitability. It is simply a way of accounting for the cost of using capital and computing profit.

b. Stockholders

Estimate approximate number of stockholders in total, with an indication of locus of control—family ownership, majority held by a few individuals, less than (for example) 5% held by any one person.

c. Employees

For certain types of organizations there may be no direct equivalents of stockholders and employees. For universities, churches, and other institutions, individuals in the assessment may be members, students, constituents. A major concern in this assessment is with the organization's relationships with those people for whom it has psychological meaning. The assessor should make appropriate substitutions that would differentiate kinds of power in the organization and varied perceptions of those who have different relationships to it.

6. Situation of the Initial Contact

There are two major categories of contact, based on the purpose for which the assessment was initiated—the formal contract (and its accompanying social contract) and the psychological contract.

As indicated earlier, an assessment requires a formal contract stating what the assessor proposes to do. Exactly how is the assessment to be conducted? After the assessor has conducted the initial exploration, he or she will propose a method. The duration of the assessment, the number of investigators, the frequency and length of the interviews, the time for dictation, transcription, analysis, and writing, and for both presentations and feedback should all be included. However, it will be impossible to establish a proposal until a preliminary assessment has been obtained. It is not unusual for plans to be altered during the course of the assessment. Therefore, the recording of this section may have to be delayed or even rewritten before the report is finished.

Sometimes in small organizations or when the assessment is limited to only a few individuals in an organization, the contract is verbal, but writing it out avoids misunderstandings, particularly about cost, and changes of mind on the part of the client.

When a large number of people must be informed about the reasons and purposes of the relationship between the assessor and the organization and the conditions of that relationship, a formal statement that can be read to employee groups must be developed. (See an example in appendix B.) Such a presentation should allow for questions and discussion to clarify the contract.

It is helpful to know why you have been chosen to undertake an assessment with the organization and what the management's conscious expectations are. The mutual conscious understanding that has been reached between the organization and the assessor is the social contract. In many instances management might not know what it really wants or, as is often the case, might specify the wrong problem.

The assessor also must specify for him- or herself (and to him- or herself) the unconscious expectations the assessor thinks the management of the organization may have about the assessor and the assessment. Those underlying, tacit expectations make up the client's part of the *psychological contract*. The unconscious part of the contract is often difficult to ascertain. The psychological contract refers to *unconscious* expectations, those people are not aware of, about dependency, about the management of aggression and affection, and the pursuit of ultimate long-term aspiration of which a person may be unaware, or ego ideal. "What ideally would you like for yourself in the future. What do you hope for?" are the kinds of questions that tap into the ego ideal.

The psychological contract comprises those unspoken, and often unconscious, expectations that both person and organization bring to their relationship. Two such expectations are (a) the mutual dependency of person and organization and the concern that either becomes helplessly dependent on the other; and (b) the amount of psychological distance people need from each other and from their superiors (e.g., "My boss is always looking over my shoulder," or "My boss is never around when I need her") to function optimally. Psychological distance includes peoples preferred ways of managing their needs for and expression of affection and aggression: "I like to work closely with a group of people;" "I want to be where the action is, right there on the plant floor." A third expectation has to do with the way organizational change, usually involving significant loss of role, status, or income, is handled by both parties.

People seek out roles that fit with their preferred ways of handling aggression: A salesperson wants to be able to manipulate customers, and the company expects him or her to do so. If the company promotes the salesperson without his or her voluntary concurrence to sales manager, where he or she can no longer manipulate customers, for the salesperson that is a violation of the psychological contract. Similarly, if the same salesperson meets some of his or her needs for affection by amusing customers with stories and jokes, he or she loses that source of gratification when instead he or she must "shuffle papers." A crucial dimension of the psychological contract is the degree to which its fulfillment enables the individual to like him- or herself for being able to pursue aspirations in the service of the organization. For example, a pastor, encouraged like most clergy to grow his or her congregation, wants also to build a massive church and to enhance his or her leadership position in the denomination. That is the pursuit of his or her ego ideal, his or her picture of self at his or her future best. When such a person is constrained by his or her ecclesiastical superiors because, though he or she is a good manipulator, he or she is insufficiently humble, for this person that is not only a contradiction, but even more, a violation of his or her psychological contract. In none of these examples are any of the parties involved aware of the tacit wishes that underlie the behavior.

One question that opens the avenue to the psychological contract is, Why did you come to work here? Another is, Where would you like to go in this organization? What will you do if you determine you can't get there? Similar questions of management, What kinds of employees or kinds of people do you want to promote? serve the same purpose.

For example, in the Powell-Kole Company (chapter 3), although the chief executive sought the assessment, he said he had no problems, only concerns that the organization was losing its family atmosphere. That he had no problems was simply denial, minimizing them by labeling them concerns. His sense of possible loss of family spirit masked his more basic concern that he would lose his tight control. He himself brought in the larger share of the business and he was reluctant to delegate that task to project heads. He did not implement the recommended delegation. He could not allow himself to depend heavily on others that he did not control. Almost all employees were "temporaries" despite his talk of "family." They had little attachment to the organization or to him. This preoccupation with control, together with denial of dependency, typical of many entrepreneurs, also reflected his psychological distance from others. An assessor could expect to be held at arms length and to keep recommendations on an intellectual level. This was not a client with whom one might develop greater psychological insight, but he might come to trust a relationship that would not threaten his control. He invested his aggression in attacking problems by computer and his affection in pleasing clients and pride in the successful products. In his fantasy, his greatest achievement would be to emulate the once financially successful Polaroid.

7. Special Conditions Affecting Validity of the Assessment

Organizations, like people, are not static. Conditions change constantly; some events may occur before or during the consultation that materially affect its validity. Among such events are strikes, the death of the chief executive, economic reverses, accidents, impending mergers, or unusually rapid growth of the market. These should be detailed here.

What are the conditions under which the assessor entered the organization? Who brought the assessor in? Why? What are the special problems in the organization? Are there any factors that might affect the assessor's or judgment of the problems? Any biases? What controls have been placed on the assessor?

8. First Overall Impressions

The initial impression should include impressions of the physical plant, as well as psychological considerations. It cannot be arrived at by measurement. The assessor is his or her own instrument. The assessor should ask, What does this place feel like? How effective and efficient does it seem to be? How would it feel to work here? The assessor should ask questions about what he or she observes and should think about the psychological, social, and economic costs and implications of what he or she observes. What are the effects of the architecture? The site? What kinds of perceptions or psychological stances do people have? What are the underlying assumptions about people? The assessor must attempt to recognize his or her first feelings about the organization, some of which will be fleeting and must be alert to momentary negative feelings because he will tend to disregard them, particularly if the atmosphere is subsequently cordial. Such feelings should not be disregarded. Chances are that the assessor's immediate and subtle feelings are shared by others who may not be able to grasp or verbalize them readily. It is from these feelings, this impact, that the assessor establishes the necessary working hypotheses about the problems of the organization. The assessor continually checks his or her working hypotheses as the assessment progresses and will discard some, reserve others, and add new ones. Here also the assessor should try to summarize the experiences from the initial tour.

B. Historical Data

To have meaning for the purposes of facilitating change, the description of any organization must be viewed in its historical context. The assessor must know not only how the organization is functioning now and why, but also how those forces evolved and what historical forces continue to influence its activity. However, one must strive for the truly salient points and not get lost in details. For example, nineteenth-century religious discrimination in the United States led to the development of Roman Catholic parochial schools; in many communities, they still maintain an outward defensive stance. Many businesses still operate with labor policies intended to deal with problems of the 1930s.

This section is devoted to systematizing the objective data that delineate the organization's development. The data incorporated should be verifiable. They provide the factual basis for all subsequent diagnostic hypotheses and for the conclusions that will follow. They form the foundation for the corrective help the organization needs now. Therefore, as in a mystery novel, this section must contain all the facts needed to substantiate the subsequent inferences. An interview form and a questionnaire for gathering some of the data are provided in appendix A.

1. Chief Complaint or Events Leading to the Initiation of the Assessment

When an organization seeks an assessment, it does so because it has one or more major problems. The chief complaint is the problem as stated by the executive or individual who asked for an assessment. The chief complaint and the events that culminated in verbalizing that complaint to the assessor should be stated here. The chief complaint is a concrete, specific component of the situation of the initial contract.

In addition to describing the direct contact in which the chief complaint was made, the assessor should try to infer the psychological meanings or implications, if any, of both the complaint and the conditions under which it was made, as illustrated in the earlier discussion of the psychological contract. These inferences should be treated as hypotheses for further testing and should be entered later in the assessment (chapter 9) under transference phenomena.

The assessor should try to infer the depth of any resistance of management to outside help and the implications of that resistance for the assessment relationship as illustrated in the psychological contract discussion. The assessor should have a mental note of this matter at this point, even though he or she may not yet fully understand it and will not formally write about it until later in the outline.

2. Problems of the Organization as Stated by Key Figures

Every organization has a hierarchy in which people holding certain positions have formal authority. In some organizations, especially law firms and consulting firms, hierarchy is masked or even denied. Some business organizations play the same game by calling clerks "associates." Nevertheless, some people have greater power than others as reflected in the concept of "reporting to" and in the fact that some can fire others. List what these people state are the primary problems facing their organization. These statements may differ from that of the chief complaint.

In many instances there are people who have de facto, rather than de jure, authority. That is, they exercise power even if they are not formally authorized to do so. These are the informal leaders. Their roles are usually discovered from the repeated references made to them in the course of interviews or when people are asked to whom they turn for help or information. View these people as key figures in the informal structure and record their opinions, as discussed in chapter 10 and B4 of appendix D. (Throughout the book such references refer to the outline in appendix D.)

"Problems as stated by key figures" might be interpreted in several ways. It might be a simple statement of what the interviewees actually say; it might be what the same persons say after a skillful interview by a psychologically oriented assessor; or it might be what the interviewer perceives that the individuals actually mean although they are not aware of the full import of their words. But in keeping with the intent of this section of the assessment, at this point the assessor lists only what the person *actually says*.

There is also the chance that the statements offered may represent the actual way top management visualizes the problem; they also may represent how the management wishes to present it because they do not yet trust the assessor. The manner in which the problem is stated also reflects the degree of sophistication with which the problem is viewed. But these inferences and interpretations must be reserved for a later section of the assessment.

The statement should be divided, separating those that are viewed as long-range problems from the short-range issues.

a. Long-Range

Problems that must be faced at some undefined future date are considered to be long-range. Developing the survival potential of the organization has a long time perspective.

b. Short-Range

Problems that must be faced by a certain known date, unless they entail long-term planning, generally are considered to be short-range. For many organizations, immediate cash flow is an urgent short-run problem. It is the assessor's responsibility to place each problem in its proper time perspective.

3. Background of the Organization

Some organizations have compiled or have written organizational histories. Others have little or no organized historical information. It would seem that the former instance should be the easier for the assessor because otherwise he or she must compile the history from talking to knowledgeable persons in the organization. However, such is not the case. The assessor has no way of knowing the degree of distortion in an organization-compiled history. Nor is history as reported by organization informants as valid as that compiled from objective sources. The assessor therefore must seek outside sources of information, if such are available, to complement both the data he or she obtains from informants and that from the record. Local newspaper files, historical society files, and similar repositories may be helpful, but they are invariably incomplete, biased, and give details rather than useful summaries. Business publications—*Fortune, Forbes, Business Week,* and others—carry articles about companies that often give adequate background and sometimes critical evaluation of performance. There are similar publications in most other fields that discuss specific institutions. The company's website is a source of useful information. Much can be learned about the facets of organizational processes and perceptions via chat rooms.

a. Key Developmental Phases

A key developmental phase is an experience that significantly changes the direction, size, effectiveness, or strength of the organization. It is a period in organizational maturation that can be located in time. It can result from

> ### CHECKLIST 13: KEY DEVELOPMENTAL PHASES
>
> - What are the key growth phases in this organization?
> - What have been the major crises experienced by the organization?
> - What major changes have there been in organizational goals and directions?
> - What major changes have there been in products or services, with what success?
> - What are its special skills or reputation?
> - What is the organization's self-image?

the development of a product or the adoption of a strategy or from natural occurrences or fortuitous circumstances, as an outgrowth of which the organization takes a new or different direction. (The assessor should distinguish between conscious choice of a strategy and one that evolves by itself.)

Such a phase may be positive or negative in the long run. A positive key developmental phase reflects growth, greater sophistication, greater maturity, greater stability through diversification or financing, or greater access to personnel or financial resources. A negative developmental phase is a type of organizational aging, regression, or failure. Evidence of such a phase might be a decline in profitability because of products becoming obsolete, declining membership, or lower quality of job applicants by virtue of uncontrollable external events. Positive or negative phases depend heavily on the organization's ability to perceive its environment objectively. (See checklist 13.)

Greiner (1998) conceptualized five phases of organizational growth and the crisis for each that precipitates the next phase, a classification I have found helpful:

Phase	Crisis	Problem
Creativity	Leadership	Founder often is not a good leader
Direction	Autonomy	Successor organization struggles to be professionally managed
Delegation	Control	Larger organization delegates authority but strives to control
Coordination	Red Tape	Increased size leads to more formalized controls
Collaboration	?	New forms of organization arise

In many organizations, especially those that are large and geographically dispersed, there is a continuing struggle about how to organize. The radical restructuring efforts often bringing about wrenching changes for the people involved as they shift from one model to another (Lublin, 2001).

Adizes (1988) conceptualized organizational life cycles as akin to human growth and development. Other management theorists occasionally refer to an organization phase or stage, usually, however, without the detailed discussion of these authors.

(1) As Reported by Organizational Participants

Organizational participants are people within the organization who have themselves experienced the key developmental phases or who have entered into the organization as a result of change. They are therefore in a position to have some knowledge of the organizational situation both before and after the event(s). Firsthand reports by political and business figures are frequently best-selling books. Their value often lies in the difference between the perceptions of the participants and those of more objective writers.

(2) As Reported by Outsiders

Such people as local political officials (the mayor, city council members), newspaper officials, business people, social service professionals, and others in authoritative observational positions are referred to as "outsiders." Persons in other companies in the same industry, parishioners in other churches of the same denomination, officials in other school systems, trade association officials, suppliers, customers, fellow professionals, and so forth are also relevant outsiders if they have information or opinions about the organization. In this instance the assessor will be dealing with a problem akin to the issue of history as written by historians versus that reported by those who actually lived the events they describe. The two accounts may differ. Thus, an observer may relate something that happened to an organization, saying, "I think this made a difference," and those within the organization may not feel that this occurrence was significant. The assessor will have to arrive at his or her own conclusions.

For example, with the advent of managed care, most psychiatric hospitals that depended on long-term patients went out of business. Staffs in those hospitals and outside observers alike attributed their demise to managed care. In one such closure, no one on the staff or among outside observers understood that the collapse had been predictable 30 years before when the management of the hospital chose a method of succession that deprived it of both managerial competence and staff involvement. An assessor who reviewed the stages in that organization's development could readily infer the sequence of events.

As with history from participants, data from outsiders can be so comprehensive and detailed that they become confusing rather than illuminating, while at the same time being neither systematic nor complete. The assessor will have to glean much information to discern trends and forces. The assessor should be cautious about the completeness and solidity of the information from which he or she will draw inferences. There is no good guideline about how to do this. In my own work, when I find I am getting the same information repetitively or when it becomes apparent that the informants do not really know first-hand, I terminate the interview. The repetition in publications also requires that the assessor value those that are documented authoritatively more highly than most newspaper stories. The heavily documented and highly regarded *Barbarians at the Gates* by Brian Burrough and John Helyar is a more widely trusted resource about the fall of RJR Nabisco than a collection of newspaper clips.

(3) As Understood by the Assessor

The assessor may discern aspects of organizational history whose import had not been perceived by persons inside the organization or by outsiders. This is frequently the case when there is high transience or radical change in the composition of the employee and managerial population.

b. Major Crises Experienced by the Organization

Major crises may sometimes be the same as key developmental phases. A crisis can precipitate a developmental phase or it can be independent of any. The vital consideration is what the crisis means to the organization.

(1) Natural Catastrophes

Natural catastrophes include floods, fires, earthquakes, explosions, and even the collapse of the World Trade Center towers when hit by fuel-loaded aircraft (though this obviously was not "natural").

(2) Loss of Key Personnel

High turnover of senior executives is usually an indication of serious problems.

(3) Labor Problems

Labor problems include strikes, slowdowns, sit-downs, lockouts, and temporary work stoppages.

(4) Financial Emergencies

Financial emergencies refers to sudden loss of bank credit, unusual cash drains, failure of clients or customers to pay their bills, loss of a lawsuit resulting in damages, or similar unexpected or unanticipated obligations.

(5) Technological Changes

Technological changes refers to change in manufacturing processes, introduction of different data processing methods, different processes for obtaining prospective students or clients, or delivering products or services.

(6) Loss of Market Share

As a result of the competition from Japanese manufacturers, General Motors lost a significant part of its share of the automobile market and American manufacturers lost the television market to Japan and other electronic markets to China. Schools and churches can lose students and parishioners to other schools and denominations.

(7) Major Changes in Response to Information and Other Technological Innovation

When IBM gave up as unprofitable the manufacture of computers, that was a major change for an organization that had dominated the field. A similar change occurred for the Roman Catholic Church when it shifted the Mass from Latin to local languages.

c. Product-Service History

The product-service history of the organization is a recounting of what key products or services the organization has offered at various times. A description of these will demonstrate how and why the key developmental phases occurred.

(1) Change and Development of Organizational Goals

What changes have occurred in organizational goals at different times and how have they developed? The problems that precipitated and were precipitated by the shift in goals indicate sources of conflict in the organization. Change sometimes means diversity for the survival of the organization. Whenever a change occurs, someone in the organization will suffer. A change in goals will always have some effect on the status, self-image, and power of different people in the organization and of the organization vis-à-vis others as the incumbents see it. The pain will be less if the people involved are themselves changing the goals. For some organizations, change has been a natural unfolding; for others, a drastic shift. The degree of strain becomes more acute when the shift has been dramatic. How much stress has the change precipitated? How has the new direction hurt which employees?

(2) Sequences of Development in Product or Service

To pinpoint who is hurting and specifically why, the assessor must know the steps of change. Who was there first, in the sense of what people with what skills and status? People who are older, have given longer service, and are more entrenched are usually more drastically affected by change. Sometimes valued skills are made obsolete. What were the technical problems? Who was involved and who acquired power when the problems were solved? What skills and talents were made obsolete? Which were pushed into the background? What contributions were no longer rewarded? How long has the resulting resentment been simmering? What has happened historically?

(3) Relative Success or Failure in Various Stages of Service or Product History

How does success or failure affect the organization? What impact did success or failure have on the people within the organization and why? In some instances success is crippling because, deluded by their victory, people can no longer learn from their errors. Contented with success, they fail to see the need for continued innovation. Or, having failed, they may lose courage. Why do things succeed or fail in this organization? Efforts may fail because they are poorly timed or inadequately studied or beyond the resources of the organization. Some people cannot tolerate success and must make "stupid" errors that lead to failure. Failure can be a mode of circumscribing one's life or a mode of learning. Some people cannot tolerate failure and must turn it into success. What happens in this organization when someone or some activity fails?

(4) Geographical Patterns

The geographical distribution of the organization's activities has great influence on many aspects of its operation. It is more difficult to maintain a sense of unity in an organization that is widely dispersed. Yet a large organization heavily concentrated in one area seems impersonal to its employees. International organizations attract more sophisticated employees because such people (called cosmopolitans) must have a broader knowledge of languages, cultural differences, and political and social forces than those (called locals) in companies limited to a small geographical area. The wider the geographical range of the organization, the more competitive it is likely to be; the greater its breadth of choices for new employees, the less the influence of local economics and politics on the performance of the organizational overall. On the other hand, the more extended the organization, the greater the problems in management, distribution, and cohesion. The delineation of the geographic pattern of the organization allows the assessor to compare aspiration against resources with the resulting strains and stresses. The geographical location of an organization says much about the degree to which it is likely to be influenced by the currents of social, political, and economic change; its relative attractiveness for certain kinds of employees; the power it is likely to wield in its host community; and even its style of management. The more isolated the locale and the more dominant the organization is in its community, the more likely it is to be paternalistic. (A paternalistic philosophy of management means that the organization tends to treat its employees as if they were children and does for them what they might better do themselves.)

(5) Special Skills or Competencies of the Organization

What does this organization do better than any other similar organization? What is its unique competence? How broad, narrow, limiting, capable of expansion are its talents? The special skill of an organization may lie in its leader, its laboratory, its depth of management, its capacity for mobilizing financial resources and making major financial commitment. It may lie in the public's identification with the image it holds forth, though its products are no different than anyone else's. Special skill is special power that can be used competitively or defensively.

(6) Performance Reputation and Record

Organizational reputation is what its publics—parishioners, students, alumni, customers, employees, competitors, financiers—think and say of it. The organization's performance record is how it actually performs. Here the concern is not with its performance on the stock market but with the way in which it serves its parishioners, clients, or customers. How much does the organization value its products? How carefully does it make them and how thoroughly does it back them up, or with what academic standards or doctrinal orthodoxy, as contrasted with what it says it does and what others think it does? The organization's reputation is a type of unwritten social contract with the public, an implicit promise to do or to deliver in certain ways. Its performance record is the degree to which that contract is kept. The effort with which the organization strives to fulfill its reputation is a reflection of organizational conscience, often epitomized by its slogan (see IIIA3d in appendix D and chapter 8). The gap between what an organization says it does and what it actually does has much to do with the organizational self-image. The greater the gap, the more resentment there is likely to be among employees and customers or clients.

Performance record can also be a point of vulnerability. As noted earlier, the more successful an organization is, the more likely it will continue to maintain the status quo and the less likely it will change how it performs. Once a standard or demand has been created, an organization feels obligated to continue to fulfill it, even at some expense to itself. This may mean, for example, conflict between a historic premium quality line and the need for products for mass sale. Thus, an organization's reputation can also suggest to the assessor where and under what conditions there are likely to be intraorganizational conflicts.

d. Organizational Folklore

Folklore is part of the culture that is preserved in beliefs, myths, legends, songs, rituals, and practices. It is an integral part of tradition and, as such, becomes an important part of the contemporary scene. Folklore arises out of common experience, often from shared events in a given location, and is frequently an effort to explain that which is otherwise inexplicable, to differentiate those who belong and believe from those who do not. Folklore defines who is to be loved and who is to be hated. Organizational folklore serves to create models, embellishing their charisma with stories of eccentricity, insight, skill, and competence, or explaining their failures by attributing them to environment, economics, or malevolent forces. It also serves to create identification symbols, convictions, and traditions that are sources of strength, and taboos. It is reinforcement for the organizational self-image.

4. Circumstances Surrounding the Assessment

In the discussions in A7 and A8 of the assessment outline, the assessor described exactly how he or she conducted the assessment and the special conditions that occurred during or before the assessment that were likely to affect its validity. Here the concern is with the broader context in which the assessment is taking place, with placing the organization in its contemporary environment. That position will influence the circumstances, issues, problems, and forces of its functioning. What major trends or forces are playing on the organization now that may contribute to its feeling that it has problems? What is happening in the industry or in this particular arena? What socioeconomic trends are affecting this organization now? (See checklist 14.)

CHECKLIST 14: WHAT HAPPENS?

- Follow a policy announcement from its origin to the lowest level employee.
- Follow an order or customer request from the time it is received until it is completed.
- Follow a news or marketing report from its recognition to its distribution end.
- Follow reports on finance, profitability, sales, trends to the lowest organizational levels.

7

DESCRIPTIVE DATA AND ANALYSIS OF CURRENT ORGANIZATION AS A WHOLE

Picking up the outline to this point, we now begin to work with the subsystem of the organization and to start our process of understanding it.

II. DESCRIPTION AND ANALYSIS OF THE ORGANIZATION AS A WHOLE

A. Structural Data

Having identified the organization, outlined its history, and defined the purposes and conditions of the assessment, the assessor now describes the organization as he or she finds it. This section, too, is largely a factual notation about how the organization is put together and how it operates but we begin to think of the inferences we will draw from them. Many of the data for this section may come from formal reports and records that the organization maintains; some of them will be formulated by the assessor from his or her observations and interviews.

1. Formal Organization

Formal organization refers to the mode of organizing and allocating functions and responsibilities and to the distribution of power. It denotes who reports (at least, who is officially supposed to report) to whom for what purposes, and the interrelationships of units, divisions, and departments. The degree to which an organization is formalized or rationalized will vary from organization to organization and sometimes even within an organization. The task of the assessor is to learn and delineate the chain of accountability and the extent to which the interrelationships of the subsystems and parts are defined (Jaques, 1996; Jaques & Clement 1991).

a. Chart

In most organizations the formal structure can be charted readily by members of top management who either have a chart or easily can draw one. It should be made clear that this is the formal chart—that is, the way the chain of accountability is officially supposed to function. In many organizations the actual chain of communication often is very different. When an organization does not have a ready-made chart, the assessor should have the member of top management with whom he or she is dealing draw one as that individual sees the situation. Under such conditions, it is also helpful to have other top executives describe how they perceive the organizational structure; conflicts in perception will be evidence for subsequent inferences and conclusions. Flexible organizations recognize the need to change the organization chart frequently. Assignments and tasks change and people move from one position to another. Employees for Lincoln Electric in Cleveland, Ohio, move rapidly from role to role as necessary, a practice other companies find too disruptive (Ellenberg, 2001). The varying assets and talents of individuals make it necessary to adapt their occupational roles to take advantage of their strengths and counteract their weaknesses.

In addition to obtaining the formal chart, the consultant should include a written description of it at this point.

b. Systems Concept

Traditional charts depict formal lines of authority and functional departments. As organizations grow in complexity, the formal charts are less useful for describing the actual interactions of people (Nadler & Tushman, 1997). Many different people are related to each other in varied ways that are not reflected on the organization chart, particularly in those organizations that alter the composition of task groups for new projects. Thus, there is a need to understand how an organization operates as a system. This can be done by constructing another kind of chart that reflects interrelationships. Such a chart might list job positions in their administrative order on its horizontal axis and a list of tasks and activities on its vertical axis. Then symbols can be placed in the squares to indicate the kind of relationship between a given task and the persons involved in that task. (See Jaques, 1996, page pair 78; see Figure 7-1.) Some charts—for example, those showing the CEO at the bottom and the employees at the top—are merely gimmicks that try to deny where the organizational power really lies.

c. Formal Job Descriptions

Many organizations have elaborate descriptions for each job, and others have none. The degree to which there are formal job descriptions reflects how carefully conceived the formal interrelationships are in an organization. It indicates also how people ostensibly are controlled, evaluated, appraised,

Figure 7-1

Role Relationships

	MGR-SUB	MoR-SoR	FLMA	PROJ. TEAM LDR-SUB	PROJ. LDR-COLLEAGUE	
Task Assignment Role Relationships (TARRs)						
	D	D	R	D	D	Veto Appointment
	D	—	R	D	—	Induct & Set Context of Work
	D	—	R	D	—	Determine Task Type
	D	—	D	D	D	Assign Task
	D	—	R	D	—	Coach
	D	—	D	D	—	Verbal Appraisal (Recognition)
	D	—	D	D	—	Positive or Negative Tasks
	D	—	R	R	—	Recorded Appraisal (Recognition)
	D	—	R	R	—	Expand or Contract Task Type
	D	—	R	R	—	Positive or Negative Pay Change
	D	—	R	D	D	Initiate Transfer From Role
	R	D	R	—	—	Assess Potential & Career Counsel
	R	D	R	—	—	Upgrade or Downgrade Pay Band
	R	D	R	—	—	Positive or Negative Transfers
	R	D	R	—	—	Promote-Demote
	R	D	R	—	—	Dismiss
	—	D	—	—	—	Appeal

Task Assignment Role Relationships (TARRs)

Accountability & Authority (A&A)

D = Decide
R = Recommend

	Prescribe	Audit	Coordinative	Monitoring	Service	Advisory	Collateral	
Components of Task Initiating (TIRRs)								
	✓	—	—	—	✓	—	—	A can instruct B to do something
	✓	✓	—	—	—	—	—	A can instruct B to stop and B stops
	✓	✓	✓	✓	—	—	—	A can instruct B to delay and B delays
	✓	✓	—	—	—	—	—	A and B disagree- A decides
	✓	✓	✓	✓	—	✓	—	A can be informed about B's work
	✓	✓	✓	✓	✓	—	✓	A can have access to persuade B
	✓	—	—	—	—	✓	✓	A can have access to explain to B
	✓	—	✓	—	—	—	—	A can call coordinative meeting with B's
	✓	✓	✓	✓	✓	—	—	A can report higher about B

Components of Task Initiating (TIRRs)

Accountability & Authority (A&A)

A = Initiator
B = Responder

From Elliott Jaques, *Requisite Organization*, Page pair 78, © 1996. Arlington, VA: Cason Hall & Co. Reprinted by permission of the author and publisher.

and charged. The detail of such descriptions may suggest rigidity; the absence of detail does not necessarily indicate flexibility. Employees in organizations that lack formal job descriptions often are confused about what they are supposed to be doing. The absence of a formal job description makes it difficult to appraise performance in other than subjective terms because there are no concise criteria for effective performance. Organizations that are composed significantly of temporary teams will have particular problems in this respect. Some chief executives prefer it that way. Said one, when asked what the company's evaluation system was, "You are looking at it. I decide who will get a raise and who will not."

2. Plant and Equipment

The assessor's interest in plant and equipment is primarily from two points of view: How do they affect the people who must work in and with them? What relationship do they have to the efficiency of accomplishing the intended tasks? The answers to both questions will have something to do with how people feel about themselves and their organizations. The description of plant and equipment may be stated in general summary terms; the assessor is not called on to write an analysis as an engineer might.

a. Location: Territory Covered

The assessor needs to make only a simple statement about where the plant or office is located; its geographical relationship to its host community; its approximate absolute size in square feet, acres, and floors; its relative size with respect to the host community; its accessibility; its architecture; and similar data that will suggest its impact on people or its effectiveness.

b. Value

Value is difficult to measure because so much of the evaluation of an organization's assets hinges on appraisal and accounting methods and on current market conditions. Therefore, the assessor will be concerned with an estimate of assets used in the business at current value. Some organizations publish a statement of their assets in their annual reports, and others do not. Fixed assets may be carried at either book value (their original cost) or current market value. It is important to know which is used and why. The way assets are listed indicates the impression the organization is trying to make. Sometimes an estimate can be made indirectly from local tax assessments. The value of an organization's assets says something about the permanence of the organization, its self-regard, the regard it has for its employees, and the way in which the community is likely to look on it. Inferences about these matters will be made in those parts of the outline discussed in chapters 8 and 9.

c. Kinds of Equipment: Size, Function

Here the assessor is interested in noting the differences in working demands and in opportunities within one organization. These may require different kinds of people as well as different management procedures. The differences may have various effects on people who otherwise may be much alike. They may constitute unique working worlds. Size and function of equipment gives one a picture of the range of activities that the organization carries on. How much of what it fabricates does the organization manufacture itself? How much is done by outsiders? What implications does this have for the organization's vulnerability because of its dependence on others; of its control of others by making them dependent? How much of an advantage is its outsourcing? What does the organization do with what it owns? In some cases equipment sits unused; in others, it is misused. Sometimes it is purchased to be "up-to-date," as, for example, electronic data-processing equipment, but the organization is, as yet, unable to use it effectively. In many instances facilities and resources are inadequate for the needs of the organization.

d. Relative Efficiency: Age, Obsolescence

The relative efficiency of equipment has much to do with how people feel about using it, particularly if they are under pressure to produce specified quantities. If machine tools cannot hold tolerances, if utility crews do not have protection from the weather in their truck cabs, if the air conditioning repeatedly fails to cool the hot kitchen, the feelings of the workers will be worn on their sleeves. One way for the assessor to infer something about relative efficiency is for him or her to question the people who are using the equipment.

e. Special Demands Plant and Equipment Make on People

Here the assessor should consider what the plant or equipment makes people do or hinder them from doing and what pressures plant and equipment exert on people.

f. Varieties of Work Environments

A garment factory located in a dingy loft with poor lighting on New York's Seventh Avenue will be a different working environment from a colorfully decorated office suite in Rockefeller Center just a few blocks away. The kitchen help and the bellmen employed by the same hotel have vastly different work environments. The varieties of work environment, the uplands and lowlands, are the context for what might be referred to as the "sociological temperature" of the organization. Degrees of such sociological temperature are related to an organization's status system and also say something about the kinds of people who can be attracted to different parts of the organization.

The assessor must note the range of environments from that of the chief executive to that of the janitor. The questions to be asked are, What does this total work area look like? How centrally located are drinking fountains, toilets, elevators, dining rooms? What differences are there in furniture, pictures, carpeting, air conditioning, parking, and so on, in the various environments. Are employees free to change their environment to the extent of hanging their own pictures? Who has to approve which changes, and what does that mean for the environment? There can be many more questions, depending on the perceptiveness of the assessor. With respect to executive offices, or other areas where an employee or work group has the freedom to construct its own environment, the question may have to do with how the office symbolizes the individual's self-image, aspirations, fantasies, and needs. In many business organizations, official approval is required before a manager can hang a picture not taken from the company collection; other companies ban pictures entirely. Some companies seem bent on suppressing manifestations of individual tastes.

g. *Age, Condition, and Effectiveness of Computer and Other Technological Equipment and Systems*

Is its condition consistent with other physical plant equipment?

3. Ecology of the Organization

Ecology is that aspect of biology that deals with the mutual relations of organisms and their environments. Sometimes it is referred to as bionomics. The concept has been adapted to sociology; it refers to that branch of sociology that is concerned with the spacing of people and institutions and the resulting interdependency. It will be used in the latter sense in this manual. Organizations are making increasing use of social anthropologists to study customer habits and practices for designing products and defining their use (Hafnery, 1999; Labich, 1999).

a. Spatial Distribution of Individuals

The consultant should determine how and where people are located within the organization and what relative distance or proximity they have to each other. Individuals may work closely together while sharing a common task, operate in a complementary manner, or work independently. They may do all three at different times. They may be scattered, as in an electric power generating station where there are few people and much noise, or as in a widely dispersed international business; they may be congested, as in a machine shop with 25 machinists in a relatively small area. Even though the machinists may be physically close to each other, each may have to watch his or her machine carefully and therefore be psychologically distant from the person next to him or her.

b. Spatial Distribution of Activities

How are different components or activities of the organization related to each other spatially? What activity is where, and what are the routes to each? The assessor should consider those questions here. The spatial distribution of activities may be different from that of people because a given activity may be carried on in several different locations.

c. Implications of the Data on Spatial Distribution

In this part of the outline the assessor should be concerned only with an objective description of the organization. By combining his or her observations on spatial distribution, the assessor can report on the implications of conditions, circumstances, or requirements that are descriptively valid. These could include clique development, nodal points within the organization, who talks or is unable to talk with whom, what empires have resulted that are then to be guarded, or the points at which invisible lines are drawn purely on the basis of spatial arrangements.

4. Financial Structure

In the case of business organizations, the assessor will want to show how the company is financed: how many shares of common stock, preferred stock, bonds, debentures, what long-term mortgages, and similar financial facts that will indicate the company's financial limits of flexibility. In chapter 6, Section A, the assessor detailed the organization's financial condition. That was a generalized statement of its assets and relative financial position. If the company is publicly held, such facts are usually presented in its annual report, in greater detail in its 10K report to the Securities and Exchange Commission (which is public), and in the summaries of investment counselors or stockbrokers. The assessor can obtain such summaries from any stock broker. The assessor can also obtain "How to Read an Annual Report" without charge from Merrill Lynch & Company. On-line resources include The Source, a global business browser, LEXIS-NEXIS, and, of course, the company's website.

If the company is not publicly held, the assessor should get a summary for a publicly held organization to use as a guide to the kind of information he or she should have. If the assessor is unfamiliar with balance sheets and the meaning of financial summaries, the assessor should ask an accountant to explain what the summary means as far as the organization is concerned. The assessor should be particularly alert to the facade the organization is trying to present in its financial reporting and the implications of its reporting practices for the way the management perceives itself, its competition, and its environment. One New England retail chain described itself grandiosely on a map on the cover of its annual report as now being beyond New England. It had one store in Albany, New York. It went broke.

Financial and control procedures for nonprofit organizations—churches, colleges, and similar organizations—are considerably different from those of business. In such cases the dues, contributions, or tax structure may be important as a reflection both of the organization's financial problems and who exerts control. Nonprofit organizations that raise funds from the public often must report to state authorities. The National Charities Information Bureau in New York issues quarterly reports on such organizations. A significant feature of their work is the amount of money each charity devotes to raising funds.

The financial assessment of noncommercial institutions is more difficult than that of business organizations. Schools may be compared on a cost-per-pupil basis with other schools; on comparative square-foot cost of buildings; on amount of money spent on libraries, laboratories, and other specialized equipment. Journals and books on educational administration offer various yardsticks. *U.S. News and World Report* publishes an annual evaluation of colleges and medical facilities. *Business Week* annually publishes an evaluation of business schools. Similarly, comparative measures can be found for hospitals, churches, and other institutions. Every institution also has its equivalent of "profit," some accrual of the results of its effort. Every institutional form has some way of judging whether it is getting its money's worth out of what it is spending, however inadequate the yardsticks may be. One must be careful in making interinstitutional comparisons because accounting systems may vary. There is considerable argument in the accountancy literature about the need for standardization. Before making comparisons within the same organization from one year to another, check to be sure there has been no change in accounting methods and also that adjustments have been made in actual figures for inflation and other forces that might alter the value of figures that are being compared. For example, if the cost of living is discussed in terms of today's dollars, a comparison with earlier years can be made in absolute terms.

Three general comparisons may be helpful: interorganizational over a span of years; interorganizational within the same industry, field, or service; comparison with other (national) trends. A different inference will be made if the organization is doing poorly while others of its kind are doing well or while all of its kind are doing poorly during an economic depression that affects everyone.

Accrediting agencies are good sources of criteria and comparative statistics. The Joint Commission on Accreditation of Healthcare Organizations in Oakbrook Terrace, Illinois, and the North Central Association of Colleges and Schools, in Tempe, Arizona, are two such agencies.

5. Human Resources

Human resources refers both to the people in the organization and the formal organization practices with respect to them as employees. At this point, the assessor should determine who the people are in the cultural and behavioral sense and how the company or institution relates to them. Some business organizations refer to their employees as associates in an effort to deny power differences. (Target Stores refers to customers as guests as if to convey the idea that the store takes care of its customers.) The structure for formal human resources relationships, or "how it is done here," is based on implicit assumptions about human motivation, social responsibility, mutual obligations, and similar issues. Both the people and the practices should be described in sufficient detail that subsequently the assessor can validate the organization's assumptions by examining the practices and comparing those assumptions with the socioeconomic and cultural facts.

a. Number of Employees

The assessor would do well to divide the personnel into different functional groups.

b. Geographical Origins and Ethnic Composition

The assessor should consider here certain aspects of the employees' backgrounds. For some employees it might be important to know their country or location of origin, which will say something about their traditions and attitudes toward work. For example, a large group of German-descended machine tools specialists settled in Rockford, Illinois. They brought a national tradition of mechanical skill, high mechanical standards, and compulsive personalities that has carried over in subsequent generations. Such features are assets for certain industries, while at the same time they might create problems when such individuals supervise others who do not share the same tradition. For other industries it might be more important to know that the employees come from the surrounding farm communities or that they have been born and reared in the city. "From" should refer to that locale which is likely to have significance for present behavior related to the organization.

c. Educational Levels

Here the assessor should determine if there are significant differences in education among people in the organization. Are such differences random or by skill; are they based on occupational responsibility or on some other basis? How many people are there at various educational levels and what are their occupational relationships to each other?

d. Average Tenure

The assessor should discover how long people stay in this organization. Does tenure vary at different levels and in different parts of the organization? Has it changed over the years?

e. Range of Skills

Here the assessor should ask, Do employees come to the organization unskilled and receive limited training? Do they arrive with a wide variety of educational and skill experiences as on a complex construction or engineering project? How well are their skills utilized? Are there a few at the top who have most of the knowledge and skill? Can the organization develop its own talent?

f. Absentee Rate

The absentee rate is a significant indicator of morale. The rates are computed within industries and can be computed within an organization for different units. Like all other rates, they may be computed differently in various organizations, so comparisons must be made cautiously. Sick-leave statistics are one good indicator, but they do not include days taken without pay. An increasing practice, supported by federal law, in business organizations allows employees to take time off to deal with family obligations and responsibilities, such as caring for newborn infants or elderly parents and other personal obligations. Rates differ for men and women and for older versus newer employees. Some people consider the absentee rate to be an index of people's withdrawal from the organization. For churches and schools, attendance rates may serve a similar purpose.

g. Turnover Rate

The absentee rate is an indication of the rate at which people stay away from the job; the turnover rate tells in what numbers they leave it. Turnover rates are compiled by industry just as are absentee rates. A high turnover rate may suggest poor working conditions, inadequate compensation, inadequate selection efforts, increased competition for scarce personnel, or a change in the social value of given work.

h. Accident Rate

Accidents may be viewed psychologically as another form of withdrawal from what is experienced unconsciously as a painful and difficult situation from which there seems to be no other escape. Accident rates are computed in varying ways. The generally accepted standard for computing this figure and the comparative industry rates can be found in the *National Safety*

CHECKLIST 15: CHART FOR ANALYZING HUMAN RESOURCES STATISTICS

	Area or Unit	Area or Unit	Area or Unit	Area or Unit	Area or Unit
Number of Employees					
Educational Levels					
Ethnic Composition					
Average Tenure					
Absentee Rate					
Turnover Rate					
Accident Rate					

News. Some organizations pride themselves on their low record of lost-time accidents. Such records should be reviewed carefully because they can often be facades; with pressure for a good record, people may be carried to the job even if they cannot do much work. Unless the employee has lost two days' time, some companies do not include certain accidents in their accident rate. The accident rate may be less relevant to organizations where there are fewer opportunities for accidents (a university contrasted with a steel mill). (See Checklist 15.)

6. *Structure for Managing Human Resources*

All organizations have established practices, policies, and programs for managing their employees. These range from highly sophisticated, professionally managed activities to informal practices derived from precedents. In this section the consultant should describe them in detail.

a. *Recruitment*

The assessor should investigate the methods the organization uses to recruit its personnel. Where does it look for what kinds of people, and what are its processes for bringing them into the organization? What success does it have with its methods?

b. *Orientation*

Here the assessor should ask, In what ways does the organization help people learn about what they are expected to do? What the company stands for? What its range of activities is? He or she should determine what process there is for the new employee to become familiar with the setting, the people, the expectations, and the politics and if there is any procedure for defining the psychological contract.

c. Training

Orientation is the attaching process. Training prepares employees to perform the work expected of them. Here the assessor should ask, In what ways does the organization help people develop the skills they will be required to use in performing assigned tasks? Training will vary with the degree of competence required of the person when he or she is employed. A nurse would get far less on-the-job training than an unskilled person employed as an orderly. Some organizations have formal preassignment training programs. Others use on-the-job training programs in which the supervisor is expected to instruct the new employee. Apprenticeship is a form of on-the-job training. Still other organizations provide no training at all or expect the employee to learn the task from other employees. The kind of training program reflects the organization's assumptions about people and also something of the organization's self-image—for example, "They won't stay anyway" or "There's no point in our having a training program. We're not very sophisticated here; anybody can do this kind of work." When a new chief executive at Florida Power and Light Co. instituted training for everyone, critics said he was training people who would go to other companies. He admitted some might, but he had to have a pool of trained people on whom to draw. Those who chose to leave would be good advertisement for FPL. Many other companies recruit managers heavily from Procter and Gamble and General Electric, who follow the same principle.

d. Developmental Opportunities

The assessor should ascertain what provisions the organization has for planned horizontal and vertical job growth. Horizontal job growth refers to scheduled training and experiences that help a person learn more about and do better at what he or she is presently doing. How, for example, does a psychiatric aide become a better psychiatric aide? What provisions are there for talking over problems on the job? For encouraging staff members to write or lecture? For keeping abreast of technical changes? Planned vertical job growth refers to systematic preparation for higher level jobs.

e. Promotion

Here the assessor should investigate what opportunities exist for upward mobility and to whom they are available. Does the organization promote from within the organization or seek outsiders? Some organizations have a covert NIH (not invented here) policy that precludes bringing in outsiders with different ideas. Others have a covert NHKA (nobody here knows anything) policy; preferred positions are offered to outsiders. How frequently are people promoted? Some organizations have regular and predictable promotion steps; some, like the military or the U.S. State Department, have an "upward or outward" policy: People are either promoted within a given period or they must leave. Still others promote erratically. Some organizations promise rapid promotion but cannot deliver; others, without adequate criteria, just think they offer rapid promotion. Promotions in some organizations are on the basis of favoritism or nepotism. In others, there are panels of superiors who make choices. In the latter case, performance appraisals are usually the basis of choice. In some organizations, particularly for higher level jobs, psychological testing is the practice.

The more farsighted the organization, the more likely it is to have anticipated its future staff needs, to have designed a program to assess potential candidates for roles of increased responsibility, and to remain informed of its human resources with some form of skill bank or talent pool—a readily available record of who can do what and who is likely to move where when. The more open, definitive, and objective the promotion policy, the more it contributes to trust and a sense of fairness.

f. Compensation

Compensation is sometimes a difficult area to delve into because some organizations prefer secrecy. That in itself says something. Closed salary practices are often rationalized on the basis that they avoid conflict. Usually they serve to suppress the conflict and to avoid dealing face to face with people. Also, compensation may be structured in such a way as to militate against productivity—for example, unit piece work that increases production of components but does not ensure the quality of the whole. Some compensation is bargained for, as in union contracts. Some is beneficent: The management bestows it on employees in such a way as to communicate its kindness. Some is based on comparative salary structures in the community. Some is incentive-based. Whether individual or group, incentive systems indicate the organization's underlying conception of work motivation. The assessor should be interested in the internal, external, and comparative aspects of the wage scale. Some organizations offer long-term financial security and use that practice to justify lower wages. Some view their employees as temporary and expendable, whereas others anticipate a continuing relationship. Charitable organizations frequently scale their wages and salaries below profit-making organizations on the thesis that they provide more stimulating work environments or that they serve a cause and the employee therefore should accept a lower wage.

Questions the assessor should ask here are, What are the wage rates and how do they compare with others in the community? What variations are there in the company? How do they compare with others in the same field? How are they established? Who decides? Who reviews the scales how and when? Who gets what increments? Incentives? Bonuses? Stock option? Overtime?

g. Performance Analysis

Performance analysis (sometimes called personal effectiveness) refers to a periodic evaluation of the employee's job performance (Murphy & Cleveland, 1991; Waldman, Atwater, & Antonini, 1998). This is a crucial process because ideally it fosters open evaluation between a person and another to whom he or she is accountable. However, in some organizations, it is not done at all; some have provisions for semiannual or annual performance reviews; a few ask subordinates to evaluate superiors. In some organizations, standards or goals are formulated by the human resources department or with its help, in others, by a person's immediate superiors. The more detailed the job description, the more likely there is to be a performance appraisal and the greater the likelihood that it will be used as a basis for promotion and compensation. More progressive organizations look on performance appraisal as an opportunity for subordinate and superior to review their joint efforts and their working relationship. Some separate performance review from salary review so that the superior does not act simultaneously as both coach and judge.

Some use 360° feedback, referred to earlier, in which comments are solicited from all who know or are in contact with the individual. This method poses problems because often those whose views are solicited do not know the technical aspects or the quality of the individual's work, so the process becomes a method of evaluating interpersonal behavior. As such, it does little to strengthen the relationship between a given person and the person to whom he or she is accountable, and the resultant need to please others fosters conformity. In some cases, the anonymous feedback can be vicious and unfair. In many companies, it is a method to evade critical evaluation by the person to whom the employee reports.

The inadequacies of performance appraisal were reflected in the large layoffs of 2000 and 2001 when many companies graded employees on a statistical curve and terminated the bottom 5% or 10%. Employees complained that such a method was arbitrary, without being based on feedback about their real performance, and that the method often was applied when there were not enough people to meet the statistical requirements of such a curve.

Judgments are always being made about performance. The more open they are, the more they are likely to enhance the relationship between a given employee and his or her manager, and the greater the opportunity for people to evaluate their own realities. Otherwise, employees tend to find out how they are doing only by the "squawk index"—that is, complaints when they err. Sometimes there may be a formal system honored in the breach or applied only at middle management levels; some systems fail because those who must appraise and evaluate others usually have feelings of guilt about negative criticism and therefore do not really evaluate. If no one helps supervisors and managers with the guilt feelings, despite repetitive changes in the appraisal forms, the system then fails (Levinson, 1984). Because of guilt, appraisal tends to be honored in the breach at higher executive levels. In that case, executives complain that they do not know how they are doing. The assessor should look carefully at the way the appraisal system actually works in practice.

h. Kind and Intensity of Supervision

Supervision is the key element in the support of a given employee or employee group, regardless of the level of the person in the organization. Even so-called leaderless groups are accountable to a higher level manager. The assessor may make a subjective judgment based primarily on his or her interviews with the organization's employees, may make inferences from a questionnaire (see the example in appendix A), or may have direct information from an attitude or morale survey or feedback effort. The assessor will want to know whether the supervision is directive, supportive, or autocratic; close or distant; regular or intermittent. Does the superior meet regularly with those who report to him or her for whose work the supervisor is responsible? Is the supervision predictable or is it intermittently harsh and lenient? Do people know what to expect? Are they comfortable turning to the superior for advice and guidance? What is the span of control or the ratio of supervisors to supervisees? How much time is the supervisor allotted for supervision as contrasted with having to take time from his or her other activities? How do the answers to these questions vary from level to level?

i. Rules and Regulations for Employees

Rules and regulations are the "laws" by which the organization seeks to control behavior. Some organizations, like Nordstrom Department Stores, have few rules, giving their employees maximum flexibility and trusting their judgment. Others have both written and verbal rules. The former usually are codified in the form of an orientation manual, a volume on rules and procedures, or a series of published memoranda. Verbal rules most often have to be elicited in interviews. Sometimes there are rules that are not verbalized but adopted by employees in reaction to a statement or reaction by a superior. (Later I will refer to the terms of the labor contract.) The assessor should note the form the rules are in, if written: book? pamphlet? How comprehensive and detailed are they? What matters do they cover? What rules are most important? Are the rules the organization's own or are they required by its customers or clients—for example, government contracts or codes of hospital practice. If there are no formal rules, are there deeply ingrained traditions that cause people to behave as if they were rules?

Throughout this part of the outline, as already indicated, the assessor should be interested only in reporting and describing. This is a compilation of raw data from which conclusions will be drawn later. The question of how closely the rules are obeyed is reserved for chapter 8. The assessor should also reserve interpretations and inferences from the rules and regulations about the character of the organization.

j. Health Maintenance Program

This refers not to an insurance program alone but also to actual prevention and treatment services. The assessor should determine if there are such services in the organization. Is there a medical department with physical facilities? Are there physicians or nurses there regularly or on call? Is there a preventive medical program that includes regular examinations of personnel, inspection of the premises for toxic and other environmental hazards? How does the medical department compare with standards for an accredited medical department? What is the relationship of the medical department to management—that is, to what extent is the physician or nurse alert to the stresses created by managerial practice, and how is that awareness conveyed to the management? With what results? Are there programs that encourage fitness, weight control, cessation of smoking or drinking, or the prevention of AIDS, and similar efforts? Who conducts them, when? Is there an employee assistance program? Who conducts it? At what professional level?

k. Environmental Program

Many large organizations now have an environmental officer who is responsible not only for the impact of the organization on its environment but also for detecting and combating internal hazards that might affect health and safety. Medical and safety departments often are incorporated in the environmental unit. The assessor should determine what the organization's formal program is. In some organizations there is a safety director. That individual maintains a continuous inspection of the plant for hazards, often working in conjunction with the company physician. If there is a large plant, or there are specific chemical hazards, there are likely to be industrial hygienists and toxicologists as well. A well-run manufacturing plant will have mechanical or chemical hazards conspicuously painted and guarded. Paths will be demarcated to avoid dangers. Safety glasses will be required of anyone entering the plant. There may be emergency drills, practice alerts, and similar training activities. Many companies have safety meetings, safety contests, first-aid training, and other devices. Sometimes the safety program is just a gesture. The program may be the responsibility of the employees, the supervisors, or the professional director. It may be systematic or sporadic, rigidly or lackadaisically enforced or ignored. The enforcement medium may be public exhibition of the offender as by placing his or her name on a public bulletin board; comparative statistics between departments; posters; interdepartmental competitions for lowest accident rates; pins and trophies for accident-free years. It is rare to find a safety program that takes into account the emotional climate of the organization as a precipitant of accidents and where there is a relationship between the safety officer and higher management to examine such forces.

l. Retirement Program

Some organizations have a formal retirement policy; others do not. Those that do usually have a published statement of the policy together with a summary of the benefits to which the employee is entitled. Some have a preretirement program to prepare the employee for retirement. Some continue to furnish medical services; send the company newspaper; invite the retired employee back to company functions; and provide legal, financial, and other counsel. Some organizations permit retired executives to use their offices, even their secretaries, or to continue to be related to the company as consultants. The Harvard Business School has an office building with secretarial services for retired faculty members. Some businesses provide offices at a site away from the company for retired executives. Many companies retire employees with a gift and a handshake, abruptly severing the tie. As a product of downsizing, many employees are prematurely retired, some without reasonable recognition of their years of service and without continuing ties to the organization.

Retirement programs vary widely, and the assessor must examine carefully the organization's policies, particularly because the psychology of the work relationship is so deeply embedded in the retirement program. For example, a person may lose retirement rights if he or she leaves the organization before a certain time. He or she may also be subject to early retirement, at lower income, at the whim of the company. The retirement program may bind the company and employee in such a way as to make their relationship inflexible. It will be important to determine how often the retirement program is reviewed and from whose perspective.

m. Recreation Program

Some companies foster comprehensive recreation activities and facilities for their employees. IBM, for example, at one time provided country clubs for its employees in the New York area. Other organizations sponsor teams and leagues, paying for uniforms or operating expenses for activities engaged in off the premises. At one time there was a league of semipro basketball teams sponsored by companies. Few companies now have such teams, or those that carry their name may be voluntarily composed by employees. Some companies now own arenas and stadiums that carry their names. The assessor should ascertain what is done in this organization. For what stated reasons? How many people participate? With what feelings on the part of the employees? Are trophies displayed? Is recreation played up in the newspaper?

n. Other Fringe Benefits

The assessor should investigate what, if any, other special benefits, perks, and conveniences are provided by the organization. Some provide stock options; others give bonuses or extended vacations. Some employ the children of their employees during the summer months. Many universities pay for the college tuition of their professors' children. Other organizations pay for medical examinations outside the company. Some provide parking facilities, and for executives above a certain level, automobiles. Others grant their employees discounts on company products. Some provide below-cost meals in company cafeterias; others, club memberships; some allow for or encourage teaching in colleges if the employee is a specialist. A few even allow their specialists to consult with noncompeting outside firms. Some lend managers to community services. Some fringe benefits have a paternalistic tradition, but most paternalism has disappeared from American companies, less so in nonprofit, especially religious, organizations.

Other fringe benefits may have a public relations motive, such as the provision in one company that employees may invite a given number of guests per month to join them for a free lunch. Still others, such as liberal severance pay and help in finding a new job, are intended to ease the process of moving people out of the organization with less anger and recrimination. In some overseas operations, particularly in developing countries, or under extreme climatic conditions as on the North Slope of Alaska, organizations may have to provide housing, food, entertainment resources, medical services, and transportation.

o. Labor Contract

If an organization has a contract with a labor union, the assessor should get a copy and append it to the case write up. The consultant should examine the contract not only for its specific provisions but also for its tone. Some contracts will be highly militant; others, innocuous. There are likely to be reasons for either extreme. A bland contract may be a "sweetheart" agreement; that is, one in which the management has bought off the union leadership. An important question is who negotiates the contract: Depending on the union, it may be done by a local committee or an international representative. A contract negotiated by an international representative is likely to be more in keeping with an industry-wide pattern than one negotiated by a local committee. How detailed is the contract? How rigidly interpreted?

Sometimes labor contracts are extremely complex and reflect mutual hostility in bargaining. The assessor may want to have an interpretation of the contract by both unionized employees (or their stewards) and outside experts who represent management in labor relations.

If the institution is a school or a university, there may be individual contracts with individual teachers. A union of teachers or a chapter of the American Association of University Professors may represent the faculty beyond the individual contract. Usually there are college-wide or system-wide provisions for tenure and, in universities, faculty senates or other consultative bodies. The relationships between employee-representative bodies and management or administration should be examined.

7. Policies and Procedures

The various ways in which an organization relates to its personnel have been described in the previous discussion. This section deals with an organization's efforts to maintain a common mode of operation. The more formal these efforts are, the greater their number, the more bureaucratic the organization. However, to label them bureaucratic is not the same as passing negative judgment because they may have to do with maintaining the quality of the product or service, with protecting the employee and the company from injury or suit, or with ensuring that the employee or customer is treated similarly in all branches or aspects of the operation. Policies and procedures ideally are the methods by which the organization accomplishes its work economically and according to certain standards.

a. Scope

Here the assessor must learn how much of the organization the policies and procedures cover. They may have to do with emergencies, such as fires and accidents, or they may cover all aspects of the activity as do policies and procedures in the military. They may be rigid guidelines as in a hospital. They may vary from section to section within a single organization.

b. Mode of Communication

Some organizations bind their policies and procedures in massive loose leaf books, and others frame them and hang them on the wall. Elsewhere they are communicated by word of mouth; some are ritualized. Some are stated on bulletin boards, in company newspapers, on public address systems. Those that are published in books are frequently revised and amended in some organizations, but ignored in others. The form in which the policies and procedures exist suggests something about how much attention the organization gives to their control. The assessor should investigate whether there is a systematic method for informing employees of the policies and procedures, or whether the organization ignores the matter. If the policies and procedures are written, who has copies of them? Are they conveniently available to all or hidden on a shelf behind a supervisor's desk? Are copies given to new employees during their orientation? Do the employees have the opportunity to learn the "why's?" What is the tone of the material: helpful? forbidding? instructive? Are they covered with dust?

c. Who Knows About Them?

In many organizations there are multitudes of policies and procedures of which many employees are woefully ignorant. People tend to forget even about such personal matters as insurance and retirement provisions if they are not immediately concerned. Sometimes there are specific policies for rare circumstances about which many supervisors may be unaware. Gaps in knowledge of policies and procedures can lead to poor customer relations and can give rise to communications difficulties, to manipulation, to projection, and feelings of injustice. The consultant should check for these situations.

d. What Discretion Is Left to Lower Supervisory Levels?

Here the assessor should ask: What degree of flexibility does the organization have with respect to its policies and procedures? To what extent must the employees follow the exact letter of the written policy or, conversely, use his or her own discretion? Where the discretion is voluntary, it may take the form of a specific statement from higher levels or be a general attitude that says that policies are only guides and are expected to be used as such.

8. Time Span and Rhythm

Many organizations are time-bound, some by season, some by inventory or book-balancing tasks, some by fiscal or academic years, some by the weather, others by manufacturing processes, still others by contractual obligations. The assessor should determine to what degree the organization is governed by time requirements, or whether there are different time constraints for different units.

a. Seasonal Cycles

If the company is bound by seasonal cycles, the assessor should ask, Do the cycles, to some extent, control the periodic peaks and valleys of energy expenditure? Do they require forward planning? Do they constitute extraordinary pressures?

b. Diurnal Cycles

In some industries, such as newspapers, restaurants, banking, and live theater, there are daily peaks of energy expenditure. The assessor should discover how diurnal cycles affect an organization.

c. Planning Spans

Here the assessor should determine the time units by which the organization plans its future. Some organizations have a 10-year plan for the organization as a whole, 5-year plans for major divisions, 2-year plans for major units within a division, 1-year plans for subsidiary units, and 6-month plans for smaller units. Taken together, these make up a consistent direction for the whole. Many organizations, however, do not have long-range plans and operate on a day-to-day basis. The more the latter condition is true, the more the organization lets fate determine its course. Some concerns must necessarily plan decades ahead. For example, lumber companies, which must have a stand of trees 50 years hence, replace the trees they harvest with saplings. A major plant investment that will take 20 years to amortize implies a commitment to a long-range plan.

d. Degree Activities Are Regulated by Time

How much are people's daily activities regulated by time? There are two major ways this may happen: by a pace process, as in an assembly line that moves at a regular rate or a machine that operates in cycles; or by piece work or other time-measured units of production. Such activities usually mean that the work regulates the people rather than vice versa and, often, that people feel subsidiary to the work process. People in executive ranks, although ostensibly they may work from 8 am to 5 pm, are usually largely free of time regulations. Typically, executives really are not paid for their time but for their results or achievements or their ability to handle complexity (Jaques, 1996).

e. Attitudes About Punctuality

The assessor should learn how the organization feels about its employees coming to work on time. What, if any, are the penalties for tardiness? Is there a time clock? Are there provisions for flex time, for dealing with personal problems, for sick children or elderly parents?

f. Urgency

Some organizations permit their work to lag until the last possible minute. Then they put considerable pressure on their employees. Some carefully schedule their activities to avoid the pressures of rushing. The consultant should determine how much pressure there is to meet deadlines. How often do crises about deadlines occur? If there is a repetitive sense of urgency, why does it exist?

g. Concern About Deliveries

Here the assessor needs to learn how strongly the organization feels its responsibility to finish its work on time. Do its delivery dates mean something or are they just there? Does it realize that if it fails to keep its commitments about time, others may be unable to meet deadlines? How much does this trouble them? For schools, churches, and hospitals, the issue relates to concern for the effects of nonpunctuality, a form of nondependability, on others. A school, for example, might be unconcerned about when it delivered requested transcripts, about returning papers to students, about examination reports. Church services may be notoriously delayed or punctual. This factor has a certain cultural bias; for example, punctuality is something quite unimportant in Latin countries.

B. Process Data

1. *Communication Systems*

A vast amount of information is available to and in all organizations, most of which abstract only a small amount of it and use an even smaller fraction of that. The system for receiving, organizing, and integrating information is usually not clear even to those who make the selections. In these days of heavy emphasis on computer-based communications, there are companies that organize information systems for other companies. Enterprise resource planning often involves the use of products (e.g., QAD, PeopleSoft) to facilitate communication.

However, such a process occurs whether the organization recognizes it or not. Observations and interviews will quickly disclose that there is a regularity to information getting and information handling. The questions for the assessor are, What does the organization 'pick up' from its environment? What from inside itself? How? To what particular kinds of communication is it especially sensitive? How is what it receives transmitted inwardly? At what point is the communication interpreted, organized, integrated, assimilated, or rejected? Having accomplished that process, however inadvertently, how does the organization respond to the data it receives? Have various computer systems—especially networks, electronic mail, and "groupware"—improved communications and efficiencies? Is everyone trained to use them?

a. *Incoming: Reception and Routing*

How much of what kinds of information actually comes into the organization? Sometimes this is difficult to determine unless the assessor asks many different people within the organization and unless the assessor observes, in various visits, the kinds of information people have on their desks, the informal discussions after they return from professional or trade association meetings, and the themes of luncheon or coffee break discussions. Typically, specialists receive technical journals that are not shared with administrators. The latter may read general management publications to which specialists are oblivious. Typically, also, various departments within an organization do not share information from the publications they receive. It is not unusual for a CEO and several other top executives to have regular meetings in which they discuss aspects of strategy, budget, personnel, finance, research, engineering, and marketing. However, it is rare for these people to bring routinely to each other, and their group as a whole, new information in their respective fields.

(1) Amount and Types of Material

Information may range widely from publications to which the organization subscribes to reports on local politics from branch managers. It may include confidential reports on competitors' market testing, informal notes on discussions at a scientific meeting, a list of good restaurants in a major city, lectures by future-oriented thinkers, long-range weather reports, and a wide variety of other data.

(2) Modes of Transmission

How does the information get to the organization? By what means are the customer complaints, the information from trade shows, the reports from scientific meetings, the topics in a given periodical, the economic forecasts, projected market changes, technical inventions information, and so on, fed into the system? By noting how the organization gets its information, the assessor can begin to formulate some conception of the nature of the input, the form it takes, and the kinds of data the organization has to work with. There are various ways of viewing how the organization receives incoming information. The following breakdown is one simple classification.

(A) Oral or Written

Oral reports can range from a simple statement of a few sentences by a colleague of what went on in a trade show to a formal conference of invited participants who would be given a systematic summary of the trade show, followed by discussion and questions. A closed-circuit television broadcast, such as a surgical demonstration, could be considered an oral input. Written reports or inputs could be items from an abstracting service, an insider's newsletter on politics, as well as a marketing intelligence summary. Information that is written or printed is more likely to be considered to be authoritative, is more permanent, and can be more easily reviewed subsequently.

Do managers in some departments feel "out of the loop?" Do individuals at lower levels in the organization have old or inferior machines? Does the organization take advantage of "groupware" that allows individuals in disparate locations to work on one project (or document) simultaneously? Does management encourage telecommuting? Does management make computers available for individuals to use at home? Does the organization provide adequate computer education and hands-on training?

(B) Formal or Informal Channels

Material that comes through formal channels and by formal means often requires some direct or indirect response by the organization. Sometimes this response may be only acknowledgment in the form of initialing the message. Sometimes it may stimulate the organization to prepare some sort of response "just in case."

Some companies have "hot lines," 800 numbers for customer complaints or similar numbers for whistle-blowers to report incidents of corruption or malfeasance. Others deliberately do not have them to avoid having to respond or act.

(3) Timing, Rhythm, and Urgency

The assessor should determine if the organization gets regular inputs of information suitable to its needs. Is the information timely for the organization's tasks? Or does the organization have a "squeaking wheel" philosophy about incoming information, getting information only when it has a problem? Does it do anything about regulating the pace and intensity of input or does it find itself from time to time overwhelmed because it did not anticipate or cannot assimilate what it is getting?

(A) According to Plan

Some organizations have a regular plan for systematically obtaining information. They depend on regular reports on styles, trends, cycles, building starts, industry-wide sales, and so on, for their own planning. If such communications occur regularly and are comprehensive in their content, they constitute a solid, dependable base for organizational action.

(B) Erratically or Spontaneously

Some organizations pay attention to incoming information or seek it out erratically or spontaneously, almost as if on a whim or fad. Perhaps a crisis gives import to data they had or were getting all the time. Perhaps an officer was stimulated at a meeting or made to feel guilty at the country club or a speaker touched a sore organizational nerve. Charles A. Heimbold, Jr., former CEO of Bristol-Myers Squibb Company, reported that his company would spend $100 million in five African countries over four years in an effort to fight AIDS in Africa when Kofi Annan, Secretary General of the United Nations, sitting next to him at a dinner party, asked what his company was doing about that problem (Waldholz, 1999).

(4) Source and Audience

With many kinds of incoming communication it will be important for the assessor to know where it comes from and for whom in the organization it is intended. This is particularly important for political, economic, and labor relations information because the origins of such information and the people who get it will have significant impact on the company's attitude about these matters. Following this communications route will help to indicate to the assessor who the influential person is on which matters. Discovery of who is subscribing to what publications and who is privy to what kinds of information will tell the assessor something about the informal power structure of the organization. A certain degree of power is inherent in possessing information that others do not have. Those who share such information form enclaves, the boundaries of which often are reflected by the routing slips on the material transmitted. Comparison of such routing slips will indicate the extent to which circles of formal information overlap and where the lapses occur.

b. Processing: Integration, Decision

Having assessed what information comes into the organizational system and by what means, the assessor should now seek to discover what happens to various types of material. Who processes it? How? For what emphases and what purposes? What material is given what treatment, by what means, and with what timing?

(1) Amount and Types of Material

Who does what to what types of material? Political data, for example, can be used as a basis for an essay by the chief executive of the organization in an organizational publication. Morale studies and attitude surveys can be muted in various ways to soften criticism of certain officials, and some can be coded to identify respondents who have been promised confidentiality (Luccetti & Murray, 1999). A prospective merger may be presented in glowing terms to anticipate and avoid possible anxiety. The daily cash register tapes of a department store may provide accurate inventory or financial information for corporate management, but comparable information about supervisor–supervisee relationships may be suppressed at the store manager level. Some companies assiduously avoid public recognition and carefully guard public pronouncements. Hospitals are bound by the law and medical ethics to control information about patients. For many years the Roman Catholic Church published no financial information about itself.

(2) Modes of Processing

Here the assessor is concerned about by what modes the information is transmitted.

(A) Oral or Written

Are the reports from sales meetings translated into written form? With questions about their import? With suggestions about who should do what about problems? With action recommendations? Are the morale study reports secreted by top management or edited into glib generalities for the company newspaper? Are the stirrings of labor organizers translated into alarm-ringing memoranda to all supervisors? Are critical statements about a product from the Federal Trade Commission shunted to the public relations and legal departments, thus denying that the employees would have any interest in them? Are the figures about decreasing seminary enrollment withheld from denominational discussion? Is the bishop unwilling to hear complaints about his or her administration and therefore much more inclined to give emphasis to "identity crises" of the ministers in the synod? Do successive layers of management rewrite subordinates' reports in keeping with what they think higher management wants to hear (e.g., Ledeen, 1999)?

(B) Formal or Informal Channels

Some organizations give heavy emphasis to controlling and directing the formal distribution of information as in company newspapers and magazines, paying no attention at all to informal channels of communication. Others deliberately try to plant information on the "grapevine." Those organizations that are more technology- and research-oriented will organize and distribute abstracts of current literature and maintain a file of such abstracts in the organization library or other repository.

The process of dealing with suggestions is a mode of handling formal communications because suggestions usually require investigation and assessment by a committee, decisions about their relative importance and value, and integration into organizational activities, as well as some statement to the person who made the suggestion. In some organizations prizes are awarded, almost randomly, and suggestions rarely put to use. Others pay cash remuneration based on value and explain in detail to all employees which suggestions were given what awards and why. Some companies use the Scanlon plan (Lesieur, 1958) or some other device for sharing cost savings with the employee population. The buzz word is "gainsharing."

In some organizations financial data are organized on a comparative monthly basis and trends are charted, but access to these data usually is limited to top management. Some organizations suppress inspection reports, taking the risk that explosion, collapse, or catastrophe will not occur. Some, as in long-range planning, deliberately seek to collate all kinds of information in such a way that it can be used for making decisions. With contemporary information technology systems there is a tendency to concentrate heavily on those data that can easily be guaranteed. This means that the decision-making process may be heavily weighted in one direction.

When information is formally distributed through regular channels, in effect, it has been given official recognition and approval. Information that must be distributed through the informal power structure may tend to undermine the established authority (or be seen that way) or else not be given the recognition, criticism, or support it needs. For example, if information that a rival company has a new product that might jeopardize the organization's survival is the subject of rumor and if that news is not dealt with officially by management, employees may panic. The contrast between the formal channels of information distribution and employee reports of where they get their information is an extremely important one because it reflects something of how much employees trust the formal information they get and to what degree management trusts employees.

(3) Timing, Rhythm, Urgency

Is there some sense of the importance of transmitting information of a routine kind at regular intervals? Of a crisis kind immediately? What is the degree of seriousness with which communications distribution is regarded? The pace of processing, integration, and decision making in many organizations is notoriously slow, partly because of procrastination, partly because of indecisive leadership, partly because of inadequate delegation of responsibility. Some have formal steps for dealing on a regular basis with information and decisions about information. Others go to great lengths to organize and integrate information that is then often ignored in favor of impulsive action. Some investigate and reinvestigate, only to enter a market or build a plant long after competition has a head start.

(A) According to Plan

Some organizations have a regular plan for distributing incoming information. The employees know the plan and depend on it. If such communications occur regularly and are comprehensive in their content, people come to respect and to trust them. If information transmission is also flexible enough to be governed by the importance of the event and people's anxieties, then that, too, will increase trust. Does the organization hold a regular weekly or daily meeting for managers? Does the manager then inform his or her department of recent developments? Are these developments and matters the basis for some kind of decision making? Are responsibilities assigned, time schedules projected, the available information "squeezed dry" and allocated to areas of greatest relevance? If there are crisis situations, can the organization process information and make its decisions quickly?

(B) Erratically or Spontaneously

In some organizations information is only occasionally or spontaneously organized and processed for the use of the organization as a whole. This may be a result of a crisis situation or the sudden interest of somebody in a high position or because of the pressure of the external environment. A chief executive, having read about the importance of performance appraisal, an abbot having heard a lecture on communications, a human resources director having participated in a seminar on organizational change, may subsequently prepare a recommendation for the introduction of a given program into the organization. Many organizations have fad-like phases of interest in given topics. There are styles and fads in management as there are in clothing (Shapiro, 1995).

Some organizations provide information reactively. That is, they report to their people when there is a crisis or an eruption of some kind. A company that takes the trouble to tell its employees of its economic circumstances only when it faces imminent unionization can hardly expect its employees to trust its communications.

(4) Source and Audience

Much of the information needed here will already have been gathered for the previous communications items. However, particularly with informal information, it will be important for the consultant to specify where such information arises and to whom it goes. This not only tells the consultant who talks to whom and about what, but it also reveals something about who uses whom. Sometimes people communicate indirectly, knowing that information eventually will reach those to whom it is directed. It is also important to know where memos or voice mail messages accumulate and on what subjects. Source and audience is equally relevant for formal inputs. For example, it is not unusual for the editor of the company magazine to draw on articles published by manufacturers' associations and chambers of commerce that then are to be transmitted to employees as, in effect, endorsed by the company. The important point here is to find out who controls the formal communications channels within the organization, to what audiences do they go, and for what purposes are they used.

This section will also say something about what aspects of the incoming communications are selected for processing, what information is given formal recognition by the organization, how that information is integrated, and for whom it serves as a basis for decision making. Here, too, the assessor should be concerned about the possible audience outside the organization for whom such information is intended. Some company publications can be veiled statements of position and policy directed to political officials. Others can serve both to increase the general knowledge of executives in the organization and a selected readership of influential persons outside it. A policy statement enunciated by the chief executive of a company may influence the political views of his or her employees who serve on city councils, school boards, and similar public bodies. Investor relations are important for a publicly traded company. How does such an organization deal with the capital markets?

c. Outgoing: Routing and Response

Once the data have been received and processed, how are they used? How is the integrated information and decisions based on it made part of the organization's functioning? What is distributed to whom and why? How does the organization learn?

(1) Amount and Types of Material

How much organized data and what kinds are put into the organization's external communications distribution channels? Do regular publications go to select audiences or does the whole business community know how the company is faring? Does the organization publish information that might be helpful in health, welfare, or economic planning—for example, health statistics published by an insurance company, car loading figures published by a railroad? Does it exchange salary information with other organizations? The answers to these and similar questions in this section will tell the consultant something about organizational secrets and will also serve to delineate the areas about which rumors are most likely to originate.

(2) Modes of Distribution

Here the assessor should determine the specific ways in which the integrated information is distributed.

(A) Oral or Written Statements

Once the data are integrated, are they transmitted by word of mouth or by some kind of written statement or by computer? The more an organization depends on oral communication, the more likely it is to be reluctant to express itself publicly and the more likely it is to minimize its public relations.

(B) Formal or Informal Channels

Some organizations have formal channels for the distribution of inte-grated data, some provide data for those who ask for them. Some crucial data are transmitted informally by prearranged telephone conference calls and individual telephone messages and Internet conferences. The more informal the transmission, the more likely the data are to be limited to a select audience and the more power is shared by those who are privy to the privileged information.

(3) Timing, Rhythm, Urgency

Some organizations provide a steady flow of processed information on the basis of which others can then take action—customers, the public, suppliers, and so on. Other organizations may provide information at regular intervals, depending on sales cycles or other time spans relevant to the organization. Still others report only when compelled to do so.

(A) According to Plan

Does the organization operate on the thesis that all its publics need to know about its activities? Does it assume that they need to know well in advance of the execution of any plan or mode of operation? Does it give partial information, leaving people to fret about its implications? Does it think of how it wants to make maximum use of information distribution?

(B) Erratically or Spontaneously

Does information sometimes burst on the respective publics who are then surprised to be receiving it? Do they complain about being told sometimes, but not at other times? Do they learn systematically about some things but only occasionally and inadvertently about others?

(4) Source and Audience

Who actually gets which information, in contrast with those for whom it is intended?

d. Processing: Integration, Decision

(1) Amount and Types of Material

What kinds of information come into the organization? Books, periodicals, reports, inquiries, data?

(2) Modes of Processing

What happens when the information gets to whomever it was intended? Is it organized for some kind of reporting as the daily news summaries for the president of the United States? It is transmitted to which others? Who decides what to do with it?

(A) Oral or Written

How much of which information is communicated orally? How much is written or published?

(B) Formal or Informal Channels

How is it transmitted or distributed? Informally or by prescribed channels?

(3) Timing, Rhythm, Urgency

With what frequency or urgency for which materials?

(A) According to Plan

Some materials in some organizations are tabbed with routing slips listing who gets them in what order. Others are routinely sent to those who have requested them, as, for example, copies of scientific papers.

(B) Erratically or Spontaneously

Much material is treated casually, like magazines in a reception room. In fact, in some organizations people may be unaware of the information available to them.

(4) Source and Audience

Where does which information come from and for whom is it intended?

e. Outgoing: Routing and Response

(1) Amount and Types of Materials

How much of which kinds of material from the organization are distributed to whom? Catalogs, reports, news releases, pamphlets?

(2) Modes of Distribution

How are they distributed? Mail, e-mail, selected distribution?

(A) Oral or Written Statements

How is the material presented: By word of mouth, as in telephone conferences with security analysts or meetings with selected customers or by printed media?

(B) Formal or Informal Channels

Are there regular channels for such communications or are they sporadic?

(3) Timing, Rhythm, Urgency

With what sense of urgency or regularity does the organization issue information? Of which kinds to whom?

(A) According to Plan

Do they have formal plans for informing certain audiences of specific product, service, or other information?

(B) Erratically or Spontaneously

Are such communications irregular or casual efforts, perhaps in response to the need for product recalls.

2. Management Information Systems

Management information systems of many complex kinds are a given in all organizations. Here we are concerned with describing what kinds of such equipment the organization uses and to what effect. Target Stores, for example, were organized around computers.

a. Age, Condition, and Sophistication of Computer Equipment

How up to date are the various management information systems the organization uses? How well do they do what they are supposed to do?

b. Groupware

How much are computer communications shared by people in different locations who can work together with the same information, meeting by computer as it were?

c. Availability and Distribution of Laptops and Other Communication Devices

How widely distributed are laptops and other devices for people to communicate with each other?

3. Current and Previous Studies in, and Reports to, the Organization

Most organizations have various kinds of reports in their files. Some are not called reports but staff studies, others are called reviews. The assessor should make a special effort to see these. They can serve as a check on the assessor's own findings, illuminate areas with which he or she is less familiar, and suggest considerations that may not previously have occurred to him or her.

a. Consultant Reports

Practically any business organization of any size and often educational, religious, and other institutions as well, have used consultants. Most consultants' reports seem to have two fates: (a) They are acted on precipitously and result in drastic reorganizations without much thought; or (b) they are placed on an obscure shelf to gather dust. The usual reason is that most consultants do not know how to feed back their reports in such a way that they become the psychological property of the organization and a basis for thoughtful, concerted action. Often consultants' reports are simply digests of what the consultants have been told by people in the organization and are therefore regarded with contemptuous cynicism by those who have been interviewed. The latter feel exploited because they cannot give their views directly to their superiors and someone else is paid high fees to report as recommendations what they themselves have said.

Despite these problems a sensitive assessor can learn many things from such reports. He or she should try to discover why management approached a consultant in the first place. What problems did the company think it had? What kinds of consultants did management employ? Why those particular consultants? For example, if the company had a morale problem and chose a communications expert, it might be inferred that the management expected to coax its people out of the problem by talking to them more effectively. However, if management employed an expert in organization structure, the assessor could at least hypothesize that the management sought to deal with this problem by clearer accountability or perhaps by compulsive control.

If the assessor discovers that the organization has had repetitive consulting reports, he or she might infer that management does not regard its own staff's capacities highly. The assessor might also infer that management tends to idealize people outside the organization.

While looking for and at previous consultant reports, the assessor can sense how the organization feels about the reports. Sometimes he or she will discover that nobody knows about such a report and that it lies untouched on the chief executive's desk. Why?

b. Special Staff Studies

Special staff reports can tell the assessor the same kinds of things as do previous consultants' reports. Why were the staff reports undertaken? By whom? What became of them? With what attitude are they regarded by the rest of the organization? What use was made of them? When an organization has many staff reports that are used in decision making, the assessor can know that top management leans heavily on its own people for gathering information and making judgments. Often such staff reports are a device for teaching staff to diagnose and make recommendations on problems. However, management can also use such reports as methods of keeping people busy or for procrastinating. This is particularly a problem in political and university circles. A special staff report can also say something about who has to please whom, how, and why. It will be important to assess the discrepancy between what is on paper and what is actually felt by those who prepared the report.

c. Marketing Studies

Here the assessor should ask, How does the organization look at its markets? How well does it define the business it is in? Does it have a broad generic concept of what it is doing? Does it know not only who and where its markets are, but also who is likely to be served by the competition? Is the organization alert to competition from unexpected sources? Marketing surveys, as contrasted with staff studies, and consultant reports, tend to be either continuous or repetitive. Consultants are called into an organization to advise on specific problems. Staff studies are usually also responses to specific problems. However, marketing surveys are asking the question, Who are the customers and how are they reacting to what the organization is doing? A school system is conducting a marketing survey when it makes its annual pupil census study. A church undertakes a marketing survey when it seeks to learn the age range, occupational status, interests, and so on, of its parishioners or of the people in a given neighborhood whom it wants to recruit to membership. Focus groups are being used increasingly by all kinds of organizations.

The firm chosen to conduct the market survey or a focus group is of critical importance because that choice reflects the organization's degree of sophistication. For example, a management unsophisticated about psychological motivation but concerned about loyalty would more likely choose a survey firm that provided relatively quick and easy "yes" and "no" answers. As with the consultants' reports, the assessor must ask if the market survey is being used for its own sake or as a device to protect management jobs. Is its prime function to keep critics at a distance?

d. Engineering Studies

Engineering studies are technical in nature and deal with the questions of plant layout, product design, time and motion studies, work feasibility studies, work simplification procedures, and similar matters. They speak largely to the technical efficiency of the organization. Important questions for the consultant to ask are, On what facets of the organization do these studies focus? How often are such studies conducted? Have the studies brought innovations? What kind? What are the underlying assumptions about the motivations of people? These questions are important because some organizations seek to rationalize production by engineering methods to eliminate the effects of people's feelings. Some implicitly assume that human beings are simply another form of a machine. Management may undertake repetitive engineering studies in an effort to avoid the underlying, more complex human problems or out of a failure to recognize them. Some companies go to considerable lengths to consider human feelings and knowledge, using sociotechnical concepts (Trist & Murray, 1993) for manufacturing planning. A typical example of the contradictory effects of such studies is the recommendation for super highways to be constructed in such a way as to funnel traffic into downtown areas and to divide the city into nonviable sections. At the other extreme, a management may be so preoccupied with other matters that it is unable to recognize the importance of mechanical efficiency. Emphasis on Total Quality Management (TQM; Deming, 1986) and similar techniques in recent years has made significant use of employee input and expanded employee control of the physical environments and even organizational structure.

e. Accountants' Audits and Reports

Most organizations have annual accountants' reports and most do regular audits. Some are checked by outside sources such as state or federal auditors that check banks. Accounting control systems have three purposes: (a) economic motivation; (b) evaluation; and (c) planning. Here the assessor must ask, How well does this organization's control system serve these purposes? An important subsidiary question is, How are the accountants' reports used? Another is, What power do accountants have in the organization? Sometimes those who manage the organizational record keeping, because of their intimate knowledge of the organization's financial status, acquire extraordinary power. They are often the behind-the-scenes power figures and, by recommending budget allocations, formulate policy without being responsible for it. Often they are more likely to think of dollars first and the nonfinancial costs of financial decisions afterward, if at all. Regardless of how reasonable the reduction is, across-the-board cuts in spending suggest that the budget has become all important and the accountants are actually running the organization. Thus, the auditing and accounting system can be used as a check, as a feedback for decision-making, or as a cudgel on programming.

Another kind of accountants' reports is often incorporated into strategic or long-range planning studies, by strategic thinkers, actuaries, or economists, that forecast long-term cost and pricing trends or that predict average ages and incomes of employees, and their implications for organizational pension plans or medical insurance plans.

8

INTERPRETATIVE DATA: INFERENCES DRAWN

Having established the basic information about the organization, the next step is to approach its meaning. There are three steps in the process: (a) to infer a hypothesis whose data are established; (b) to interpret that meaning from a conceptual point of view; and (c) to integrate the interpretations into a consistent whole or conclusion.

III. INTERPRETATIVE DATA:
INFERENCES DRAWN FROM THE ANALYTIC DATA

A. Current Organizational Functioning

The data gathered to this point have been almost wholly factual. It would be easy to obtain agreement about the data if several disinterested parties were to undertake the same search. Those inferences that may have had to be made at various points were but limited extrapolations from the data and could be made by most people without specialized training.

Now, however, the assessor must begin to exercise his or her professional judgment. Different assessors using this manual may arrive at different inferences, depending on their training, experience, and theoretical orientation. Regardless of these factors, every assessor should be aware that he or she is dealing with inference and must be prepared to offer evidence for the inferences and the conclusions he or she reaches. Only by offering evidence can the assessor specify the sources of knowledge, indicate how well he or she has tested the hypothesis advanced, and differentiate and identify speculation and opinion. There is nothing wrong with speculation or opinion, with intuitive hunches or global judgments, if they are appropriately identified. However, the assessor should keep facts separate from inferences. If the assessor fails to do so, he or she not only defeats the value of the scientific attitude, but also fails to take advantage of the opportunity to teach him- or herself consciously.

Current organizational functioning refers to how the organization learns, thinks, feels, and behaves, if it can be said that an organization does these things. In chapter 7 we discussed its structure or the equivalent of its anatomy or sociology. In this section we will be talking about its functioning, the metaphorical equivalent of its physiology and psychology.

1. Organizational Perceptions

Organizational perceptions refer to how and what the organization senses, both within itself and in its outside environment. Perception is the active receiving system of the organization.

a. Degree of Alertness, Accuracy, and Vividness

Here the assessor should be concerned with the extent to which, and with what effectiveness, the organization recognizes and uses that information that is available to it. The bombardment of stimuli may range from newspaper reports stating that for the past five years summers have been arriving earlier and lasting longer to the most recent Supreme Court decisions affecting parochial schools or organizational mergers. An alert organization may realize quickly from weather and sales curves that it should have its fertilizer on the market earlier next year, or, in the course of a law suit, that it may have to adopt different business or enrollment practices. An acutely alert organization will be open to perceiving potential threats— such as regulatory, environmental, and technological discontinuities—to exploit them to its own advantage (Grove, 1996). Conversely, an organization may be insensitive to the import of its environment or may misinterpret or perceive external stimuli only dimly, as happened with IBM, General Motors, and Eastman Kodak in the 1980s (Levinson, 1994). An organization's actions subsequently will be based on what it is able to perceive.

The assessor must make subjective judgment about "degree of alertness." An experienced assessor may be able to compare this organization with others or may be able to contrast the way people speak with the way they act. *Alertness* refers to the number of antennae the organization has out and the degree of sensitivity it has to their vibrations. It also has to do with the *kind* of antennae, because the organization cannot "hear" what its sensing instruments cannot resonate with.

Accuracy refers to the judgment about the correctness of the interpretation of the stimuli. For example, some metropolitan city officials often heard early rumblings of a potential riot. However, just as often, they failed to interpret what those rumblings meant and often mistakenly attributed the cause of the riots to outside agitators. If a competitor announces an expansion into a new region, is this signal a ploy intended to preempt its competitors from entering that region or market? A regular reading of the financial press would have answered the question of whether it has lines of credit in place to finance the announced entry. The projection of long-term population trends and the continuing constraints on power plant expansion should have alerted California state officials many years before blackouts occurred that they were going to face a shortage of power.

Vividness refers to the detail with which the stimuli are interpreted. Inadequate differentiation of detail results in a fuzzy conception of the situation, which in turn culminates in responses that do not effectively resolve the issue, or shotgun responses. Such public programs as rehabilitation of the unemployed and efforts to deal with juvenile delinquency flounder for just such a reason. The failures of the former programs were the result of politicians assuming the unemployed would be forced to work if welfare payments were constrained. But they did not see the problem clearly enough to recognize that some welfare mothers could not work without child care and that others were mentally ill. Similarly, efforts to increase the penalties for juvenile offenders by requiring the courts to treat them as adults do little to rehabilitate those who are impoverished or caught up in gangs.

It is theoretically possible to be alert without being either accurate or vivid. For example, early on many people could see new-fangled inventions like automobiles, airplanes, electricity, and computers. Failing to perceive accurately their implications for social change, few felt such inventions would last. Even fewer differentiated special commercial possibilities.

(1) To Stimuli From Within the Organization

How does the organization know what is happening within itself? Specifically, how alert is it to what is going on? How accurate and vivid are its perceptions?

(A) From Personnel

By this time the assessor will know what the processes of communication are within the organization and what the structures are for relationships among personnel. He or she should be able to make a judgment about how internal communications are received by the organization's management. For example, management may conduct a morale study and receive a report that its employees want more communication. Does management hear this as, "We must tell them more," "We must sell them more," or "This is an agitator-generated employee complaint?" Much of what management hears is determined by what it wants to hear. The assessor will have to judge how accurately and with what understanding management is listening to its personnel. For example, in 2001, both Yale and Harvard experienced organized student protests against raising wages for lowest paid employees. Both universities had long seen their compensation policies as more than fair and the student protests as unnecessary, but they yielded in the end.

i. Employees to Management and Vice Versa

When top management makes unilateral decisions that threaten employees and management presumes employees will simply accept them, it ignores employees' feelings. Employees characteristically are suspicious of top management's decisions and increased pressures on them about which they have not been consulted.

ii. Supervisor to Subordinate and Vice Versa

How well do supervisors perceive subordinates' feelings, wishes, and problems? And how do employees perceive those of their supervisors?

iii. Departments to Each Other's Needs

Often there is insensitivity and even conflict between departments within the same organization. The most common conflict occurs between production and sales departments. Such conflict usually exists in direct proportion to the pressure on each from higher management. As a result of such pressure, communications between departments decreases, empires are guarded, one group refuses to assist another for fear of having trouble with higher management. Conflict also occurs because of differences in values or objectives. A finance department values predictable cash flows; sales values new customers; technology values new technology that could pay off big in the future.

(B) From Physical Plant

People in the organization receive a variety of stimuli from the physical plant. Some are more easily identifiable than others. Smoke, heat, shabbiness, dirt are within everybody's purview. Lighting, decorations, quality of machinery, statistics of equipment breakdown say something—for example, whether the management cares or not. In chapter 7, A2, the assessor examined the plant and described and analyzed what he or she observed. Here the assessor interprets the effects of what he or she saw and the effects of things he or she did not notice then but has seen since or has had reported to him or her. The assessor should begin by asking, How are such things experienced by those in the organization?

(2) To Stimuli From Without

(A) Primary External Stimuli

Most factors that are basic to the organization's survival—where and how it buys and sells, sources of labor, how markets are going to change, and so on—are primary external stimuli. Some reference has been made to these earlier. Here the assessor must infer. How alert is the organization to the implications of these factors and the trends, pressures, and data that relate to them? The assessor must make judgments about the organization's response to nuances, its alertness to the accuracy and differentiation of subtle external stimuli.

i. Industry and Marketing Conditions

The assessor will need some knowledge about the markets for the particular organization to judge its degree of alertness, accuracy, and vividness with respect to them. The web is a useful tool for quickly gathering information about market conditions. In addition, the assessor can obtain such information from NEXIS-LEXIS, ABI-Inform, and other research engines available through university libraries, from trade journals, from annual reviews in such publications as *Forbes* and *Fortune,* from summaries in *Business Week*. Population trend data, social class data, insurance data, and similar information will yield the same bases for judgment with respect to schools, churches, and hospitals. *U.S. News and World Report* annually evaluates hospitals and universities.

ii. Purchasing Conditions

The ease or difficulty of buying supplies, obtaining raw materials or components, also will affect an organization's chances for long-run survival. Many organizations have established closer ties to their suppliers, both to maintain quality levels and to ensure just-in-time deliveries. Some involve suppliers in the design of their products—to hasten product development cycles. Some competitors have joined forces to purchase supplies on the web.

iii. Labor Conditions

Here the assessor should be concerned with the organization's sensitivity to the supply of potential employees, their preparation and training, their willingness to be employed, and the conditions under which they find employment acceptable.

Many organizations have a long history of labor conflict and repetitive media exposés of poor working conditions. There is so much information about such issues and other conditions that affect organizations that the assessor will have to limit his or her focus to those that seem most relevant to the present assessment. For example, the long history of industrial warfare in the coal, steel, and railroad industries makes fascinating reading, but only the inferences that one can draw from that history for their effect on today's problems will be worth the assessor's attention.

Other organizations have had equally long eras of positive relationships with their employees. There have been repetitive books and articles on the best organizations to work for, elaborating the conditions and practices that make them so good. For example, in 2001, Cisco Systems undertook to retrain members of the Communication Workers of America who were its employees and who otherwise would lose their jobs when those jobs became more technical and there was no longer a need for their former roles.

(B) Secondary External Stimuli

Here the assessor should ask, What are the organization's perceptions of other environmental factors that influence it but do not immediately and directly affect its survival? Often organizations react to secondary external stimuli as if they were primary. For example, some business people spend much time and effort fighting the "big government" when most would also recognize the need for nationwide standards and controls for many aspects of business.

Teachers' unions vigorously fight efforts to evaluate teachers and against incentives to reward good teaching despite the fact of increasing social pressures to do both. The Cuban refugee organizations in South Florida are still carrying on their vendetta against Castro, and the rest of the country is moving closer toward accepting him. The assessor will want to interpret such arguments that appear to be less than immediately salient.

i. Legislative (Regulatory, Tariff, and Tax Laws)

How alert is the organization to what the Congress, the state legislature, the city council, and various other regulatory bodies are doing? Some organizations exist by means of government protection—tariff, subsidy, or facilities. The rates others may charge are regulated. The operational standards of still others may be regulated by half a dozen different bodies. Some maintain powerful lobbies; some public utilities used to maintain continuous suits before regulatory bodies that enabled them to adjust their rates at will "pending the outcome of the decision." Some pay minimal attention to government. Others are highly sensitive to advantages given to competitive businesses by means of governmental regulation, as, for example, tax preferences, import quotas, and fixed prices. Florida for years governed its universities by a central board to prevent duplication of effort and to maintain consistent standards. When that board was abolished in 2001, the president of Florida Atlantic University publicly expressed his pleasure that his university was now free to compete with all the other state institutions.

ii. Transportation

Changes in transportation facilities, networks, schedules, and modes affect the use of all kinds of institutions and organizations. Some are alert to the implications of such changes, and others are oblivious until long after they occur. A distributor of computer peripherals in Syracuse, New York, sought to improve his competitive position by speeding up deliveries to his customers. He moved his distribution center to Albany which, because of the United Package Service routes, delivered his products a day earlier than from Syracuse. Many industries in small communities protest the loss of air service that diminishes their economic importance. Centralizing small rural high schools made for longer bus rides for the students but provided a wider variety of courses and extracurricular activities.

iii. Competitors

Does the organization maintain an awareness of what is happening in the rest of the industry or field? How does it understand what its competitors are doing? The issue of competition is just as important for churches, schools, hospitals, and other institutions as it is for businesses, because each competes for constituency, endowment, resources, and staff. In the Powell-Kole case, that awareness was obvious. Writers about religious institutions, noting the decline in membership of mainline Protestant churches, point to their failure to engage the emotions of many parishioners who have turned to more fundamentalist churches.

iv. Research Developments

Some organizations are alert to what is being accomplished in universities and are aware of current financial trends. Others are not so attuned. Some organizations do not use the fruits of their research, preferring to get patents on the discoveries and inventions of their laboratories solely to prohibit others from also discovering and using the ideas. Some license others' patents or buy other companies rather than invest in research in a given area. Some relate their research to current research trends; others seem unaware of them. Some churches revise their authorized translation of the Bible in keeping with contemporary archeological findings; for others, it is as if such findings did not exist. Some continue to deny scientific findings with theological arguments. It is important that the assessor learn his or her client organization's attitudes in this area.

v. Economic, Social, and Political Trends

The United States is moving toward an increasingly affluent, highly educated society. This means that its people are more sophisticated, want greater choice of product and service, and want to be more fully informed about them. These are only a few gross social trends. There are many others. The assessor should determine to what extent the organization is aware of such trends and with what clarity.

At the same time, the assessor should be aware that occurrences and trends in other countries can affect any organization based in any given country. The competitive marketplace is global. Although this is especially important for organizations that operate in foreign countries, it is equally important for those whose products or services may be replicated in other countries and sold in this one. As indicated earlier, for example, growing sophistication about computer technology has led to proliferation of data processing services in India, and greater manufacturing sophistication to the production of all kinds of goods in China. Statistics about better mathematics performance of Japanese and European high school students has stimulated efforts to improve those in American high schools. The success of the

American free enterprise system has led many underdeveloped countries to try to emulate it.

b. Direction and Span of Attention (Selectivity)

Here the assessor should learn, of all of the perceptions an organization has, what it concentrates its attention on and how wide its focus is. To what stimuli does it give exquisite attention; in what direction is its organizational radar turned? For many in Orthodox Jewish communities and some in Mennonite communities, there is no television nor do they go to movies. These same Orthodox Jews are heavily oriented to religious education and political efforts to preserve the integrity of their communities, even in some cases isolating themselves from surrounding communities. For years, railroad managements thought of themselves as being in the railroad business rather than the transportation business. Thus, narrowly focused, they were outflanked first by buses, then by aircraft, and now have difficulty competing with long-haul trucks.

(1) Dominant Foci of Interest

Many school systems are preoccupied with having students pass achievement tests. Organizations of Wisconsin and Vermont dairy farmers are intensely preoccupied with maintaining their subsidies to preserve the smaller farms against the growing competition of large dairies in Western states.

(A) Long-Term Framework

All organizations concentrate selectively year in, year out, on some aspects of their environment. In some organizations this is formalized in the form of "organizational planners" or "consultants in long-range planning." These organizations typically evolve statistical trends, projected years into the future. Other organizations may not plan formally in the same sense, but because of the training and experience of the leadership they continuously concentrate on those issues that are important to that leadership. What are those foci in the client organization?

Jewish organizations project trends on intermarriage and methods of preserving the integrity of the faith. Contemporary petroleum companies are concerned about the declining domestic oil sources. Federal health agencies are concerned with the increasing weight of Americans and efforts to get them to lower their calorie consumption.

(B) Short-Term Framework

Short-term framework refers to those matters with which an organization concerns itself that are likely to be relevant within the next year or two. It may refer to the fact that the organization focuses only on short-term issues.

Those petroleum companies that do not have their own production facilities and must buy their oil on the spot market, or that which is available from others as they need it, are continuously attentive to OPEC maneuvers, government oil reserves, and consumption statistics. Supermarkets and retail pharmaceutical chains keep a careful eye on the ads of their competitors, and some department stores send "shoppers" to report on what others are doing.

(2) Significant Neglected Foci

Having abstracted and interpreted what the organization pays attention to, now the assessor must make a judgment about those matters that seem to him or her relevant or that appear to be relevant in the eyes of others, although the organization is not attuned to them. Those factors that an organization does not heed—if they are relevant to its survival—ultimately will be the source of its downfall. If an organization cannot recognize relevant stimuli, this suggests impairment or pathology in organizational functioning that must be further investigated.

Once prominent Brooks Brothers, respected purveyors of conservative men's clothing, appeared to be unable to recognize trends toward more informal male dress, resulting in its decline. Communications companies that invested heavily in fiber optic lines found themselves in an economic morass as more communications were carried on by wireless methods. The then CEO of Digital Equipment Company, highly successful with sophisticated computers, did not foresee that computers would become almost as widely purchased as refrigerators (Fraker, 1983).

c. Assessment of the Discrepancy Between Reality and Perceived Reality

The assessor must now assess the organizational perceptions he or she has documented. Is there a difference between reality as the organization perceives it and as the consultant (or informants) sees it? An organization may be accurate in its perception of some stimuli but be incorrect in its interpretations of them. Sometimes an organization has become inept in a certain area; with new leadership, it may rise to unforeseen heights, as was the case of Louis V. Gerstmer, Jr., at IBM and Chrysler when Lee Iaccocca took over.

The converse is also true. Sometimes an organization precipitates its own difficulties and then must live with the results. The boards of two nonprofit hospitals, Good Samaritan and St. Mary's, in West Palm Beach, Florida, were accused of mismanaging them into misguided amalgamation and multimillion dollar losses. They were then sold to a hospital chain (Galewitz, 2001).

(1) Of Reality Within the Organization

If an organization has trouble understanding itself, the assessor will know that subsequently he or she must use subtle therapeutic or quasi-therapeutic methods to help the organization understand itself better. Such will be necessary when the disparity between what goes on in the organization and what it perceives comes across sharply to the assessor. For example, at the height of its clinical reputation in the 1950s, two new forces began to impinge on the Menninger Clinic: the development of group and family therapies and the advent of psychotropic drugs. The Clinic, still preoccupied with its heavy emphasis on individual psychotherapy, was slow to respond. Belatedly, after such new methods had established their usefulness elsewhere, they became integrated into the Clinic's treatment program (Stamm, 2002).

(2) Of Reality Outside the Organization

If an organization can perceive accurately what is going on inside itself, the most difficult kind of perception, but cannot see clearly what is happening outside, presumably the assessor can improve the situation by cognitive educational methods. Sometimes distortion of external reality is a matter of the personality orientation of the leader. For example, Sewell Avery led Montgomery Ward to near failure in the post-World War II years because he thought a depression was imminent (Vittert, 1997). That decline ultimately resulted in its collapse in 2000. Henry Ford in his later years failed to accept the reality of union organization. During the 1980s, John Akers, then CEO of IBM, and Kenneth Olsen, then CEO of Digital Equipment Corporation, among other CEOs, failed to respond to changes in the marketplace (Gannes, 1988). The distortion and perception may be a matter of simply not having sufficient education, broad enough perspective, or specialized knowledge to gauge the situation. Whatever the case, the assessor will have to make a statement about his or her understanding of this issue.

If the assessor finds the organization has difficulties in perception both within and outside itself, the assessor will have to raise serious questions about the kinds and quality of the assets available to the organization for its rejuvenation. Some problems cannot be solved, particularly if the same people remain in the organization or behind-the-scenes controls inhibit effective adaptation. That is what happened with the Good Samaritan-St. Mary's example.

2. Organizational Knowledge

In chapter 7 we discussed organizational communications channels, modes, sources, and targets. In the preceding discussion of perceptions we were asking, in effect, what is the organization's capacity for receiving stimulus input? We then sought to assess the effectiveness of the organization's perceptions. In this section we are concerned about what the organization *knows*. What body of information does the organization possess on which and with which it can act? Such a body of information is usually transmissible in the form of techniques, history, experience, specialized competence, research data, and project reports. How an organization acquires and makes use of knowledge is an indication of its adaptability. Here we must be careful to distinguish between that gross input called communication, which is a transmission of perceptions, and internalization, that information that is organized, integrated, and anchored within the organization as one of its strengths. Perhaps an analogy might be helpful. A college student may take a wide variety of courses and achieve good grades in many. The student may quickly forget what he or she has learned in most of the courses after completing the final examinations. However, the student usually will remember and integrate into a systematic body what he or she has learned in major courses and those that have had the greatest relevance for him or her. The student has, then, perceived many topics; indeed, the student may have communicated at great length about them. However, the student's knowledge is the integrated crystallized residual of all those data, which he or she can draw on for problem-solving and adaptation. The task of the assessor at this point, then, is to interpret from the previously noted data what the organization learned and how. In short, what has become its core competence?

a. Acquisition of Knowledge

Here the assessor is concerned with how the organization learns. CEOs of the General Electric Company reinforce their leadership practices in discussions with each entering class of managers at its Crotonville, New York, training center, a place where they live while they learn from visiting professors and each other. Some organizations turn interdisciplinary teams loose to learn from each other while they solve organizational problems.

Many organizations regularly send their people to both academic and technical training programs, to conventions, professional meetings and public programs. Some reimburse tuition. Some bring in outside experts on a regular basis. Increasingly, religious and health care organizations are involving their executives in managerial training. Academic organizations often provide for sabbaticals so that teachers can refresh and extend their knowledge. Some organizations have extensive libraries, others have computer-based teaching programs. Physicians at some distance from medical schools may check into computer-based consultation for immediate support of their diagnosis and treatment in local hospitals. Engineers in Acindar Industria Argentina de Aceros SA, a steel company in Buenos Aires, traveled all over the world to keep abreast of steel making. Florida Power and Light Co. sent managers to Japan to learn Japanese manufacturing methods, as did many other companies. Many organizations rotate their managers through a range of different jobs in different locales to broaden their experiences and enhance their adaptation to different cultures.

(1) Methods of Obtaining New Knowledge

(A) Related to Personnel and Plant

How and where does the organization acquire knowledge about personnel and plant (or its equipment)? Does it analyze and use regular audits and reports, such as morale studies and attitude surveys, as contrasted with those that are made and filed? Does it have a human resources staff, a human resources library? Some human resources departments are continuously aware of what is occurring both within and outside of their own organizations. They maintain their own training programs into which they bring outside authorities. They also participate in university seminars and other activities in related areas.

Some organizations, especially those in the pharmaceutical, food processing, and health care industries, are subject to regular government plant inspections, as are aircraft, ships that visit American ports, railroads, and financial institutions. The 2001 Ford-Firestone SUV tire crisis allegedly was caused by tires that were made in one plant. Firestone said that it did not understand the problem that way but subsequently closed the plant. A CEO of a pharmaceutical company resigned when that company's manufacturing processes could not meet government standards. Meat packing plants are often in the news for inspection violations. Other organizations conduct regular safety, environmental, and engineering studies of their facilities and equipment.

The same methods that are used for learning about human resources considerations may also be used for learning about the plant. Supervisors, plant managers, office managers, and others who subscribe to journals, attend conferences and seminars, do considerable outside reading in their fields, and who have to be sources of organizational guidance will be far more alert to human resources and plant problems than those who do not. In addition, many equipment manufacturers have consultants who will help their customers learn the most effective ways to use their plants and equipment. The assessor's concern here is not merely with noting where information comes from, but, more important, with interpreting its integration into a body of resource and practice.

(B) Related to Products, Services, or Competitors

There are various ways of gathering information about products, services, and competitors. Some stores hire shoppers who compare competitors' prices. Others, even automobile manufacturing companies, buy competitors' products and test them in their own laboratories. Some invent, test, and evolve their own products. Some discover what customers want and prepare or manufacture products accordingly or develop new services. Some employ marketing consultants and keep a careful check on competitors. Some are heavily involved in trade and professional associations. Some subscribe to a range of information sources.

(C) Related to Financial Resources

How does an organization discover what sources of financing are available to it? Can it turn innovation in funding to its own advantage? Does it engage in hedging, trading in foreign currencies, leveraged buyouts, or similar financial maneuvering? Does it conduct surveys before undertaking financial campaigns among its members, parishioners, alumni, or the community? Does it engage consultants to advise it about new stock issues or whether to float bonds? Does it have continuing relationships with banks and lines of credit?

(D) Related to Forces and Trends Affecting the Organization

Earlier the assessor was concerned with the various political, economic, and social forces that affect the organization. Here the assessor is concerned with how this organization becomes proficient in its knowledge about the various external political, social, and economic trends that might affect it, as contrasted with learning about them. Some organizations are constantly alert to government commissions of a tentative and exploratory nature, anticipating that in time they may become firmly established parts of government. Others "tap into" regulatory bodies to keep a constant check on changes. Some organizations extract their information from the newspapers. Others assign one person to the job of watching a state legislature or maintain lobbyists. Some companies keep statistics about new housing developments, new light and water meter installations. Still others send their executives to monthly chambers of commerce luncheons. Others make it a practice to have their executives play golf regularly with selected people. Some subscribe to economic reports, labor relations reports, and similar services.

(E) By Whom (Sources Within and Outside the Organization)

Here the assessor must determine who acquires the knowledge about the four items just delineated: human resources and plants; products, services, or competitors; financial resources; forces and trends affecting the organization. Is it done by individual specialists who then communicate it to others? Is it done by outside consultants who report regularly or on assignment? Is it done by internal discussion among employee groups? Does the organization attempt to use what its people at the operations level have learned about the most effective ways to do their tasks? Is it or has it been involved in Total Quality Management, Six Sigma or reengineering, or similar internal self-renewing, cost-cutting, and quality assurance efforts?

(F) Reservoir of Intellectual Sources

What is the pool of intellectual sources for this organization (Stewart, 1997)? How much of such sources does the organization have to depend on? Some organizations draw on regular university faculty in different disciplines who are on retainer. Some depend regularly on outside consulting firms ranging from accountants and lawyers to technical experts in obscure disciplines central to their work. The assessor must make a judgment of quality and quantity at this point.

i. Talents and Skills Within the Organization

Most managements do not know much about the range of skills and talents among their employees. Often, if they are known, management takes them for granted and tends to ignore them, unless the organization has programs or problem-solving mechanisms that call specifically on some of those skills. Some companies, conversely, will buy other organizations just to get some of their talent. The late Sir Ian K. MacGregor, who rescued British Coal and Steel for British Prime Minister Margaret Thatcher, previously had been head of Amax, Inc., an aluminum company. He reversed the process: He made it a practice to seek mergers with corporations that were larger than his but whose top managements were so weak that he could expect soon to accede to their leadership (Levinson & Rosenthal, 1984). What talents and skills are available within the organization for its use? Is there an up-to-date inventory of them? Who keeps track of whatever additional competencies people develop?

ii. Consultants

An organization often will use outside consultants when it does not have anyone within the organization who can solve a particular problem. In addition, it may use such consultants to reinforce the in-house specialists, or it may use them for greater objectivity, or because it does not value its own people. One incoming CEO asked a management consulting firm to size up the company before he took over its leadership. Rather than coming to know his own organization, he simply followed the consultant's recommendations. The company failed. Some organizations use consultants as an act of desperation, as in the case of the two hospitals cited earlier. How does this organization use such consultants, in what areas, and with what success?

iii. Affiliations With Specialized Institutions or Universities

Most organizations have their own particular field of university specialists to draw on if they wish. Historically, farmers and farm bodies drew on land grant colleges and universities. Pharmaceutical companies have relationships with medical schools and chemistry departments; hotels with hotel management schools. Such affiliations serve as sources of knowledge by sending relevant bulletins, offering refresher training and consultation on specialized problems. Organizations may sponsor university-based research from which the organization may benefit (e.g., technological innovations).

iv. Library Facilities and Services

Is there a library in the organization? If so, are it and its related functions part of the resources of the organization? Is it well-supplied, current, used? Is it staffed by professional librarians? Do those librarians support the work of the staff? Are the employees allowed to check out material for the usual duration? Is the library open throughout the day? Does it have a good interlibrary loan service? A library can truly serve as a repository of knowledge, or it can simply be a repository of books and journals. In addition many metropolitan libraries now have specialized services to support the industries in their communities. In some states there is a state library that backs up local library facilities, and in many cases, historical societies as well.

v. Computer Networks

In addition, with contemporary computer networks, companies can draw on library resources worldwide. What is done here?

(2) Degree of Receptivity to New Knowledge

It is one thing to have systematic methods for acquiring knowledge and another to want to integrate it for organizational action. For example, some managements deliberately, although unconsciously, refuse to make use of knowledge about new sources of money. They may fear loss of control, as, for example, in selling their stock publicly. A church may understand that it readily can raise money simply by increasing its dues or tithes but may prefer to use a heavy mortgage as a device for binding parishioners to the organization. Many managements are aware of sophisticated psychological knowledge about motivation but seem unwilling to translate it into organizational practice despite the costly, often self-defeating consequences of continuing to manage as they currently are doing. An organization may know of ways to expand on its product–service mix, but may be reluctant to do so because it requires expanding the organization or because management is spread too thin already or because it will mean bringing in new people with other identifications and values. Conversely, some organizations are always alert to new knowledge and try to use it before they have the experiential maturity to do so. For example, in the early days of computer technology, many companies installed computers before their managements understood how to use them for better management.

(A) By Whom

Here the assessor should determine who the people are who are stimulated by the new knowledge. Who seems to be notably curious? Who is impatient with the failure of others to use the new knowledge? How much do they want to know? About what? Who does not want to know what? Why?

(B) To What

What subject matters attract greater interest? Lesser interest? No interest?

(3) Level and Range of Knowledge

How sophisticated is the organization and over what range of phenomena? An organization can be knowledgeable about one area and naive about another. For example, a bank may be ultrasophisticated about financial matters but impoverished in its thinking about human resources practices. A monastery may be erudite about theological matters and not have even a glimmering of contemporary managerial conceptions. Many early computer companies that failed—Digital Equipment Co., Data General Co., Prime Computer Co., Wang Computer Co. among them—were strong in engineering but poor in marketing. As one critic put it, "They didn't listen to their customers."

(A) Concerning Themselves, Their Products, Their Services, and Related Factors

Some organizations are ignorant about themselves as organizations. In some, knowledge about products is limited to the specific people who make or market them, and the same is true with services. Others are informed about every aspect of their history and operation. Without a grasp of their organizational history and organizational image it is difficult for employees to adhere to a commonly shared set of values. Some understand their products but do not know their customers as well, a fact they discover when their customers turn to another company's products. College professors who know their subject matter very well may be poor teachers.

(B) Outside Their Immediate Area of Interest

The more enlightened and sophisticated the people in the organization are about the environment in which their organization operates, the more able they are to take advantage of that knowledge for adaptation. By widening the range of their information, their sources of input and gratification, an organization stimulates its employees to greater flexibility and more resources for creativity.

b. Use of Knowledge

Here the assessor should try to discover how knowledge is translated into a basis for organizational action and usefulness and what happens to it after it has been so translated. Are new products and services evolved? Does the organization do a better job of attracting parishioners, community support, endowments? Is marketing more focused and refined? Is research stimulated? Does the organization get more of the kind of public attention it wants? Is its prestige enhanced among competitors, regulators, customers, clients?

(1) How Is It Brought Together?

Knowledge may be formalized in the form of proposals, long-range planning projects, committee task-force reports, administrative decisions, and interpretations of annual reports. The assessor must determine what this organization does.

(A) Who Thinks About It?

How is the knowledge considered for its import and usefulness? Does the executive appoint a committee? Does the chair of the board expect a report? Where are the nodules of concern? Is all innovation left to the top? To the research laboratory? To changes in chief executive? How much employee discussion is there about new knowledge? What are the expectations of stockholders, faculty, the press? What task forces and project teams undertake analyses and recommendations?

(B) Level of Abstraction

Concrete knowledge usually goes hand in hand with short-term planning. Both in turn suggest reaction to external stimuli and forces rather than mastery of them. Concrete knowledge about elementary biology is relatively useless in high school courses today because, to meet the demands of college entrance examinations, students must acquire higher levels of proficiency. Contemporary developments in communication made it anachronistic for AT&T to think it was in the telephone business. Schools of business increasingly have had to shift from teaching business skills to teaching management conceptions and team-based problem solving. The work of Jaques (1996) has made it imperative to think of conceptual capacity, the level of ability to handle abstractions, for the various levels of managerial work. Stewart (1997) calls attention to the intellectual capital of an organization.

(2) How Is Knowledge Organized and Systematized?

The assessor should examine how the organization incorporates the knowledge into a viable condition. It can be "packaged" in the mind of an individual, a committee, a consultant, different committees having a variety of interests. It can be placed in computers and be given multivariate analyses. It can be publicly announced, or transmitted in manuals. It can be taught in internal education programs or filmed. The way in which it is organized and systematized says something about how much it is "owned" by the organization as a whole and how rich a resource it is for the organization.

(A) Committee System

Some organizations have transdepartmental committees. Harvard University, for example, has developed committees from its different schools to confront complex problems that transcend the domain of any one school. Others have specialized committees in given subject areas. Some use committees only to facilitate administration or to handle special projects. Others have standing committees that are formally part of management such as the committee in an insurance company that passes on claims or that in a bank that decides on major loans. Some use committees to block actions, others to facilitate them.

(B) Records and Storage System

The assessor must separate the formal records *of* the organization from the formal records *about* the organization. The formal records *of* the business will include data used in chapters 6 and 7. Those that are *about* the organization will include reports on new techniques, discussions of innovation, current market surveys, changes in tax information. The assessor's concern here is with the functional usefulness of the acquired knowledge, using the following three points as guides:

- *Accuracy:* How much of the knowledge is factual? How much of the detail can be trusted? How much is speculative?
- *Availability:* Where is the information stored? How is it filed? Is it convenient to check out? To whom is it accessible? Can it be recalled for repetitive use?
- *Comprehensiveness:* Does the knowledge represent thorough data or is it incomplete? Is it annotated? Does it contain errors, bias?

(C) Other Modes of Organization and Systematization

Some organizations make films of their products or services in action. Others make public announcement of the performance of their products, as for example when automobile companies recall vehicles. Some, as certain religious institutions do, pass on much by word of mouth or traditional observances. Ancient tribes and other native societies would pass knowledge from generation to generation through song or story or on stone tablets or hieroglyphics drawn on the walls of caves.

(3) Amount and Kind of Use (Retrieval)

Who has access to the formalized knowledge? How do they then inject it into organizational thinking? How much of the knowledge is confidential? How much is available in day-to-day awareness? Who can learn from it? To whom is it forbidden? Nurses, who once could not prescribe medications, now may do so if properly trained. Fire fighters, once limited to fighting fires, now also have become communities' agents of emergency first-aid.

(4) Organizational Conditions Affecting the Use of Intellectual Sources

Given the knowledge, what circumstances enhance or interfere with its application by the organization? In some organizations enthusiastic endorsement by prominent persons facilitate applications. The proliferation of books on management by famous lecturers is a case in point. Farmers were moved to try new methods when county agents succeeded in getting those prominent and respected among them to be the first to do so.

In some cases there is not enough money to hire specialized teachers for handicapped individuals or to provide social services for poor individuals. In other cases, shortage of trained personnel makes services unavailable. In still other situations, reluctance makes some people obsolete and unemployed. Further, religious prohibitions may forbid certain surgeries or blood transfusions.

(A) Ability to Deal With Abstract Problems

The ability to deal with abstract issues is an increasing problem for many organizations, often posed by people who are using computers naively, who do not know how to view their businesses more abstractly than they have in the past. Some organizations are highly abstract in their considerations. A component of the ability to deal with abstract problems is the facility with which the organization can contend with the selection of a target on which to focus its efforts. This is a growing concern because of the plethora of new information and the need to have some basis for selection. Frequently the problem is not a matter of selection but rather one of organization of the information around a given core, such as an enunciated organizational purpose. The questions, What is our core competence? Who is our customer (audience)? arise with increasing frequency as technologies and demographics change. The head of an engineering project to build a nuclear electricity generating plant must be able to look ahead 14 years, taking into account social and political issues as well as the technical problems that are likely to arise because it will take that long to complete the project.

(B) Flexibility

Can the organization change itself or open itself to new kinds of knowledge? For example, some companies, heavy with engineers or financial types, find it impossible to make use of contemporary advances in personality and organization theory because, both in terms of the personalities of the individuals in the organization and the nature of the work, they are psychologically unable to make use of anything other than formulae or to take into account people's feelings. Others are so entrapped with a "hard sell psychology" that, although they may hear the words, they are unable to shift from their style of operation to apply new conceptions usefully.

(C) Characteristic Style and Variations

If an organization exhibits a characteristic style of behavior, it often runs the risk of hardening of that style into a rigid psychological stance (Levinson, 1994). A frozen characteristic style can inhibit the use of new knowledge by circumscribing, distorting, or uncritically accepting new information. For example, many authoritarian executives encourage the development of personnel and training staffs and the teaching of psychological knowledge in their organizations, provided it is focused on making lower level management more effective with line employees. Some organizations are composed of dependent people who have difficulty when asked to assume initiative or to be amenable to ideas that will require them to act independently or that will stimulate conflict within the group. Some can be outwardly aggressive but passive and conforming within the organization as, for example, a police department. Some can be passive outwardly and aggressive inwardly as, for example, a college faculty torn by political bickering. Characteristic style and variations might be equated to the dominant mode of attack and the number of plays of a football team. Some teams are passing teams while others play a running game.

c. Dissemination of Knowledge

Having observed, described, and interpreted how and what kinds of knowledge are acquired by whom, the assessor must determine whether the information is used as an organizational asset. How is it dispersed? Does it serve the organization maximally? The assessor should not be concerned here with the communications network as outlined previously but rather with an identification network or some kind of capillary-like process. To illustrate how knowledge is disseminated by identification, the late, famed biologist Konrad Lorenz reported an experiment in which one young chimpanzee was removed from a cage full of chimpanzees and trained to obtain bananas by following an elaborate number of steps to which the chimp had been conditioned (Lorenz, 1966). When he was returned to the cage, the other chimpanzees saw him obtaining bananas as he was trained to do, and even ate some of them, but they did not learn how to obtain them by watching him. However, when an older chimpanzee was similarly trained and returned to the cage, the other chimpanzees not only observed him as they had observed the younger one but also they learned to follow the process.

Are authority figures consciously used as models in disseminating knowledge? Is new knowledge stated in memorandum or procedure form with the assumption that people will then apply it without the need for models or instruction? Are people formally trained to use new knowledge? If so, who does the training? How quickly and completely is it assimilated by what other parts of the organization?

3. Organizational Language

Organizational language tells people what is going on *in* the organization. It is therefore important to note and interpret the meaning of how the organization speaks. In this section, the assessor should analyze the style, content, syntax, figures of speech, attitudes, and values that appear in organization communication. He or she should be particularly interested in the feelings that are disguised by the language used, the degree to which the organizational language is a barrier to discourse within the organization or between the organization and others, and the degree to which it constitutes a cultural or industrial boundary. That is, people unfamiliar with the localized or intraorganizational jargon may not be able to understand the communication. The French complain about the infiltration of their language with computer-related English words. Popular magazines like *Time* often publish lists of words and their meaning that have become the in-language among adolescents, athletes, or sci-fi aficionados. Recent articles report the infiltration of Yiddish words into everyday language.

a. Themes and Content of Employee Publications

In many house organs the themes are (a) produce more; (b) serve better; (c) look how good we are to you and our customers. The content abounds with personal data: births, deaths, unusual hobbies, and achievements. Usually there is very little news pertaining to unpopular policies and difficult, complex problems with which the organization must deal or which might threaten people. Mining company publications, for example, do not discuss the historic pollution problems mining causes and the hostility of local communities to the contamination of their water supply. Thus, most house organs are quite "newsy"; however, they tend to hide the realities of the organization and place a smiling organizational face before the readers, who usually disregard it. Such propagandistic publications are generally disguises for paternalism that, in turn, veils underlying authoritarian attitudes.

Some employee publications are clearly political, intended to represent the viewpoint of the management or administration. Usually house organs are relegated to editors who are well-controlled by several administrative layers above them. Dissent, debate, criticism therefore rarely are found in them. The assessor should be aware that although this need not necessarily be so, it is nevertheless commonplace.

b. Organizational Ideology

The dominant set of beliefs of an organization is considered its ideology. The theme and content of employee publications reflects the organizational ideology. In general, the assessor will infer the organizational ideology from the forces or factors given attention or ignored. One can interpret from these the stance the organization assumes toward the outside world, how it conceives its reason for being, what it sees itself to be, and who it perceives to be its opponents. Labor publications usually repeat the theme that management is the enemy. For years, in much of the literature of investor-owned electric power companies, the foe was government ownership of public utilities. Many industries share a political ideology of individual independence that often is at variance with their efforts to seek government support and regulation of the competition.

Organizational ideology can also be inferred from the kinds of public relations activities an organization will support or finance. For example, some business organizations often will contribute to the support of economic education in high school and college courses, but will not contribute to programs that might teach minority group members how to organize themselves to strengthen their own neighborhoods. Many leading church people espouse an ideology of justice but act as if their responsibility stops before acting on that ideology.

Within the organization there is almost always a relatively congruent set of values. If a dichotomy arises, which is often the case with mergers and acquisitions, or the advent of a new management, major steps will have to be taken to breach the schism or the split will be disruptive to the organization. For example, with the decrease in regulation and the corresponding need for its managers and executives to be more competitive, AT&T publicized its change from maternalism with the slogan, "Ma Bell doesn't live here any more."

c. Advertising Themes

Advertising themes are relatively self-evident. They are as relevant to the understanding of colleges, monasteries, hospitals, labor unions, and churches as they are to businesses. Colleges advertise by their catalogues, recruiters, alumni associations, publications about overseas campuses. Denominational schools speak about their parochial atmosphere. Christian monasteries promote Christian vocations and Buddist monasteries contemplation. Regardless of the particular kind of institution, advertising themes are public relations gambits that more often represent pretensions than facts.

Advertising themes often represent the organizational self-image as the top management of the organization ideally would like it to be. Frequently they reiterate the dominant value that the organization wishes the public to believe it to hold or to be striving toward. *Consumers Reports* frequently punctures advertising claims and the federal government polices drug, to-bacco, and liquor advertising.

The assessor must be careful not to take a condescending attitude toward advertising themes as a result of being able to observe the gap between fact and fiction. No human beings fully live up to the aspirations they hold for themselves, nor does any organization of humans. However, this is not to say that the assessor should not make inferences about dominant values, organizational self-images, and aspirations. The assessor will want to be alert to elucidating, enunciating, and clarifying advertising themes sufficiently to be able to differentiate between illusion and reality, because the greater the gap, the greater the intraorganizational difficulty. Imagine how the employees of Sears, Roebuck and the General Electric Company, both companies that championed their trustworthiness, felt when even small components of both companies were reported in the press to have cheated customers (*Detroit News,* 2001). Many of the predominant features of an organization's self-image result from the incorporation of values that origi-nated from pretensions. Public utility companies, for example, had to identify themselves as service organizations to combat the residual public hostility toward giant holding companies when in the early 1930s those combines were fractionated. The effort to live up to this concept of self has been a vital component of the organizational self-image of some public utilities for many years.

d. Organizational Symbols and Slogans

Here the assessor should ask, What is the organizational symbol and why has the organization chosen this particular one, maintaining and nurtur-ing it? Symbols range from abstract designs, to inanimate objects, to animal images. The symbol of an organization says something about the relative strength and mode of handling aggression as viewed by the people in it. The University of California Golden Bear and the Princeton University Tiger are different from the Hornet of the Emporia (KS) State University. Antioch College has no such symbol. The cross is the universal symbol of Christian churches and the Star of David of Jewish synagogues.

The organizational slogan tells the assessor what the company feels itself compelled to be or what it sees itself as being. The slogan is the way a company projects its image to the outside world. The assessor should note the extent of that projection: How far does the organization push this slogan and into what areas? For example, does it say the same thing to a scientific audience as to a lay audience? To physicians as to patients? To wholesalers as to retailers? If not, why not, and what difference does it make? Unofficial slogans should also be included in this section. Sometimes slogans are used like security blankets: Some people feel secure as long as they can mouth a certain set of words, including

- Comprehensive four-year liberal arts college
- *E Pluribus Unum*
- People are our most important products
- Live better electrically
- None may enter who can pay; none may pay who enter
- Research for Life
- Maximum benefits at minimum cost—with the best possible service
- Avis tries harder
- So we may better serve
- To the stars through difficulties
- A city in motion

e. Language of Policies as Distinct From the Policies Themselves

Pursuing organizational language, the assessor should review the way in which organizational policies are stated. The tone of directions given inwardly more often conveys the true feelings predominating in the organization than those words that are spoken outwardly. The contrast between the language of policies and the manner in which the company speaks to its respective public reflects a gap that may have important psychological significance. The greater the emotional distance between the language of policies, as opposed to the language of advertising, ideology, and themes of employee publications, the more likely the latter is to be a facade and the greater the likelihood of internal conflict. The language of policies informs the assessor about the manner in which the organization envisions its employees. How does it look on them? Is the language condescending, forbidding, commanding, reasonable, obtuse, pretentious? Does the language address the employees as human beings? Is it so complex that the employees will not look at the message unless they absolutely have to? Must explanations be followed verbatim? Some organizations make their policy statements in a superficial manner, as if to say, "You won't feel this if we gild it." This is the "orange juice in castor oil" treatment.

Policies often vary in their tone from institution to institution. For example, hospital policies are likely to be formal and specific because of the relationship to legal obligations and treatment protocols. However, even under such circumstances there might be variation in policy that would indicate the flexibility of the institution according to the requirements of the situation. It would indeed be a flexible hospital that would say, "If you are the nurse in charge of this section, the visiting hours are 2 pm to 4 pm. At times, when the patient needs extra support or when the patient is a child and would profit from having his or her mother close by, use your own judgment." Another policy statement might say: "Do not use any bottle in which ether has been stored. Break and destroy. Failure to adhere to this rule will result in immediate dismissal." In some organizations all policies carry the same forbidding quality whether they concern minor or major matters.

f. Language of Customs, Taboos, Prohibitions, and Constrictions: Direct and Implied

The language of customs refers to the wording of special events, methods of worship, and modes of behavior. The language of address in some churches is "sister" and "brother." Priests are addressed as "father." The custom of Yom Kippur is self-abasement and atonement. The "language" of this custom would be, "If you plead enough, father will forgive." In the army, before the advent of female officers, the male company commander was referred to as "the old man" by his subordinates. Some companies require employees to address each other as Mr. and Ms., but far less so than in the past. Some require them to dress in certain ways because the dress has certain implications for the customers, patients, parishioners, and others. Here the assessor is interested in what the customs, taboos, prohibitions, and constrictions say about the organization. Does the emphasis on dress, for example, reflect a pretentiousness or a facade on the part of the organization? Does it deal with the realities of the organization's situation? Is dating among employees prohibited because it will create problems within the organization or because the chief executive officer believes it to be immoral? Are women not promoted at the same rate as men because custom says, in effect, "Women are less competent and less adequate and therefore cannot accede to these roles?" What do the customs, taboos, prohibitions, constrictions say about the fears, concerns, myths, and problems of the organization?

It will be more difficult to deal with taboos because most are implicit. A taboo is proscribed verbalization or behavior. Often there are no written rules governing a taboo, like drinking alcohol on the job, but, at least in most instances, the behavior simply does not happen. Sometimes there are published rules with punitive consequences for their violation. For example, in the armed forces, officers are prohibited from socializing with enlisted personnel; in the business world, a subordinate ordinarily does not invite superiors to home for informal social purposes. For many years at IBM, there was a taboo against drinking alcoholic beverages both on and off the job.

4. Emotional Atmosphere of the Organization

The emotional atmosphere of an organization refers to its tone. Characteristically, factories where there is great pressure for production likely are hurried and harassed in emotional tone. There people work quickly. They may speak loudly and use their hands and other body movements to facilitate communication. By contrast, the emotional tone of a museum is more reserved. The emotional atmosphere can be hectic but congenial, noisy and joyous, or loud and hostile. It may, in effect, say to people, "Be on your guard and control yourself," or "One slip and you're out," or, as at Southwest Airlines, "Enjoy, enjoy." In other words, the assessor wants to learn how it feels to work in the organization. Is it warm, pleasant, and supportive? Is it rejecting, hostile, and threatening?

a. Prevailing Mood and Range

What is the dominant emotional theme? What is more characteristic of this organization and how widely does its emotional tone vary? The range of emotionality is narrow in a funeral establishment. There is little occasion for laughter. In the case of a newspaper editorial office, the mode may vary from excitement on election night to sadness on the eve of war. Reporters and editors in a news room are freer to swear out loud and have less consideration for those who may hear them than might be the case with government officials in a state office building.

Here the assessor is interested in the tone of the dominant emotional theme or feeling and how widely it fluctuates.

b. Overall Stability or Variability of Mood

How rapidly and how widely does the mood in the organization shift? For example, how "hot under the collar" can people safely become? How free or constricted are they to say what they feel? How *strongly*, how *much*, in what *direction*, under what *circumstances*, and for what *duration* can the people within the organization express the range of their feelings? These factors may be difficult to judge. Perhaps the best subjective yardstick for the assessor is the question, How appropriate is this expression of feeling?

(1) Intensity of Reactions

The adjective "intensity" speaks for itself. The assessor should be interested in the strength of the feeling. Is the hostility jocular or is it deadly serious? Does the joking serve as a basis for relationships; is the laughter in response overexaggerated and suggestive of something else?

(2) Duration of Reactions

How long do these reactions last? If people are happy, do they stay reasonably happy or are they quickly disillusioned? If they are hostile, are there lasting residuals of hostility or is the hostility dissipated quickly as it might be among rival partisans in the audience of a football game? On one hand, if feelings last a long time, they may reflect stability of mood, basic solidity, or a positive quality. On the other hand, if minor provocations precipitate feelings of great intensity that last long periods of time, the assessor might suspect continued aggravations and chronic hostility.

(3) Appropriateness to Stimulating Factors

Are people appropriately pleased and happy because their accomplishments and achievements lend themselves to such feelings or because they are whipped up into a false sense of achievement? If the latter is the case, then they will again and again have to be whipped up to that level, and ultimately the effectiveness of that kind of motivation will decline. For example, the top management of Wal-Mart meets every Saturday morning to review its achievement and renew its spirit.

If employees can take many minor frustrations without becoming disillusioned in their leadership, then this speaks well for the kind of affectional bond and trust existing between the leaders and their subordinates. If reactions are disproportionate to the events that precipitate them, then the assessor must seek their source. Everyone is familiar with the experience of being angry with a spouse or friend after being criticized by his or her boss. Disproportionate angry reactions are likely to be displacements from discontents that cannot be alleviated at their source. The reverse can also happen: Sometimes there are those who are irrationally enthusiastic after a positive but innocuous remark from one's superior or respected public figure.

c. Intraorganizational Variability

Different parts of an organization often will have different emotional tones. Some parts may feel discriminated against by others. Some may feel they are the favorites. Some may feel oppressed. Some parts of an organization are laconic in their pace and conservative in their mood. Others are frenetic. The assessor must determine how the emotional atmosphere varies in the organization.

(1) By Hierarchical Level

Variability by hierarchical level refers to the nuances in feelings and attitudes from level to level. People in top management may know that the organization is going to disintegrate and feel depressed; people at the bottom are not concerned with this because either they do not know about the situation or feel that they easily can get other jobs. In a merger, top management may want to get its money and get out; middle management may be frightened of the change because of the effect it could have on their jobs; line workers, as at Powell-Kole, may be unconcerned because their jobs are temporary.

(2) By Department

In addition to varying by hierarchical level, the emotional atmosphere within an organization often will vary widely from one department or one unit to another. This may have to do with the leadership of that unit, with the pressure on a particular unit, with the partiality shown toward one unit or another, with particular problems in a given unit, and many other factors.

(3) Other (Geographical Location, Profession)

Emotional tone or mood will also vary from place to place within the same organization, or it may vary widely depending on skill level, competence, and similar factors. Sometimes higher management deems a unit to be unrelated to its central thrust and allows it to deteriorate. The resulting mood in that unit will be depressed.

One can sense the differences in mood by entering two different stores of the same company. One may be meticulously kept, merchandise attractively displayed, and service personnel friendly, whereas another is unkempt and the clerks hostile. The same comparison may be made of different classrooms.

5. Organizational Action

Here the assessor is concerned with how the organization acts, its characteristic style of behavior. Sometimes organizations are described as fast moving, lean and hungry, bumbling, and so on. Each of these words or phrases captures a nuance of what we mean by organizational action. Microsoft is alleged to try to absorb the activities of its presumed partners, like Eastman Kodak, preempting their innovations. In that view, it is aggressively all-encompassing (Wilcox, 2001).

a. Energy Level

What is the pace of the organization? With what degree of enthusiasm or lethargy does it pursue new products, different markets, innovative technology, new parishioners, diverse students? How aggressive is it in its competitive efforts? No longer constrained by a State Board of Regents, Florida Atlantic University is actively developing new departments and campuses. In speaking of the degree of "vigor" of an organization, the assessor will be making a value judgment. Implicitly or overtly the assessor will be comparing this organization to another, in the same or in a different field. For clarity's sake, the assessor may want to state his or her yardstick if the assessor has one in mind.

(1) Consistency or Variability of Application (Rate of Discharge of Energy)

Here the assessor is concerned with whether the organization applies itself continuously and diligently to whatever it perceives to be its tasks, whether it operates from crisis to crisis or in response to some form of pressure. Some organizations operate continuously at high pressure and fast tempos, others are very quiet and sedate.

(2) Points and Periods of Peak Expenditure of Energy

For some organizations, there are particular times when they must be especially vigorous. They may be deliberately slow-paced at other times to allow sufficient reserve to cope with the peak periods. How and when they move into action says something about the organization's capacity for adaptation and also its point of great vulnerability. When the Federal Emergency Management Administration did not move fast enough to cope with the aftermath of Hurricane Andrew in 1992 in Southern Florida, it was drastically reorganized.

b. Qualities of Action

If by "energy level" we mean *intensity*, by "qualities of action" we mean the *form and consequence of the behavior*. What did the organization do and how did it do so? With what outcome? General Motors was slow to respond to Japanese competition and lost significant market share.

(1) Degree of Directness

To what extent does the organization confront problems head-on? Does it attack the real problem or create substitute targets on which to focus its energy? The degree of directness with which an organization deals with its problems is contingent on the sophistication available to it for recognizing problems and being able to confront them. If the organization has sophisticated resources available to it that enable it to delve into the core of a problem rather than by attacking the superficial aspects of that issue, the assessor must raise a question about the reasons for blind spots.

(2) Degree of Flexibility

Some organizations respond to any problem with a predictable pattern. Others have a more task-oriented focus and will respond in different ways, depending on the problem. Here the assessor should be concerned about flexibility of action or modulation of organizational behavior.

(3) Planning and Timing

Some organizations let events happen to them. Others make things happen, master their own worlds, and compete aggressively to survive. Planning refers to how the organization uses itself as a mastery device. It refers not only to scheduling but also to anticipating change, mobilizing resources, and applying resources with maximum thrust at optimum moments.

(4) Degree of Persistence

Here the assessor should be concerned with whether the organization finishes the tasks it sets for itself or abruptly leaves them to pursue other objectives. If a project is unsuccessful, does the organization readily disband it? Persistence can be either useful or costly.

(5) Effectiveness

Here the assessor is concerned with how well the action works. It may be effective though stereotyped as, for example, when a management threatens to move its plant every time it appears that unionization might be successful. Effectiveness has to be judged in financial terms, in terms of the reputation of the organization and its position in its field, in terms of its stability and capacity for long-term survival, and in terms of meeting its own goals. The question of effectiveness throws into relief the issue of whether the organization knows what its goals are. The assessor, however, must be careful not to misjudge temporary achievement for long-range effectiveness.

(6) Constructiveness or Destructiveness

Here the assessor may want to make a value judgment about the organization's actions vis-à-vis its goals. In what ways does the organization's action undermine its long-run purposes? How does it hurt or support the community? How does it entrench itself firmly in the social fabric? These issues may well have been fully covered by information gathered for the preceding item ("effectiveness"). If not, the assessor should examine the organization's actions in detail.

In this chapter, the assessor has begun to give meaning to the factual data he or she has gathered. The assessor has begun to define subtleties of process, nuances of difference, in preparation for developing an understanding of those forces and factors that distinguish the client organization from others, no matter how similar to others it may seem. It is these subtle distinctions that allow the assessor to feed back to the organization the kind of information about itself that the organization can use. The inferences the assessor has made in this chapter constitute the bases for the interpretations the assessor will make in the next.

9

INTERPRETATIVE DATA: ATTITUDES AND RELATIONSHIPS

Part III of the outline (see appendix D) follows. The division into chapters is arbitrary and to ease the reading.

B. Attitudes and Relationships

In chapter 8, we discussed the organization's perceptions, attention, knowledge, language, emotional level, and modes of action. When these aspects of the organization are integrated, they result in characteristic attitudes and relationships. We speak of these characteristic attitudes and relationships as the organization's psychological stance. Having made inferences from the factual data about the many ways in which the organization is functioning currently, the assessor now must synthesize his or her inferences into statements about an organization's psychological stance. What feelings lie behind the ways the organization functions? The focus here is on enduring psychological postures or perspectives that give unity, cohesion, and consistent direction to organizational behavior or, conversely, that may be disruptive to it. These are reflected in attitudes toward major dimensions of existence: attitudes toward self and others, toward time, work, and authority. Although the assessor has already referred to attitudes in many of his or her examples, here the assessor must give them explicit attention. It is imperative to understand attitudes and relationships because they represent ways of coping with enduring implicit or explicit problems. Also, any attempt at organizational intervention or change will necessarily involve an alteration in the configuration of the organization's attitudes and relationships. It is this configuration, rather than isolated variables, that must be dealt with if changes are to be effected and effective. In chapter 10 we will consider the systematic interrelationship of many factors and the configurations into which they fall in the concept of organizational integrative patterns.

1. Contemporary Attitudes Toward, and Relationships With, Others

What is the organization's conception of and relationships to those persons, forces, and institutions outside itself? Toward some it may be truculent; toward others, supportive; toward still others, hostile. An organization may build permanent working relationships with other organizations. It may be transient in its relationships. It may be expedient: now friendly, now hostile, depending on the problems. Some businesses may have joint ventures with other businesses with which they are also competitive. If the assessor examines these attitudes and relationships, he or she will learn what the organization perceives to be the source of its problems, on whom it is more likely to project blame, how it regards the emotional quality of its environment, and, ultimately, its style of behavior.

a. Range, Diversification, Depth, and Constancy

The *range* of its attitudes and relationships reflects the complexity of the organization. The greater the number of attachments, the more secure the organization will feel. Companies that build aircraft or ships buy components from a geographically wide range of suppliers. When threatened with the loss of government contracts, they mobilize protests from the many different congressional contacts whose districts will be affected. The wider the scope of gratification, the greater is the likelihood that the organization receives stimulation from many different sources and the more energetic it is likely to be.

Diversification in this context refers to varied relationships. Some organizations insulate themselves from the economic and political world, limiting their activities to suppliers and customers; others invest themselves heavily in trade associations, a range of specialized publics, educational institutions, and community activities. Coca-Cola seems to be ubiquitous.

Depth refers to the degree to which the organization becomes involved in its relationships. For example, some organizations, like an airport terminal newsstand, can be casual in their relationships with their customers; others, like hospitals, must become deeply involved, literally in life and death matters. All become more deeply engaged with, or related to, some persons, institutions, or activities than others. Depth of engagement will tell which relationships are more important to the organization.

Constancy is the other side of the coin of dependability. Constancy of attitude characterizes the stability of the organization's perceptions and stance and the enduring nature of its relationships. It also says something about the degree to which the organization can be counted on and by which other persons, organizations, or publics.

(1) Customers, Clients, Students, Patients, Parishioners

There is a business axiom that the customer is king. In some organizations the customer may be regarded as almost a nuisance. A customer (patient, client, parishioner, student) presumably is the person for whom the organization exists. The organization's relationship to its customers is a vital index to the kinds of problems it has or is likely to have.

(2) Competition

Competition between organizations, as between individuals, arouses rivalry, hostility, and, more covertly, fear. The manner in which an organization relates to its competitors, competes with them, and reacts to their competitive behavior reflects the stability and security of the organization. There can be a range of diversified relationships with the competition, depending on the history of such relationships and the behavior of the competitors. As noted previously, many large corporations have joint ventures or other partnership efforts with components of their corporate competitors. These diverse relationships will reflect some of the values of the client organization.

(3) Employees

Attitudes toward, and relationships with, employees may vary with hierarchical level, geographical dispersion, history of the plant, and many other circumstances. Much of the time an assessor might be tempted to assume these to be constant, just as he or she might assume parents to act in exactly the same manner toward each of their children. At this point in the assessment, differentiation is important. Some organizations are paternalistic with respect to their line employees but exert severe pressure on their executives. In some businesses, the customer is always right and the employee always wrong. In some church denominations, the pastor is always wrong when there is conflict between the pastor and the congregation. In still others, there is a latent attitude that the employee could not be very good or he or she would not be working in this organization.

(4) Occupational Associations and Representatives

Occupational associations range from trade associations and professional societies to labor unions. Here the assessor should infer whether the organization looks on such associations as allies that can help with recruitment, maintenance of internal standards, and similar needs, or views them as competing for employee loyalty. Some trade associations and professional societies enforce standards among their members. Are there varying attitudes toward different groups? What is the degree of accommodation in union–management relations? How well does the grievance arbitration process function? What is the character and degree of union challenge and management response?

(5) Stockholders

Stockholders are to be equated with owners at this point in the outline. They literally may be stockholders or members of a cooperative, the citizens who own a community's schools, the religious denomination that supports a hospital, or the contributors to a charitable agency. Here the assessor should ask, Does the organization feel answerable to its "owners?" If so, how? Is it open and straightforward? Does it manipulate them? Does it exploit them? Some organizations go to elaborate lengths to inform their stockholders of exactly what is happening within the company. Others conduct their annual meetings in inconvenient locations, furnishing a minimum of information, and using annual reports as window dressing. This is an area that the assessor must scrutinize because many organizations wittingly or not try to deceive the "owners" so that the management will be freer to run the organization. For example, in one organization's annual report, an increase in profit and decrease in dividends was reported; however, the organization never stated why this condition existed. One had to presume that the increased profits were diverted back into the organization. Another organization heralded its employee pension plan. What was not mentioned was that the pension fund owns a controlling interest in the company's stock; the company executives are the officials of the pension fund and therefore, for all practical purposes, are free agents.

(6) Legislative Bodies

Most organizations of any size necessarily must have relationships with legislative bodies because they are so easily affected by the actions of city, county, state, and federal legislative bodies. Some organizations maintain formidable lobbying efforts through trade associations or public relations counsel; some have direct relationships with specific legislators; others mobilize a significant number of voices whenever necessary. Earlier the assessor examined the *attention* given to external legislative and regulatory bodies. Here the assessor is concerned about *attitudes* toward them. Are they held in esteem, fear, respect? Treated forthrightly or maneuvered?

(7) Executive and Regulatory Bodies (Governmental)

Banks, savings and loan associations, transportation businesses, public utilities, pharmaceutical companies, schools, hospitals, colleges, and many other organizations are immediately and almost continuously involved with governmental executive and regulatory bodies. Such bodies often set rates, standards, performance requirements, make inspections, renew licenses, award franchises, and, in fact, hold almost life and death power over the organizations they regulate. The organization's attitude may be one of accommodation at one extreme or be more direct and aggressive at the other.

(8) Control Bodies (Internal)

A control body regulates and restrains an organization. It may be either a board of directors, a board of governors, or a group of trustees. It is usually differentiated from the executive group which runs the organization and from the public regulatory bodies that enforce public controls on the organization. Control bodies range from those that exercise little control to those that are intimately involved in the organization's management. In the case of the two West Palm Beach hospitals discussed in chapter 8, the respective boards were publicly accused of micromanaging and, because of the rivalries among the board members, could not integrate the hospitals.

(9) Suppliers

Suppliers may provide goods and services, personnel, students. They may refer patients, provide data, or manufacture complementary or component units. Some organizations are heavily dependent on suppliers. Others organize themselves and shape their activities to not to be so dependent, such as having captive suppliers (ones that they own). Some organizations have a wide range of suppliers so that they will not be at the mercy of any one. Some exploit their suppliers. Wal-Mart, Sears, and automobile manufacturing companies are notorious for their pressure on suppliers. Others build enduring relationships. The more the organization dominates a given market and the more it controls a given product, the greater is the dependency of the suppliers on the goodwill of the organization.

(10) Financial Community

The financial community comprises official sources of funds. These may be banks, brokerage houses, fund-raising agencies, insurance companies, and similar groups.

(11) Host Community

The relationship of an organization to its host community can vary from one in which the organization is the single dominant force and controls the host community to one in which it is isolated from it. Some organizations are intimately related to a community politic; others are involved in hostile town–gown debates. Harvard University has gone to great lengths to rid itself of the hostile resentment of Cambridge and Boston. Costco's expansion into Boca Raton was vigorously opposed by many in that community as was the continued expansion of Florida Atlantic University. The manner in which an organization relates to the community often contributes to the growth, sophistication, responsibility, and integration or conversely, the stifling of the community. Many small communities fought against the abolition of subsidies for sugar cane farmers, arguing that sugar mills were the only industries in town and the abolition of subsidies meant the end of their communities. Similar arguments are made for other single-industry communities or where one institution dominates.

(12) Dealer Organizations

Dealer organizations are the go-betweens for the manufacturers and those who actually sell the product to the public. For example, an association of Ford retailers is a dealer organization. The Ford retailer is also a dealer organization. The salesperson who sells a Ford car represents the dealer rather than the Ford company. Some companies go to great lengths to build up and support their dealer organizations or their franchisees; others manipulate them; still others control them rigidly. The dealer organization, in effect, if not literally, holds a franchise to represent the parent organization. The equivalent groups for colleges are departments or schools; for a diocese or synod, the local church; for a school system, the individual school. There is an implication here that the dealer organization has a degree of autonomy from the larger organization of which it is a part and which may be the subject of assessment. If this is not the case, as often it is not with respect to schools or branch stores, the individual unit must be viewed as part of the whole and not be regarded as "a dealer organization."

(13) Plant Builders

Growing organizations do much building and rebuilding of their physical plants. Some have continuing relationships with architects, contractors, land planners, and others. Other organizations have no consistent relationships with such people. Obviously, in the former case, those who plan and build the organization's facilities can be intimately knowledgeable about the organization's business, personnel, and problems. They can be working partners. Those who operate more casually and expediently will not have the advantage of such a partnership.

(14) Consultants

Consultants are literally helpers from outside the organization. Some organizations will treat consultants as aliens, to be used and discarded as quickly as possible; others will see them as threats; still others will use a range of consultants who are specialists in various areas to compensate for the organization's limitations. Some will go so far as to use consultants repetitively so that, for all practical purposes, the consultants make the major organizational decisions. How have they been regarded and what has been their influence?

(15) Unions

Relationships with unions historically have been fraught with conflict, sometimes with armed conflict. Many companies go to considerable length to remain union-free, charging their directors of human resources specifically with that task. Others have worked out more cooperative relationships. Some have developed "sweetheart" contracts, buying off the union leadership to avoid labor troubles. Even nonprofit organizations are not necessarily free of conflicts with their unions. Many municipal and other governmental organizations are heavily unionized and sometimes collective bargaining efforts become vitriolic. In recent years the administration of a Roman Catholic Hospital operated by a church order in Port Jervis, New York, endured a nurses' strike that resulted in the unusual involvement of the Church administration of the diocese (Greenwald, 1995). In 2001, both Harvard and Yale students demanded that their university administrations increase the pay of their kitchen help, who were already represented by unions (*Harvard Gazette*, 2001). The assessor should look beyond the literal union contract to the nature of union–management practices.

(16) Others

If there are other outside groups with which the organization has relationships, the assessor should discuss the nature of those relationships here. Some organizations, for example, are frequently involved in consortia. These are associations of companies to do together what no single one could do alone—for example, petroleum companies who form joint ventures for overseas projects. Other organizations are involved in joint ventures, like various electric power companies that jointly build atomic energy-generating units or railroads that jointly operate a terminal. Some are experimental, like pharmaceutical companies that together undertake testing of new drugs. Some organizations, like the military, have relationships with employees' families. Hospitals, schools, colleges, and other institutions often have to deal with accrediting bodies that have no official (governmental) status.

b. Major Attachments

Here the assessor is still concerned with the relationships in the preceding discussion. But now his or her attention should focus on with which of the relationships the organization has the strongest connections and feelings. That is, in the eyes of the organization, which of these is the most important to it?

(1) Positive

The major attachment of a hospital staff may be to patients and reputation. Staff and employees alike talk about the need to serve the patient and their wish to do so, as well as their need to increase their effectiveness and reputation. The makers of greeting cards speak proudly of their imaginative cards and of their CEO who creates them. Pharmaceutical companies lavish expensive attention on physicians.

(2) Negative

In 2001, the major negative attachment of the Enron Company was to the Securities and Exchange Commission. The company simply did not want its activities to be regulated. Nor in 2002 did the Hewlett and Packard families want the new CEO of that eponymous company to acquire another and vigorously fought the idea (*Los Angeles Times*, 2002).

c. Masculine–Feminine Orientation

Organizations evolve orientations and styles of behavior, some of which have already been discussed. Here the assessor should view these on a masculine–feminine continuum.

(1) Of Organization

(A) Masculine

C. Northcote Parkinson (1962) pointed out that a male corporation is to be identified first of all by its rough exterior. The layout is more practical than pleasing, he noted, the machinery unconcealed, and the paint more conservative and drab. He noted that combined with this rugged appearance is an assertiveness in advertising, a rather crude claim to offer what is at once the cheapest and the best. Finally, the male organization he described is extroverted, outgoing, and inquisitive.

The more masculine the organization, the more it will tolerate its own aggressive behavior and that of others; the more militant its posture, the less sensitive it is likely to be to the feelings of its customers and employees. Heavy industries like coal, steel, railroads, petroleum, and lumber that historically required muscular men and exploited the environment for natural resources are examples. Their characteristic insensitivity to people's feelings led to bitter strikes, despoliation of the environment that often led to government-compelled corrective action, and much of the contemporary conflict about environmental pollution.

(B) Feminine

The more feminine in style and orientation an institution or organization is, the more likely its control is modulated, the more sensitive it is to feelings, and the more concern it manifests for people. Organization management is becoming more feminine as executives learn to have greater sensitivity to their employees, customers, and communities. The continuing movement toward greater group participation in the decisions that affect people, the increase in managerial team effort, and greater awareness of conditions that affect morale and motivation, all soften the historical hard-nosed management style. But a more feminine orientation does not mean softness in management. Greater awareness of people's feelings leads to wiser management. Feminine organizations are likely to be more caring—some, like hospitals, literally so.

(C) Degree of Achievement

Here the assessor should ask, How well does the organization achieve its apparent sexual orientation? How much conflict is there between a masculine and feminine orientation? How well is the conflict between the two orientations compromised?

(D) How Pervasive

The achievement of the underlying masculine–feminine orientation may be highly developed in one part of the organization, less so in another. If the two functions are in competition, conflict may develop. For example, corporate training programs may teach managers contemporary concepts of motivation and leadership, but higher management's insistence on pressing for results may put managers in conflict. Conversely, monks in a monastery may be so preoccupied with their food producing activities that they do not adequately manage their institution.

(2) In Relation to the Industry

The orientation achieved by a particular organization has meaning for the organization's role within the industry. It has implications for organizational survival, for industry-wide leadership, and similar issues. When a major cigarette manufacturing company decided to accept the scientific reports of the damage cigarette smoking was doing to society, other cigarette manufacturers rejected its participation in their deliberations.

d. Transference Phenomena

As discussed in chapter 2, transference means unconsciously bringing past attitudes, particularly those toward family members, into present situations. Transference phenomena are symbolic recapitulations of earlier relationships within the family. By tacitly assuming that a superior will be hostile, caring, punitive, or supportive in the current working relationship, a person unwittingly transfers to his or her superior attitudes that the person established very early in life with his or her parents or others with power over the person. At the peer level, transference occurs when a person assumes that his or her peer is a competitive rival, or the psychological equivalent of brothers and sisters. Sometimes a hospital staff will treat patients as if they were naughty children, or the manager of a company will behave as if his or her employees were delinquent, unappreciative children. Conversely, the employees implicitly can regard the CEO or their immediate manager as a good or bad parent.

(1) Related to the Assessor

The attitudes of interviewees toward interviewers are frequently metaphors for how the interviewees perceive authority. They may look on the assessor and his or her staff as spies, friends, allies, saviors. The more irrational the expectations behind such images, the more difficulty the assessor is likely to have and the more easily disappointed the organization will be.

(2) Related to the Organization

Members of an organization implicitly or explicitly have transference images of the organization. These take many forms. Most often the images are parental. They look on the organization as carrying out maternal or paternal functions with respect to them, sometimes "big brother" functions. They also characterize the organization as benevolent or malevolent in referring to the way it behaves toward them (Schwartz, 1987). These transference phenomena relate to what people need psychologically from the organization, to what degree they get it, and how they perceive themselves with regard to the organization. For example, before its first drastic reorganization in the 1980s, AT&T employees used to speak of "Ma Bell," and refer to the benevolent supportive qualities of the organization.

(3) Related to Each Other

In addition to the transference reactions from the employees to the organization, there is frequently the reverse. This is most often reflected in the competition between the older and younger employees. The older ones frequently will speak of the inadequacy and incompetence of the younger ones, complain that they are not interested or do not care or are unwilling to uphold cherished values or that they simply are not experienced enough. The greater the gap in competence or power between the ruling clique of an organization and those who carry out its functions, the more vividly will the transference phenomena become visible. The more members of a family are involved in a given organization, particularly if they are literally parent and offspring, the more frequently will ancient family rivalries continue to be pursued (Kets de Vries, 1996; Levinson, 1971). In some organizations there is a "splitting" phenomenon: Certain people, by definition, are good and others are bad; certain divisions or departments may be good and others troublesome. When such splitting occurs, the group usually will idealize its leader and project its hostility on another leader or group or on distant malevolent forces.

2. Relations to Things and Ideas

In the preceding discussion of attitudes, attachments, orientation, and transference, the assessor was concerned with human relationships and with psychological stances toward other humans and toward the personification of the organization. Here the assessor is concerned with relationships to concrete objects versus abstract ideas, nonpersonal versus interpersonal issues. That is, in what things and ideas does the organization invest itself psychologically? For example, analyses of Apple Computer Corporation at its economic low point in the early 1990s attributed its difficulties to its idealized attachment to "Mac," its computer. While beginning to become engrossed in "Mac," Apple Company was more intrigued by another computer possibility named "Lisa." "After Steve Jobs visited the Xerox Palo Alto Research Center in 1979 . . . the 'Lisa' took on a distinct personality that made it possible to become the ultra-computer that Apple needed" (Weyrich, 1992, p. 1). Critics of IBM's late 1980s decline attributed that decline to its attachment to mainframes, its large computers (Gannes, 1988).

What differences are there in investment or attachment to objects and ideas within the organization? Do these complement or conflict with each other? Do attachments to objects or ideas transcend attachments to people? What psychological purposes do such investments serve? Beyond ideals, what other abstractions have meaning for the organization and how?

a. Quality and Intensity of Relations to Plant, Equipment, Raw Material or Supplies, Product, and Services

(1) Symbolization

Plant, equipment, product, and service can symbolize a variety of things to the people who are involved with them. A product may be viewed as the "baby" of the person who created it. A piece of equipment may be seen by one person as an extension of him- or herself; by another, as his or her master. A building may be a haven or a prison. For a person who distributes supplies, these may be his or her devices for purchasing affection. For one member of clergy, the service rendered to his or her parishioners may be just that; for another, part of a crusade.

(2) Unconscious Personification

Transference, as used here and discussed in chapter 2, is the tendency to look on the organization unconsciously as a contemporary representative of power figures early in the life of the individual. Here the assessor is concerned with what kinds of human qualities are attributed to plant, equipment, and product or service. Sometimes a building or a piece of equipment is even given a sexual identification—"he" or "she" (boats are always referred to as "she"). A service can also be personified, for in rendering it one can view him- or herself as acting in the image of someone else. A priest, for example, may see him- or herself as the vicar of Christ on earth.

b. Time: How Is It Regarded?

In chapter 7, the assessor was concerned with the time span and rhythm that governed work. There the assessor saw time as an external force that had its controlling effects on behavior. Here the assessor is concerned with how people implicitly regard time. For some, only the past has any meaning and the present is merely an appendage to it. For others, neither yesterday nor tomorrow have significance. For still others, only the future has meaning.

(1) Past, Present, Future Orientation

When people talk about the organization spontaneously, what is the implicit time focus of their conversation? Do they talk about its glorious history or refer to tradition as the basis for their perceptions? Do they talk about what the organization is planning for the future? Or do they talk about right now? Those who revere the past will tend to cling to it and have difficulty anticipating the future. Conversely, those for whom the past is irrelevant will lose whatever value there is for the organization in its history; they will be oblivious to the momentum from the past and the effects of organizational experience on present and future activities.

(2) How Is the Future Planned For?

Some organizations engage in formal long-range planning; many do not. Even those that do not plan formally are, in effect, planning for the future by making no plans. Implicitly, they allow themselves to be governed by external and accidental forces and to that extent are less the masters of their own fate. The act of planning has been mentioned before. Here the assessor is concerned about attitudes toward it.

(3) Value of Time as an Investable Commodity

Some organizations regard time as a commodity that is investable and therefore valuable. Because time per se is seen as a resource, blocks of it are purposely invested with the expectation that they will yield benefit to the organization. Organizations devote time to team meetings, retreats, planning, celebratory events, social activities, and even organizational assessments because they expect a profitable return for doing so.

(4) View of Work Cycles

Are work cycles seen as problems or opportunities? Does the organization consider deadlines oppressive barriers to be overcome, or does it view work cycles as providing opportunities alternately for rest and for intensive activity? Some organizations appear harried and hurried, and others are relaxed and confident that the work will be done. Daily newspapers, for example, are under relentless time pressure.

c. Space: How It Is Conceptualized

In chapter 6, the assessor was concerned with the use of space and its direct impact on the individual. Here the assessor is more concerned with what and how the organization implicitly thinks about space as an abstraction. For example, to some organizations space has no meaning at all. If the staff is increased, more partitions are erected or more machines are added or new buildings are constructed close to existing ones. To such organizations, space is not something to be lived in, mastered, controlled, or used to serve. Space simply exists. For other organizations, space is a part of its thinking, whether it is a church board that plans the design of a new building to have a vaulted arch symbolic of the ascent to heaven or a community park department that seeks to use every inch of available ground within the city limits for a recreation area.

(1) As a Local Concern

How much attention does the client organization pay to the use of space in its buildings and grounds? Is it something to be capitalized on or economized on? The assessor can discuss the economic aspect by asking questions such as, Does the organization deem it worthwhile to spend money just for space, or does it limit itself to the bare minimum needed? How expansive are the grounds? What effects are sought? Many large legal and accounting firms lease expensive quarters in large cities to be close to their financial clients and to hold out an image of their status.

Real estate values and the scarcity of space in given locations would not appear to be pertinent because organizations that value space highly reflect that fact in the way they manage their space resources. One of the underlying psychological issues is the degree of freedom in the organizational atmosphere as reflected in its thinking about space.

(2) As a Cosmopolitan Concern

Space may be conceived of not only as an immediate setting within which an organization operates, but also in terms of how the organization views itself with respect to the broader world. Some organizations perceive the entire world to be their "oyster." They view themselves as having legitimate interests in all or various parts of the world and see their activities as being international or cosmopolitan, even worldwide. National boundaries for such organizations have as little meaning as state and county boundaries or even city boundaries for other organizations. Some organizations may be international in their operations but do not think in terms of international complexities. The assessor should determine how the client organization relates itself to its space possibilities and what it conceives its life space to be.

d. Meaning of Work for the Organization

Work has different kinds of psychological meanings for individuals. For some, it is a means of attack on the external world; for others, it is a means of justifying their existence; for still others, it is an instrument for maintaining a place in the social community or acquiring power. For all, it serves deep-seated psychological and cultural needs. Because people tend to affiliate themselves in and with organizations that serve their psychological needs, work will come to have meanings for the organization. One or more such meanings may be more prominent than others.

(1) As a Device for Coping With the Environment

Work as a way to cope with the environment is particularly evident in highly competitive business organizations. Their race to be first bespeaks a wish to be on top. To be other than big or the biggest can seem to be a threat to them of ultimate annihilation. Indeed, the practice of hostile takeover is now a familiar business threat and mergers of large corporations commonplace even across national boundaries.

(A) In Economic Terms

Growth and size are equated with power and stability and compel the attention of the outside world. Such large and expanding organizations see their strength in either their monetary resources or control of raw materials that enables them to deal with governments as if they were equals. Some large corporations are more wealthy than some nations. In the late 1990s and into the twenty-first century, many massive organizations undertook acquisitions and mergers to increase their already monumental size; Exxon and General Electric are cases in point.

(B) In Terms of Skill

Some organizations implicitly experience work as a way of mastering the external environment by means of their special skills. They speak about what they can do, how they are going to improve their competence, what contribution that competence may make to society. Microsoft Corporation is illustrative. The assessor might ask, Why does this organization exist? What does it do better than anyone else? What does it do to make itself better?

(C) In Terms of Thinking

For some organizations, thinking is a way of coping with the environment. Ideas are the roots of power; concepts are devices for mastery. With the increased pressure for innovation, employees are being encouraged to "think outside the box." Training programs to help them do so have proliferated. Many contemporary employees are referred to as knowledge workers since Machlup (1962) coined that term.

(D) In Terms of Psychological Defense

Work is not only a means of coping with the external environment, but it is also a means of dealing with feelings. Sometimes it is disproportionately a mode of managing feelings as, for example, when one is a work addict. Then work is seen to be a defense against the discomfort that would otherwise arise. Under such circumstances it is likely to be too intense or unremitting or in conflict with what the person says he or she wants to do. Organizations can give primacy to work as a defense by fostering workaholic behavior or perpetuating work practices that serve to deny the anxieties of employees (Menzies, 1960). Another question is what behaviors the organization undertakes that seem to conflict with what it says it is trying to do and what behaviors it cannot give up even though they are no longer functional. For example, an organization may keep compulsive time schedules even though they serve no economic function. Thus, time is being used for a defensive function. It has been demonstrated that some management styles are less efficient for certain kinds of businesses than others. Yet some organizations cannot make changes that economics dictate. They are imprisoned by their own style of doing things. It is when an organization insists on continuing to operate in ineffective and inefficient ways, on denying the realities of the information it has about its own performance, that we speak of the organization of work as a defense (Jaques, 1955; Levinson et al., 1962).

(2) As a Device for Fulfilling the Psychological Contract

The psychological contract, as explained in chapter 5, is a set of mutual obligations and expectations between employees and organization that arises out of the needs of both. Some aspects of the contract are conscious, most often referred to as the social contract, for example, return of loyalty and service for guaranteed employment. Many writers confuse the social contract with the psychological contract.

Here the assessor also should determine the degree to which work serves as a device for meeting the organization's expectations of what it ought to be. These are most often stated in the form of mission, obligations, purpose, or, put another way, in terms of values, rules, aspirations, and self-judgment. But put in concrete terms, the staff of a hospital, respected for its exceptional treatment of cardiac patients, is serving both its individual aspirations and those of the hospital as well. The staff of the Salvation Army, devoted to rescuing the homeless, simultaneously meets both personal and organizational aspirations. Together, in my jargon, pursuit of both personal and organizational aspirations could represent pursuit of the organization's ego ideal. Of course, if that ego ideal is unrealistic or unattainable, that would be a violation of the psychological contract (Schwartz, 1987).

(3) As a Device for Channeling Energy

Some organizations are composed of people who feel driven without thinking too clearly about where, why, and what for. This is particularly true of young, ebullient organizations that are expanding rapidly and acting on many fronts at once. It is also true of organizations that have been involved with some kind of internal revolution and have neither crystallized an organizational structure nor tied their activity to well-defined purposes, tasks, or objectives. There is a sense of business without clear focus.

(A) Constructively

Many businesses that have become diffused are now shedding components that are not consistent with their present competitive thrust and attempting to define their core competence. In recent years, hospitals have tried to limit their services to short-term conditions and have referred patients who need rehabilitation or longer convalescence to rehab or nursing facilities. For some organizations there is pressure to do something good, useful, or important immediately, if not sooner. Some are compelled to demonstrate what they are and can do well. Has this organization refined its dominant effort?

(B) Destructively

Some organizations and some organizational activities seem disproportionately to serve the purpose of discharging aggressive or destructive energy. They seem always on the attack. Sometimes they are in a continuing path of hostile takeovers. Sometimes they are accused, like Microsoft Corporation, of swallowing and absorbing the techniques of other corporations like Eastman Kodak who sought corporate alliance to advance their products, not takeover.

(C) As a Process of Regression

Regression is a reversion to an earlier, less controlled form of behavior. In some organizations work is a means of "letting go," of acting, at least temporarily, in less than mature ways. In some organizations, on Friday managers can dress casually. Some have management meetings in vacation resorts where the managers can drink, play, and bond with each other to strengthen their working relationships. Some organizations provide regressive opportunities after busy meetings, such as bars, night clubs, and similar entertainment activities. Others foster regression as a part of their function, such as the informal social activities at trade and professional association meetings and collective attendance at sports events. Permissible or sanctioned regression relaxes people and fosters their pleasure in each other. That's why comedians are so popular. Impermissible regression, like coming to work drunk or dressed in ways others find offensive, is not acceptable.

i. Within the Work Setting

Regression within the work setting is a phase or activity of work that permits or sanctions a socially acceptable return to a more relaxed or childlike form of behavior, either as a part of the work process or in conjunction with it. The movement to "dressing down" or casual apparel in otherwise more formally dressed managers is an example. Southwest Airlines encourages relaxed, humorous behavior on the part of their flight attendants and other staff, both to make the work more pleasant and to ease the anxieties of passengers. In some work groups there is a lot of bantering, in others a practice of practical jokes. What happens here?

ii. In Nonwork Activities

For some people, work is a means to an end, not an end in itself. It is something they have to endure to have certain pleasures. Those pleasures may involve participation in a wide variety of social, religious, and community activities that are described as relaxing. There are organizational holiday parties, picnics, and other social events. Sometimes also businesses take over entertainment complexes for a whole day and their employees' families are invited to enjoy the facilities.

e. Authority, Power, and Responsibility

Authority is the potential for action, or capacity to act. *Power* is the degree of force of the action. *Responsibility* is derived from both authority and power, because any attempt to grasp responsibility without power is difficult, if not impossible. An organization's right to exercise initiative, to exert power in its self-interest, must be recognized by the corporate self, by those who are in the organization, and by those who are outside of it. Where there are conflicts about power, the organization may be inhibited in its actions. Where it is diffused, organizational actions flounder. Where power is used without concern for its effects, sooner or later there will be negative consequences. (Kets de Vries & Zaleznik, 1985; McClelland, 1975).

(1) How Does the Organization Regard Power?

Within the organization power may be glossed over, denied, or shunned. It may be something to be undermined, controlled, feared, manipulated, or used. Participative management techniques may be trumpeted but not practiced. In some religious orders the monks call each other brother or sister and superiors are elected. The more autocratic and rigid an organization, the greater the likelihood of manipulative effort to exploit loopholes and otherwise evade controls. What happens here?

(A) The Power of Others

Others can be competitors, regulatory bodies, politicians, dominant community groups, or even managers of the economy. How does the organization look on the power of others?

Some organizations, like tobacco companies, fight government restrictions. Some, like associations of farmers, lobby for legislation to support subsidies. Some, like the Roman Catholic Church and some fundamentalist conservative Protestant organizations, fight for public acceptance of abortion prohibition. Some, like the Nature Conservancy, seek to protect the environment. Recently some business organizations have joined environmental protection efforts, and some pharmaceutical companies have sought governmental advice before proceeding with marketing efforts. What does this organization do about which outside forces may threaten it?

(B) Its Own Power With Regard to the World Outside

Lumber, mining, ocean shipping, and broadcasting industries frequently dominate the governmental agencies that are intended to govern them. Wholesale electric power-generating companies, following the 2001 blackouts in California, were accused of manipulating prices and selling their power out of state. Some organizations view themselves as more powerful than outside forces, some as helpless in the face of them.

(C) Power Internally

How do people in the organization view the power that is exercised within its boundaries? Is it benign, paternalistic, inhibited, diffused? Is it taken for granted, feared, benevolent?

i. Generally

Is power exercised appropriately by superiors who are taught their role behavior and held accountable? Are there avenues for appeal, for dealing with special problems like discrimination or sexual harassment? Are there morale studies that evaluate managers? Do human resources departments exercise initiative to ensure fairness?

ii. By Ranks

Reactions to and concern about power may vary from one level to another in the organization. General officers are treated more leniently for violations than are enlisted personnel. The same is true for other organizations: High-level ecclesiastical authorities whose misbehavior has been publicized have been eased out of their roles less punitively than their subordinates; corporate executives are penalized less punitively for malfeasance than are low-level employees.

(2) How Does the Organization Handle Authority?

We have differentiated power from authority—authority being the permission or responsibility for action; power being the exercise of that permission. However, authority can be used in ways other than for direct action to compel somebody else to do something. For example, when a highly respected educational center makes a pronouncement about methods of education, it speaks as an authority. It has *social influence*. When a medical center calls attention to clinicial hazards, it, too, speaks as an authority. Those who accept that authority will guide their own actions accordingly. With this in mind, the assessor should investigate how the organization thinks in respect to itself: Does it recognize its own authority? Does it act as if it has a certain authority? How comfortable is it in such actions?

(3) How Does the Organization Handle Responsibility?

Here the assessor should ask, Does the organization carry responsibilities commensurate with its powers? Is responsibility avoided, rejected, unrecognized?

(A) Outside the Organization

Does it carry its weight in the community? Does it use its influence for social good? After years of town–gown conflict, Harvard University has embarked on a comprehensive cooperative effort with the cities of Cambridge and Boston to protect their neighborhoods, improve their schools, develop more adequate housing, and support their economic development. Many poor countries in Central America were exploited by the American plantation owners until the late Eli Black, who was then CEO of United Fruit Company, reversed course to improve housing and schools.

(B) Inside the Organization

The rapid turns of economic events in the forms of contraction, merger, and even organizational collapse have caused many to lose their jobs and even whole communities to lose their economic base. Some organizations have developed retraining programs, out-placement programs, mutual support programs, opportunities to transfer to other units, guaranteed continuing health insurance, and other measures to protect those who were affected. Some have given warning long in advance. Others have terminated their people abruptly. One company that for years had paternalistically overpaid unskilled workers decided to terminate them all with lump-sum financial settlements for people who had never learned to manage large sums of money. They were not only vulnerable to exploitation but also were unprepared for new jobs. Instead, the company, recognizing that it had handicapped the very people it had tried to protect, could have paid these employees in increments contingent on their getting trained for new roles, thus protecting them financially and occupationally.

f. Positions on Social, Ethical, and Political Issues

Sometimes explicitly, but more often implicitly, organizations take a stand on contemporary social, economic, and political issues. Some companies invest a tremendous amount of time and effort in economic education, and others actively promote concepts of democratic management. Some contribute heavily to political campaigns to ensure against enforcement of government practices and policies. Some public officials are said to represent the dominant political power in their communities and therefore fight for the interest of those institutions. In Boston, the alliance of several medical schools means that members of Congress lobby for research funds while in Seattle, Boeing carries the same weight for its interests. Still others are concerned about management's responsibility to the community. The assessor should determine what stance the organization takes on specific issues and, particularly, in what *manner* it does so. This is especially important if the organization takes a tacit stand but works behind the scenes, because that activity then becomes a skeleton in the organization's closet. For many years, tobacco companies denied that smoking caused cancer despite their own data. One large tobacco company is now claiming to be in the healthcare industry while continuing to produce cigarettes that are referred to within the company as "nicotine delivery devices."

3. Attitudes About Self

The self-image of an organization, like that of an individual, does not materialize suddenly. It is a result of years of interaction with others and with the environment in which it develops. The self-image relates to how the members of the organization see themselves collectively, how they see themselves in relationship to other organizations, to their host communities, and in their multiplicity of interactions and relationships.

a. Who Do They Think They Are and How Do They Feel About It?

Feelings of dismay were the pain of members of religious organizations when their clergy were indicted for sexual peccadilloes, for example.

b. Where Do They Think They Are Headed and How Do They Feel About It?

The collective feelings in an organization about the future have much to do with its present motivation. Those who see the realities as forbidding and overwhelming are likely to be depressed; those who see them as advantageous may be naively optimistic. Strong leadership that communicates imaginative plans and takes appropriate actions to implement them are likely to sustain high morale. That leadership that vacillates or undertakes what employees believe to be "pies in the skies" will soon be deserted by its more capable people. However, realities can serve as solid bases of motivation and hope.

c. What Are Their Common Aspirations?

Here the assessor is concerned about shared values and modes of achieving the goals implied by those values, together with people's feelings about their own aspirations and values. The assessor might ask where the interviewee thinks the organization is going, both in terms of its direction and economically, and how he or she feels about that. The assessor might also ask where the interviewee ideally would like to go in his or her life and how that dovetails with his or her values and where he or she thinks the organization is going. Would this individual want his or her children to work in this organization?

d. How Do They Look to Themselves?

Here the assessor is concerned with self-image, or perception of self. The assessor must infer the information from the way people personify the organization and from what they say about the kind of people who would join the organization and why they would join. This view incorporates, but goes beyond, the earlier masculine–feminine orientation to include what they think of themselves for working here. Kansas Power and Light employees often expressed their pride that they were in a company that provided an essential service, was respected in their communities, and they were regarded highly for having steady jobs at a time when few people enjoyed this stability.

4. Intraorganizational Relationships

Previously the assessor described the key people, different work group levels, and other bases for classifying people and units. Here the assessor must interpret specifically the emotional relationships among these people.

a. Key People in the Organization

Psychologically who are they? The assessor should write a brief historical character sketch of each key individual that will be a summary statement of (a) his or her characteristic behavior (e.g., a salesperson who relates to others through the use of humor; the sad clown smiling on the outside, crying on the inside; the meticulous comptroller); (b) his or her transference paradigm (attitudes toward power; some people are obsequious, some are obliging, and some behave as if there were no differences in power); (c) his or her style of handling individuals and conflicts in the organization; (d) his or her reaction to what goes on in the organization consistently bothers him or her; and (e) his or her methods of communication.

b. Significant Groups Within the Organization

Here the assessor should specify what he or she thinks are the most significant groups in the organization and what are the relationships between or among them. For example, there might be a technical group on the one hand and a marketing group on the other. They may be hostile to each other or may cooperate cohesively. In a church the most significant groups might be conservatives versus liberals; in a community, three or four ethnic groups; and so on. Community groups frequently fall into social class categories. In business, they may be divided according to management levels.

In specifying the groups that he or she thinks important and delineating their relationships, the assessor should look particularly into their points of difference and conflict in an effort to understand why they differ. In some cases, groups will differ because of their geographical origins, as in the case of former Kentucky hill folk who had difficulty with lower middle-class ethnic supervisors in Detroit automobile plants. In other cases, they will differ because of varying value systems, ethnic differences, divergences in goals and aspirations. Often groups with power, such as managers, will be contemptuous of those without power, such as their subordinates, and act accordingly. Conversely, highly unionized and cohesive work groups may well be contemptuous of management.

In assessing the relationships between or among important groups, the assessor will want to look at how they communicate with each other, what nonwork activities they undertake together, and under what conditions they mobilize against a common outside threat. The assessor's understanding of the significant groups in the organization will be crucial for his or her subsequent recommendations and change efforts.

c. Implications of a and b

What differences in terms of organizational functioning do these relationships make? This might be summarized in the form of a paradigmatic statement like this one:

> The Stemble Company was formed by one man. It is a product of his own drive for the recognition and extension of himself by organizing a group of people concentrated on and specialized in a product with a limited market. The market is limited partly because other companies manufacture similar products and partly because the product must be

used in conjunction with other equipment. The company is carried on by his son, who is still struggling with his own problems of resolving his dependency on his father. The son is not particularly equipped to run the business. His power derives from owning the assets and thus being able to direct or persuade others that something should be done. In addition, the son has the support of his father who also is able to persuade others to move in certain directions. As an extension of the son's struggle, there is no concise policy for the continuation of problem solving; the company must grapple with each crisis on an ad hoc basis. There is a tendency for the subparts of the company to be isolated from each other; people identify with their own unit rather than with the company as a whole. The dealers who sell the products are uncertain about whether to commit themselves to the company and its products. There is a pervasive air of pessimism in the organization. It is as if the company is saying, "We have men and machines. We build, or will build, something for you. However, we can't sell it ourselves; we don't have patents, and we don't have brilliant innovators. We depend on others. We do not know what to do about this." The son depends on the father and the chief accountant. The company is wrestling with the questions. Can it depend on the son? Who is running the company? Who is innovating now? Can the accountant? Can the son?

5. Management Information Systems

These days all organizations are required to obtain and sustain a wide range of information, particularly that which can be maintained on computers. These data may vary from the list of names, addresses, and contributions of parishioners in a small church to patient histories in a hospital now available no matter where the patient may be, to the vast array of computers that characterizes a space mission or a complex worldwide commodities trading operation. Increasingly organizations seek to computerize their operations. Even much of manufacturing an automobile is now managed by computers. What is done here and with what competitive implications?

- In general, are computers and other technical devices embraced or are they objects of fear and loathing? (Do people talk regretfully about the old ways of doing things?)
- Are computers and related technologies used as divisive mechanisms? Are some managers "information rich," and other managers "information poor?"
- Does management view computer technology as a dynamic tool to encourage creativity and innovation?
- How do managers view the management information system (MIS) or information technology function? Are MIS managers and technicians responsive to the needs of "users?" If not, how

does their apparent unresponsiveness impede the flow of work within the organization?
- Do people working in information technology feel a part of the organization and its major thrusts or do they feel subordinate and servile?

I am indebted to Robert Krock for these questions.

10

IN CONCLUSION

Now it is time to tie together all of the data the assessor has collected following the continuity of the outline (see appendix D).

IV. ANALYSES AND CONCLUSIONS: INTERPRETATIONS FROM INFERENCES

This chapter provides a framework for the assessor to selectively interpret the identifying, historical, and examinational data. The conclusions at which the assessor arrives will establish a basis for his or her understanding of, and intervention into, the affairs of the organization. Because there is no consensus on established criteria either for assessing an organization or for defining modes of intervention, the assessor's conclusions and recommendations necessarily will be based on subjective interpretations and selections. They will reflect his or her professional orientation and, as such, will be that part of the assessment in which there will be the greatest diversity of interpretation. Because of the variety of theoretical orientations, the assessor must approach the selection and understanding of these data with an open mind and yet with firm conviction about the ways *he or she* interprets the data, based on *his or her* professional orientation.

With these qualifications, this organizational assessment method provides guidelines for obtaining data from which interpretations can be made by practitioners of various disciplines. The validity of these interpretations will depend on their consistency within the particular frame of reference of a specific discipline.

Extracting and distilling the data necessary to arrive at a useful body of conclusions is analogous to the making of fine wine. Just as the vintner selects and processes the grapes, presses them, and filters out the extraneous matter and opacities to produce wine of brilliant clarity, so the assessor, from his or her accumulated data, must select and condense those that will reveal the essence of the organization's vitality. The assessor must describe comprehensively the dynamic organizational processes, taking into account both internal and external interactions, to delineate and clarify the multiple determinants that bring about the organization's current adaptive behaviors. The dynamic processes that this organizational assessment method elicits are a reflection of the conflicts with which the organization contends in its efforts to survive. From this assessment, therefore, the assessor can determine the various organizational strengths and weaknesses as they enhance or interfere with its ability to cope with its stress.

This chapter first considers the data in terms of the ecology of the organization, the interaction of the organization with the forces external to it. It then considers the data in terms of the internal structure and processes of the organization itself.

The questions always before assessor are, How does this organization hurt? How do I interpret what the key people cite as their main problem? How do I interpret what other employees speak of as their main problem? The pain may be literally what the informants say it is or it may be symptomatic of something deeper. How does the organization experience its problems? That is, how severe do the problems appear to be to the organization? And how well does the organization relate them to basic causes? These are vital questions because the degree to which the organization experiences pain is one measure of how ready the organization is to accept help.

A. Organizational Integrative Patterns

In this section of the outline, the assessor must continue to exercise professional judgment. The assessor must be careful particularly to indicate where and how, in his or her judgment, the organization is not integrating effectively. In making these observations and judgments, the assessor must not assume a pejorative attitude. The assessor's concern is not to seek out evil or to find the person who is wrong; he or she must instead seek out failure and potential failure (as well as strength and potential strength) for the purpose of helping to remedy or strengthen those situations. There is a tendency on the part of consultants to look for culprits—the cause or the person—and to substitute invective for consideration. Such actions can only blind the assessor to the realities with which he or she and the organization must deal. To repeat, the assessor constantly must be aware of the fact that he or she is dealing with inference, that he or she must be prepared to offer evidence for interpretations and conclusions, and that he or she must regard his or her statements as hypotheses to be tested.

To review organizational integrative efforts is to discuss the manner in which the organization is functioning cohesively and effectively, as well as where it is disjointed, where it stumbles, where it falls, where it errs repetitively and where it dissipates energies.

1. Appraisal of the Effect of the Environment on the Organization

The assessor cannot understand the organization in a vacuum; he or she can do so only in the dynamic setting in which the organization functions. In this section, the assessor should assess the relationship and interaction between the organization and forces external to it. The assessor should take into account what the host environment has done to and for the organization, both in terms of the environment's response to the organization and the organization's response to the environment. Of course, the assessor will be making a somewhat arbitrary distinction by separating the effect of the environment on the organization and vice versa, but doing so will help him or her to analyze the operating forces.

The assessor's first step in this section should be to elicit and describe the significant points and sequences in the organization's past interactions with its environment so that the assessor can state, These things have happened; this is true of the organization today. To do this requires knowledge of the historical external influences on the organization, both real and as perceived by the organization. Although the way in which the environment is perceived by the organization is an integral part of this section, and because this phenomenon will always influence the interaction, the particular psychological needs determining both qualitative and quantitative dimensions of the organization's perception of its environment must also be discussed. They will be taken up further in the section of the conclusions that deals with the organization's internal functioning. Making this appraisal also necessitates inferences drawn from past behavior and functioning, just as one infers from the rings of a tree stump those periods of drought, fertilization, freezing, and other events that influenced the growth of that tree.

To avoid biased selections that would lead the assessor astray, he or she must be as comprehensive as possible in making this assessment. A parallel pitfall that would lead to erroneous or misleading conclusions would be to accept too easily seemingly obvious explanations of cause and effect. This would ignore the principle of multiple causation and result in overly glib, one-to-one, causal explanations rather than recognize that the same outcome may arise from multiple and different determinants (for example, ascribing the decline of the railroad passenger business *completely* to economics and competitive factors, while ignoring the influence of long-standing railroad management attitudes that neglected the necessary service functions, those having to do with taking care of people, an attitude rooted in the hypermasculine origins of the railroad industry).

This retrospective view of the organization's development and change in response to environmental influences must consider both immediate and long-term effects if the assessor is to be able to assess what changes produced stable steps in the organization's evolutionary process. War, for example, may increase a particular market; a specific demand for a new product may bring an immediate growth. In these instances, however, the short-term success may be dangerous for the organization's survival if the organization's response to it is at the expense of long-term growth and diversification. Conversely, what might appear, at first, to be harmful environmental stresses, may, at the same time, open onto avenues that will foster organizational growth. The demise of the trolleycar, for example, forced electric utility companies to become involved in, and actually to develop, new community and public uses for electricity. At the same time, the government attacks on public utility holding companies in the 1930s allowed both the birth and development of independent utility companies.

The ongoing and reciprocal nature of the organization's relationship to its environment involves both past and present considerations and can produce an attitudinal climate among the public that often is a stimulus of strong potential force. An illustration is the neglectful misuse of natural resources that may go unnoticed for a long time. When the exploitation finally is brought to the attention of the public, the enormity of such contemptuous behavior, together with its chronicity, may evoke strong feelings and unduly restrictive countervailing legislation. A similar example might be the way the public reacted to its perception that, for many years, the automobile industry disregarded safety features in cars. However, there is the danger of ascribing oversimplified, one-to-one, causal relationships when other facets of the industry's image and interaction with the public influenced public attitudes and response. To take this illustration a step further, if the assessor were to try to assess a contemporary environmental response, he or she might not yet be able to say whether a given ecological phenomenon will foster or hamper the survival of any given organization.

Another example of organizational climate that elicits a positive rather than a negative environmental response is the protective alliance stockholders form with those large, stable companies that have outstanding and reliable dividend performance. Many stockholders of AT&T, before its breakup, rose in righteous indignation in response to antitrust investigations or attempts at restrictive legislation.

The following section of the formal outline divides the ecology into three main historical groups—past, present, and predicted future—with subgroups for qualitative assessment in terms of beneficial and harmful aspects (that is, those that may foster and promote organizational survival versus those that may be destructive to the achievement of that goal). There are, necessarily, overlapping and interrelated classifications. It becomes necessary, therefore, for the assessor to be flexible in this part of the assessment so that, at this juncture, the accuracy and validity of those interrelationships are not hidden by a rigid need to "split hairs" regarding time and qualitative judgments. The focus should be on the genetic forces that have resulted in the current state of the organization and those that will determine its future.

The items to be considered, as covered in the outline (geographical and natural resources; economy; market, long-term and short-term; staff power; labor movements; legislation and regulatory agencies; supplies and suppliers; competition; and cultural forces) similarly are exemplary rather than all-inclusive. The limitations of these items will be determined more accurately by the data that are included in the body of the assessment.

    a. Historical

        (1) Beneficial
        (2) Harmful

    b. Contemporary

        (1) Beneficial
        (2) Harmful

    c. Anticipated

        (1) Beneficial
        (2) Harmful

2. Appraisal of the Effect of the Organization on the Environment

    a. Historical

        (1) Beneficial
        (2) Harmful

    b. Contemporary

        (1) Beneficial
        (2) Harmful

    c. Anticipated

        (1) Beneficial
        (2) Harmful

3. Reactions

    a. Of the Environment

Whenever an organization injures its environment by withdrawal, assault, aggressive relationships, or random adaptation efforts, inevitably the environment must react. This process of stimulation and reaction tells the assessor something about the organization's characteristic mode of adaptation, at what point it is likely to be in conflict with its host environment, and the need for the organization to observe this pattern of provocation and reaction.

  (1) To the Injury
  (2) Toward the Source of the Injury

  b. *Secondary Reaction From the Organization*

How does the organization react to the environment's reaction? Does the organization understand it? Does it recognize its contributions to precipitating conflict in the first place?

4. *Appraisal of the Organization*

The assessor must recognize, at the outset, that any "appraisal" is just that—an estimate, a value judgment that is made in terms of the assessor's professional orientation and that is influenced by certain biasing factors unique to both the discipline and the individual.

For example, business-oriented consultants would think in terms of "assets" and "impairments"—positive and negative factors, strengths and weaknesses, pluses and minuses. From the standpoint of survival and growth, what one consultant might see as an organizational impairment—such as the *inability* to function without federal support, as in the aerospace industry—another analyst might view as an asset—such as the long-established tradition in the aerospace industry of interdependency with the federal government.

In the fields of psychiatry and clinical psychology (here seen as part of the field of the healing arts), the orientation traditionally was to the "pathological." The focus of interest was heavily on curing or ameliorating the impairments (the disease, if you will), sometimes to such an extent that a person's assets were not always accurately or adequately recognized. Because this organizational assessment method has been extrapolated from a clinical case study method, the assessor using it must recognize the need to guard against overemphasizing the impairments at the expense of the assets— thereby skewing, or distorting, his or her assessment.

In this section of the outline, the assessor will succinctly evaluate the organization. The assessor should do so in terms of its survival and growth, how the organization has functioned in the past, and how it will be able to continue to function in the future. In making such an appraisal, the assessor will have to make positive and negative value judgments with regard to the organization's assets and impairments, and in doing so from a consulting orientation, what he or she chooses to call "assets" and "impairments" will be related to the proposed intervention to follow—that is, *consultative intervention*. As a consequence, the assessor will pay special attention to such organizational qualities as points of vulnerability, points of necessary intervention, and points of useful intervention. Consultants from other disciplines may adhere to different principles in their appraisal of the organization.

A second difference that usually is more apparent than real is that the assessor will think of assets and impairments in both *material* and *functional* terms.

a. Special Assets

(1) Material or Tangible (Financial, Patents, Physical Plant, Equipment, Geographical Distribution, Transportation, Communication, Personnel)

Material assets and impairments are definable quasi-permanent elements that form a relatively enduring part of the organizational matrix; they are, or are treated as, nonhuman elements. In the 1930s and the early 1940s, the dark green delivery trucks operated by Marshall Field and Company of Chicago were perceived by the community as sources of help in emergencies. During their regularly scheduled delivery rounds, the drivers often became side-tracked on errands of mercy—getting a kitten out of a tree, returning a lost dog to its home, hastening a mother-to-be to the nearest hospital, putting out a fire. These events occurred so often, and the drivers of the dark green trucks became so well-known for their humanitarian qualities, that it was as if these qualities resided in the *trucks themselves*, rather than in the individuals who drove them. It was the *truck* that was sought in times of emergency.

Items to be considered, as listed in the outline, are examples, not a complete list: financial status, patents held, physical plants and equipment, geographical distribution, transportation facilities, communications, personnel (that is, their particular talents—such as the *number* of engineers in a construction firm).

(2) Functional (Including Leadership and Mental Set, or Attitude)

The qualities the assessor looks for in the functional assets of the organization are human in nature. They are dynamic; at this point the assessor should think in terms of the organization "being alive"—"being able to respond." In appraising the "functional" assets and impairments, it becomes impossible to exclude an assessment of organizational key figures, and it is difficult to separate the assessment of such figures in their own right from the assessment of the organization as an entity. However difficult such an appraisal may be, it must be made. What is an asset to the individual may well be an impairment to the organization; the reverse also is true. In differentiating the positive and negative qualities of the *key figures'* behavior the assessor might ask, What is the cost to the *organization* of this individual's behavior?

(A) Reality Orientation

One dimension of a functional asset (or impairment) is seen in terms of the organization's orientation to reality (or lack thereof). Here again the distinction must be made between the organization's ability to perceive and judge the world around it as opposed to perceiving and judging the organization itself. Robert Burns's famous lines about the importance of being able to see oneself are as germane for organizations as they are for individuals.

> i. *To External Environment*
> ii. *To Internal Environment*

(B) Values and Ideals

Another dimension for assessing the assets and impairments of an organization concerns its values and ideals and the degree to which they are institutionalized or have become part of the organization itself (rather than remaining solely those of the individuals within the organization). How much are they part of the organization itself? This is difficult to define and detect, but the assessor should think in terms of the perpetuation of something that the organization stands for—something that is adhered to regardless of changes in personnel, economic and marketing conditions, and world events. Freedom of speech is such a value in the United States. In addition, the assessor must ask, How congruent are these values and ideals with the organization's internal and external reality (as an indication that they are an asset)? or, How great is their disparity with the organization's internal and external reality?

> i. *Degree of Institutionalization*
> ii. *Congruence With Reality*

(C) Task Mastery

The assessor can look at task mastery as an additional dimension of a functional asset or impairment.

> i. *Psychological Contract Fulfillment or Violations*

What is the psychological contract in the organization? To what degree is it recognized and fulfilled? (Please refer to the discussion of the psychological contract in chapter 5.) It is postulated that when the three issues of affection, aggression, and dependency are effectively dealt with, and both the individual and the organization feel themselves to be moving toward a conjoined ego ideal, the reciprocal relationship between the person and the organization tends to be such that it promotes health and more effective individual and organizational functioning (Levinson et al., 1962).

These questions may help:

- How comfortable is the client system about its dependence on the assessor?
- Who in the system depends more heavily?
- Who rejects his or her dependency on the assessor?
- Where in the system is there reasonable interdependence?
- How do senior managers and executives express or inhibit their aggression toward the assessor?
- How warm and friendly are their relationships with each other? With their subordinates? With the assessor?
- Do employees feel respected and regarded?
- What do people wish for themselves and the organization in the future?
- What cautions must the assessor consider about his or her feelings of affection and his or her own feelings about who is in which roles of authority recognized in the organization chart? It is said of some executives that they fall in love with each candidate they interview and it impairs their judgment. The assessor can "fall in love" with preferred interviewees or the organization itself. The assessor also might have feelings about the effectiveness of certain managers and executives and wonder why they were chosen, or having been chosen, why they continue to be in their present roles.

ii. Growth and Survival

What has been the past history of organizational survival and growth? What are future prospects along this line?

iii. Task-Directed Behavior

Finally, to what extent has this organization demonstrated, and does it now demonstrate consistently, the ability to direct its behavior toward task performance and problem solution? Or, conversely, to what extent *must* this organization resort to defensive maneuvers and regressive behavior?

b. Impairments

  (1) Material or Tangible (Financial, Patents, Physical Plant, Equipment, Geographical Distribution, Transportation, Communication, Personnel)

  (2) Functional (Including Leadership and Mental Set, or Attitude)

  (A) Reality Orientation

    i. To External Environment
    ii. To Internal Environment

(B) *Values and Ideals*

    i. *Degree of Institutionalization*
    ii. *Disparity From Reality*

(C) *Task Mastery*

    i. *Psychological Contract Unfulfillment*
    ii. *Growth and Survival*
    iii. *Task-Directed Behavior*

c. *Level of Integration*

When organizational integrative efforts fail, emergency activities are instituted in proportion to the severity of the threat to the organizational equilibrium. These activities are attempts to maintain the organization's equilibrium. All coping activities "cost" energy. As the organization's equilibrium progressively becomes more precarious, the organization will apply increasing energy to shore itself up.

The level of integration is reflected in adaptive coping efforts or emergency activities that the organization expends. These can be catalogued according to their effectiveness and the amount of energy they require. However, it is difficult to distinguish levels, so such labeling necessarily will be arbitrary. Karl Menninger and colleagues (1962) categorized coping devices for maintaining individual equilibrium according to similar considerations of effectiveness and energy requirements. A comprehensive list of organization adaptive activities modeled on that list is in appendix C.

When increasing amounts of energy must be devoted to coping activity, this energy is deflected from its potential discharge in the forward motion of the organization. In a sense, an organization is like a space capsule that maintains its equilibrium using jets of gas. If it uses most of its fuel maintaining its equilibrium, it loses forward momentum. Furthermore, the greater the use of the jets, the more likely the capsule is to be defected from its forward course. The same is true with individuals and organizations. Thus, the very nature of these coping activities is that too frequent use impairs the organization's relationship to reality while demanding greater investment in the coping mechanism. As the organization becomes increasingly disordered, it acts less successfully on its problems. It also achieves less return for its investment in coping activities.

The decreasing efficiency of these counterbalancing activities is characterized by increasing amounts of energy invested, increasingly less successful coping efforts that provide less adequate results and less gratification. Contemporary downsizing activities that do not increase productivity or profitability are cases in point.

Once the organization goes beyond the normal adaptive activities it is headed for danger. Each time an organization moves to a more severe degree of dysfunction, it becomes easier for it to regress to that level. It is as if a psychic path were being worn in a field. There is a commonly used analogy in physical medicine: When a person dislocates his or her shoulder, it is easier for that individual to sustain the same injury another time. Each successive dislocation makes the individual more susceptible to a future dislocation under *less* stress. Another factor in this phenomenon is the frequency with which the person dislocates his or her shoulder: If the second dislocation occurs relatively soon after the first, the chances for an additional dislocation is further increased. All the ligaments and muscle bands in the injured shoulder become stretched and never fully recover and, therefore, cannot protect against a future dislocation.

This analogy applies to the organization's use of various orders of defense. Because stress is not quantitatively or qualitatively the same at all times, the organization does not operate on any one level of defense at all times. Rather, it has to "dip down" in its level of functioning to meet increasing stress. Therefore, an organization operates with normal activities; frequently with first-order activities; sometimes with second-order activities; occasionally with third-order ones. Keep in mind that with coping activities, the emphasis is on the *discharge of aggression* toward attacks on problems or efforts at mastery. In most instances it is the inappropriate discharge of aggression as a defense that provokes difficulty.

(1) Normal Adaptive Activities

Normal adaptive activities permit some discharge of energy toward problem resolution and, concurrently, offer some provision for gratification to compensate for the threat the organization experiences. In addition to helping to deal with whatever arouses anxiety, they also serve to assuage the anxiety.

(2) First-Order Adaptive Activities

First-order adaptive devices are more intensive versions of the normal activities an organization undertakes to set things right when it is hurting just a bit. These are exaggerations of the normal regulatory coping activities of the organization in everyday life. They are temporary and are used only when needed to meet a given situation. They offer some provision for gratification to compensate for the sense of threat and guilt feelings. Often, first-order activities seem to reflect a feeling in the organization that it is under attack by hostile forces and therefore must become more guarded or more self-centered. Hostility (aggression) in this sense serves either to whip the organization into shape or to attack the purported enemy. Self-centeredness serves to diminish in importance the external information that is threatening to the organization. Nothing is allowed to prick the organization's self-inflated balloon, as it were.

(3) Second-Order Adaptive Activities

Second-order devices usually are a means of coping with time-bound stress. They tend to a massive focusing of energy on some particular task or problem at the expense of the on-going activities of the organization. Examples include responses to fires, tornadoes, and earthquakes. In that sense, they are disruptive.

Another example is the Coca-Cola experience. When in 1999 CEO M. Douglas Ivestor did not respond effectively to the Belgian upset over allegedly toxic Coke, the company's image suffered. Coke's board of directors reacted by replacing Ivestor with Douglas Daft.

The difference between second- and third-order adaptive activities is that the former are responses to temporary glitches from which the organization can more readily recover. It is like the difference between having flu and having pneumonia: Both are upper-respiratory infections, but the latter potentially is much more serious.

(4) Third- and Fourth-Order Adaptive Activities

The difference between third- and fourth-order adaptive activities is that those of the third-order tend to be intermittent or episodic in nature, whereas those of the fourth-order have a chronic or continuous quality.

In considering coping activities, an organization can go from second-order to fourth-order without touching third-order. The first episode can lead to a continuous fourth-order level of integration.

d. Overall Effectiveness and Facade

Some types of disorganization or discomfort will not be manifested in markedly lower competence. The façade that prevents inner problems from becoming noticeable may be a great asset or a great liability. There should be some attempt to appraise this facade. For example, during the dot.com heyday of the late 1990s, some mutual funds scrapped their more conservative investments to capitalize on the dot.com opportunities. With great enthusiasm, they trumpeted their increasing success to prospective clients. Their managers did not think of the need for fall-back positions. When the dot.com bubble burst, they suffered rapid decompression. They had not protected their customers against inevitable downturns in the market.

B. Summary and Recommendations

The summary and recommendations section considers the data first in terms of the ecology of the organization—that is, the interaction of the organization with the forces external to it, then in terms of the internal structure and processes of the organization itself.

The data the assessor has gathered and interpreted thus far have provided him or her with the material he or she needs for viewing the organization and its external and internal environments from both longitudinal and cross-sectional points of view. From this dual perspective, the assessor can make a definitive statement of the present status of the organization. Finally, an explanatory formulation will provide the assessor with the dynamic and genetic understanding of the organization's present status. The assessor may state prognostic conclusions based on perspective, present status, and explanatory formulation.

1. Present Status

In this section of the outline, the assessor makes a statement that conveys a cross-sectional description of the organization in its environment and at one point on the time spectrum—the present. This statement should be a summary and integration of the material discussed in the first section of this chapter. Although it need not be lengthy, the statement should contain those pertinent facts and inferences needed to capture the essence of the current situation in which the organization finds itself. This statement, diagnostic in nature, should contain a complex set of conclusions: descriptive, analytic, and evaluative. It should describe an organization, an environment, and their interaction; it should pay particular attention to those aspects of the interaction that seem to be unsatisfactory, costly, inefficient, painful, or full of conflict. Such a statement will always be polydimensional, multidescriptive, and continuous. Theoretically, such a statement cannot be recorded because no sooner has it been written than it begins to be out of date. Therefore, the quality of continuous change must be recognized and the statement of "present status" must be understood to be *dated*.

2. Explanatory Formulation

Once the assessor has described the present status, he or she should offer an explanation of how that status was reached; that is, the explanatory formulation. It is in this section of the outline that the assessor is called on to demonstrate the consistency and validity of his or her particular discipline and the theory of motivation he or she assumes.

a. Genetic

For the assessor who has a psychoanalytic orientation, the explanatory formulation must have a genetic dimension. It must explain the present status in terms of the entire life process of the organization. Such a longitudinal explanation will take into account those specific events in the organization's life span that have molded, shaped, and influenced its present state.

b. Dynamic

In addition to the genetic dimension, the explanation must have a dynamic dimension for the psychoanalytically oriented assessor. It must explain organizational behavior and the environmental response in terms of energy systems, defensive maneuvers, conscious and unconscious conflicts, and multiple causation and motivation. It must see the organization as being moved by forces of which it is often unaware and continually making compromises and adjustments to achieve the best level of functioning in light of the forces coming from within itself and from the environment.

3. Prognostic Conclusions

Here the assessor must weigh those factors that help the organization, help the assessor help the organization (if that is his or her goal), or help the assessor help the organization to help itself against those factors working against it. The assessor must first consider those forces or circumstances that seem to work *against* improvement and ask him- or herself such questions as,

- Are the prospects for improvement limited beforehand by unalterable factors: for example, the advent of the automobile to a company that can make *nothing* but buggy whips or the loss of financial resources or a dominant leader?
- Are the prospects for improvement impaired by conditions unlikely to be altered: for example, the advent of a "throwaway" society to a company that makes equipment for repairing shoes, hats, and typewriters; or the development of successful preventive effort for tuberculosis to an organization devoted to raising money for just that purpose?
- Does the organization's life history indicate that its aggressive impulses are difficult to deflect, modify, placate, or direct into task performance and problem solution: for example, the history of militant labor relations in some heavy industries; the continuous attack on socialized medicine by the American Medical Association in the face of public pressure for more comprehensive medical coverage.
- Is the organization's self-centeredness so extreme as to preclude the capacity for establishing new, gratifying relationships: for example, the investment of a maternal organization in "taking care of her own flock" (IBM, Eastman Kodak, AT&T before 1990); associations of dairy farmers in Wisconsin and Vermont devoted to protecting family farms against the inevitable movement westward toward larger, more economical operations.
- Are the indirect satisfactions from the present level of integration in excess of the price paid for them: for example, aerospace

industry being "on the government dole," constantly vulnerable to government budget cutbacks; communities that try to preserve obsolete military bases rather than seek new competitive industries?

- Is there apparent acceptance of self-destructive behavior within the organization: for example, the militant fight of the cigarette companies against the obvious, documented scientific evidence of the negative effects of smoking?
- Is the environment within which the organization must function frustrating, corrupting, or otherwise harmful: for example, county governments and the patronage system? Likewise, the assessor must consider those forces or circumstances that seem to work toward improvement that are capable of being exploited in that direction.
- How much does the organization's discomfort motivate it to seek a more favorable compromise?
- How painfully does the organization sense the loss of satisfaction?
- How well-endowed with competence is this organization?
- Does the organization show some propensity for acquiring and using relationships with other individuals, groups, or organizations?
- Are there latent capacities for diversification or consolidation from which gratification can be achieved?
- Is self-punitiveness such a marked feature that the substitution of other forms of penance or realistic restitution are possible, as in some form of public service?
- Are there undeveloped potentialities for creativity and innovation within the organization?
- Are there preferred environments within which the organization can function that are attractive and health-promoting? Some organizations are better off for everyone within them if they are in a larger organization whose thrust they fit. Some are sold that are no longer in existence because their major product did not fit their acquirers' dominant thrust. Anyone remember Ipana toothpaste?
- Is the organization's temperament basically optimistic or pessimistic?

The assessor must also recognize that any prognostic statement must be expressed in terms of degree of probability. Because no one actually *knows* about the future, one can only say what the trend seems to be.

Finally, again it must be emphasized that even the prognostic conclusions of this organizational assessment are made from the assessor's point of view, primarily as precursors to consultative intervention.

4. Recommendations

Recommendations are part of the assessment proper. They are not the report to the client, which is discussed in chapter 11. These recommendations are intended to be a summary of proposed modes of intervention, based on a review of all of the previously integrated data. Ideally, the assessor should be able to point to a series of reasons as the basis for each sentence in this section and to reject alternative actions on the same basis. If his or her reasoning is tentative, the assessor should so indicate. If his or her proposed actions are trial efforts, that should be indicated, too. Recommendations are still part of the assessor's road map. If the assessor errs, they permit him or her to retrace steps and reexamine actions, to formulate and try alternative hypotheses. The more detailed the recommendations, the more hypotheses the assessor has to test.

11

THE CLOSURE PROCESS

Having completed and written up the assessment, the next task is to begin the closure process by feeding back the results. This involves two steps: preparing a report to the client and presenting the report to the client system.

However, these are only the mechanical steps. The closure process is a complex and subtle endphase negotiating process. The way in which it is handled will be the most significant influence determining whether the client will proceed further on the issues discerned.

PREPARING THE REPORT

The report to the client should be a summary of those findings abstracted from the write-up, together with recommendations for actions. (See the example in appendix B.) It should be no longer than what can be read aloud in an hour. The summary should describe what the assessor did, how the assessor got his or her information, and the period of time covered by the assessment. This will enable the client to put the report in perspective and to understand its sources and its limits. It should then state what in the judgment of the assessor are the essential findings. These should be couched in such a way that those hearing the report can say, "Yes, that's the way it is here. You have reported our feelings and experiences accurately and with empathic understanding. You appreciate our struggles." That is, the assessor should consider carefully the education, level of understanding, degree of interest, and opportunities for action the audience has and, therefore, what they can hear. While being factual and empathic, the report must not be dishonest at one extreme or an indictment on the other. The report must be tailored carefully to those who will hear it and have to deal with its consequences. The assessor should be careful not to overwhelm the client with negative findings that leave the client with disproportionate feelings of helplessness and therefore unable to act.

For example, in one situation, the subordinates of an executive told the assessor a great deal about the executive's aloofness and authoritarian manner. Some of their feelings about his authoritarian style stemmed from his aloofness from them. The assessor recognized that the executive could not change his personality significantly and that part of his aloofness resulted from not knowing how to get closer to his people. The assessor reported to the executive that his subordinates looked to him for leadership and support and wanted to see more of him. The assessor recommended regular meetings with the subordinates about the common problems they faced. Had the consultant merely told the executive he was authoritarian, the executive would have been left with criticism, which he could only reject because he saw himself not as authoritarian but fatherly. Once he rejected the assessor's findings, there would have been no way for the assessor to help him further. In this particular instance, the assessor was in a position to help him learn to relate more effectively to his people and to mobilize them toward their mutual tasks.

The assessor should be guided by the questions, How much of what kind of information can the client (executive and organization) accept? How must the client be told?

The findings should give appropriate emphasis to the strengths of the organization and its assets for coping with its problems. They should provide a balanced picture of the organization and its problem-solving efforts. They should be stated in such a way that organization members, by following the same process the assessor followed, would return the same findings. In technical jargon, the findings should have "face validity."

A statement of recommendations should follow the presentation of the findings. The recommendations should offer *specific* avenues for confronting the problems disclosed in the findings, and they should be in keeping with the strengths and assets in the organization. There is little point in making recommendations that are beyond the capacity of the organization to undertake. Too often consultants assume that the organization can readily use the strengths it has. Most, however, will need help in using strengths—help in the form of delineated steps toward more effective functioning, together with support from the assessor or someone else in taking those steps. Often management will be fully aware of its problems but not know how to go about beginning to cope with them. And often the assessor's recommendations are too general to be useful.

PRESENTING THE REPORT

Once the report has been prepared, the actual feedback process can begin. And the first step is to present the report to the executive who was responsible for the assessor's entering the organization. It is important for the assessor to recognize that the client has the right to be in charge of what is happening to him or her. Therefore, I prefer to read the report to the client executive. I ask him or her to set aside the last two hours of an afternoon to meet with me alone. I indicate to the client that I would like him or her to listen to me read the report, to make whatever notes he or she wishes while I am doing so, and to consider how the report will sound to the others in the organization when they hear it. I want the client to be particularly alert to my use of words, to be sure that I do not convey meanings I do not intend, and to see that I do not inadvertently become trapped in organizational politics. I want the client to be sensitive to the way I present matters so that he or she does not find him- or herself in embarrassing or difficult circumstances because of the way I have phrased things. (Once I used a word in a report whose source the CEO immediately identified.) I make it clear that I cannot change the substance of my findings, but I emphasize my need to have the client's help in stating what I have to say in the most advantageous way.

I then read the report aloud, slowly. When I have finished reading it, the client executive is then free to ask whatever questions he or she wishes, to discuss any items or implications, and to advise me on language. I also seek the client's advice on the next steps in presentation.

After the initial two-hour session with the client executive, I give him or her the report that I have read and that we have discussed. I ask the client to read it that evening and to meet with me again for the first two hours the next morning to review the report and discuss it further. *It is extremely important to follow this arrangement exactly.* Any such report is likely to have some disturbing implications for the executive no matter how much he or she needs the assessor's help or how willing he or she is to seek constructive consultation. The client will tend to perceive definitions of problems as criticism of him- or herself and to magnify that criticism in his or her own mind. The client therefore will have many hostile feelings about the report and the assessor, particularly when he or she has had an opportunity to read the report and to think about it. Unless the discussion is resumed *immediately* the next morning, these feelings will fester, and could result in hostile rejection with possibly devastating consequences. The client may decide that the report is no good or that he or she does not want to go any further with the project or that the assessor has been unduly critical. When such feelings are talked out immediately, the client has the opportunity to reestablish a more accurate perspective and to assist the assessor in planning the next steps in the feedback process. *This phase is so critical the consultant should not undertake feedback to the executive client until an afternoon–evening–morning schedule can be arranged.*

For one CEO, I had to repeat this process five times. Each time we carefully reexamined words and phrases that reflected criticism of his highly paternalistic management. He could not understand why his people questioned his behavior when he was trying so hard to be a good leader. Later, his vice presidents, scientists all, criticized my method when I recommended that they move their offices from their ivory tower suite closer to their people.

For the next step in the report feedback to top or senior managers, as I indicated in chapter 2, the assessor should provide numbered copies of the report for each of the listeners to follow along as the assessor reads it aloud. At the end of the presentation, the assessor should collect the copies to prevent premature leaks or inadvertent misuse of the information. For lower levels in the organization, it may not be necessary to distribute copies. However, visual aids will be important.

Ordinarily I prefer to present the report to others in the organization in the same sequence I followed when I entered the organization. However, sometimes it is politically wiser to alter course. For example, in one assessment with an organization that was scattered in several communities, it was important to take the second step in the feedback process in a community other than the headquarters because the group there was more closely related to decision making than others at lower levels in headquarters. The chief executive's advice on this matter saved us both considerable difficulty.

Sometimes the client executive will want to distribute the report widely. As I indicated in chapter 2, the assessor should help the client think about the implications of doing so. In some cases, there are those who would exploit any such material for their own advantage. The assessor must protect the client by raising appropriate cautions.

Charts and graphs will complement the presentation. Such concrete reference points can counteract the distortions that are likely to occur in listening to this kind of verbal presentation. They also facilitate questions and discussion. Each group to whom the assessor reports should have the opportunity to suggest changes in the wording, but not the substance, and offer suggestions about presentation to those who next will hear the report.

Usually the feedback process follows a consistent psychological course. At first the listeners tend to be tense and hostile, as if fearing the worst. Then they become more attentive. Once they become more relaxed, they will frequently voice approval during the reading. Finally, the questions that follow, directly or indirectly, say, Are we really going to do something about it?

The discussion that follows the reading also tends to take a predictable course. During the first stage there is criticism of the report and of the assessor, and even sometimes argument with the assessor about the validity of his or her information. Often there will be debate within the group about the findings and implications, as well as about the recommendations. Such debate is frequently a form of intellectualization, which constitutes the second stage. People will then begin to talk in the abstract about the problems, using clichés from the literature or their particular field. This third stage is projection, the tendency to seek scapegoats or someone or something to blame for the problems. This is followed by rationalization— "things are that way because. . . ." Next, the group usually wants to know how their organization compares with others as a way of assuaging their feelings of guilt and inadequacy. This is followed by an expression of feelings that problems are the inevitable lot of being human; they "own" these problems and they should take steps to correct them. Statements of acceptance of the report and support for its recommendations usually then follow. The last stage often includes remarks directed to the assessor indicating greater openness on the part of the group and sometimes comments intended to appease him or her for earlier hostile remarks.

Seen another way, there is usually an initial defensive, hostile phase that includes efforts to escape psychologically; a discussion of feelings and issues stage; and a stage of consolidation behind the report.

The assessor should let the report stand on its merits. By this I mean the assessor should make certain his or her method of gathering information is understood with all its limitations and that the interpretations and inferences are clearly recognized as his or hers and subject to critical examination. The assessor must be sure it is understood that his or her recommendations are matters for the group or organization to consider. There may be many optional ways of solving the perceived problems. The assessor's recommendations, however comprehensive the assessment and however logical the conclusions, are of only one person. They are to serve as an impetus to the organization's problem-solving efforts, a way of getting problems and possibilities out on the table for organizational consideration. The assessor should make it clear that he or she is not there to tell them how to run their organization. The assessor's job is to gather and organize information; to summarize and interpret that information; to offer recommendations derived from that information based on his or her training and experience, to facilitate action.

The feedback procedure will be the scene for the mobilization of powerful feelings within the groups to whom the assessor is reporting. Some will feel chagrined that the assessor has discovered organizational secrets; others will gloat in their satisfaction. Some will feel guilty for having "squealed" for what they now feel is an indictment of their superiors. Some will feel attacked, some deserted by the assessor from whom they had expected much more. Some will complain that the inferences drawn from their statements were exaggerated, that the issues raised are not that important. Some will want to know if top management has heard the report and what they will do about it.

Struggles over these and many other feelings will come to the fore during and after the feedback presentation. Sometimes they appear in the form of dead silence. Sometimes factions within a group will argue with each other. Frequently the attack is directed at the assessor.

The assessor should not become defensive. The assessor has put forth what he or she has learned and how he or she understands it together with what ideas he or she has for dealing with the problems. It is now the job of the groups to whom the assessor is reporting to work with that material and with the assessor to define its usefulness to them and what they want to do about it.

If some are chagrined or guilty, the assessor can raise the question of whether such feelings are appropriate to the situation. If some feel attacked or indicted, the assessor can help them express their resentment and then ask what aspects of the presentation seem to constitute the attack or indictment. If some feel their point of view to be inadequately represented or the conclusions to be inadequate or distorted, they have the opportunity to counterbalance the findings by the corrections they have been asked to make. Those who are concerned about whether top management has seen the report need to be reassured. The groups should be told what top management plans to be the next steps, if there are such.

Throughout the presentation, the behavior of the assessor should be a model for how he or she wants the organization to go about its problem-solving activity: by joint engagement with authoritative leadership around open examination of mutual problems for collective solutions toward more effective organizational functioning. The assessor must demonstrate that he or she does not fear hostility; that he or she stands confidently for the findings despite differences, that he or she is willing to be cross-examined about what he or she has learned and how he or she has learned it, together with the assumptions he or she has made; that he or she is willing to be appropriately corrected and to have his or her conclusions modified by new data.

Sometimes the information the assessor brings will be at a level never before considered by these groups. They will be uncomfortable. They may believe such information inappropriate for their level. They need to know they have top management's "permission" to hear and to think about these issues.

It is often helpful for the same groups to have a follow-up session with the organization's vice president of human resources or someone in the same relative position. That person then can ask, with the assessor no longer present, what the employees think of the report. If they still believe it to be valid, then the organization representative might ask them what problems should be taken up and in what order. I prefer to have organizational groups assume responsibility for defining priorities rather than having management assume the responsibility for solving all problems indiscriminately. First, no management can do that, let alone do it well. Second, to do so contradicts the principle that people who share problems together should be responsible for helping to solve them. Third, it is self-defeating paternalism. Once problem priorities have been defined, then management, with the help of the assessor, can evolve mechanisms with employees for their solution.

Sometimes chief executives feel too threatened by the report to open up the possibility of discussion at lower levels. The assessor will have to work with the executives at some length on the problems that trouble them—fear, rigidity, anger that their people do not love them, helplessness, lack of knowledge about what to do and how to do it. Only when they are more comfortable and feel supported by the assessor will they be able to take the necessary steps. Some will need additional support from their boards, which then also will have to hear the report.

Some chief executives who, out of helplessness or fear, want to deny they have problems do so by avoiding the issues. They assume that once the feedback has occurred, that in itself should solve their problems. And, they conclude, people should be talking better with each other and everyone will love everyone else. Usually such executives are afraid to take authoritative action and are uncomfortable with confrontation. Most often they need greater direction from the assessor about where to begin and they need support from the consultant when hostility arises from their subordinates. Some executives need restraint, particularly if their subordinates do not immediately become deeply involved in responding to the feedback.

The executive may want to force them to respond. The assessor should ask the executive to agree before entering the feedback situation that he or she will take no action during the feedback but simply let the participants speak as they will. If they do not participate, then executive and assessor together should try to ascertain why, perhaps even to have the assessor conduct additional interviews with some of the participants, and plan the subsequent steps accordingly. The same restraint will be necessary if the executive wants to proceed immediately and unilaterally to implement the recommendations. No matter how good they may be, in such circumstances, the recommendations are bound to be rejected in subtle, if not open, ways.

When the assessor is finished, he or she should review all of the diary notes on the feedback process, together with those of the whole assessment, specify on paper for him- or herself what he or she thinks has been learned, what mistakes he or she has made, and what he or she would want to do differently next time. Unless the assessor is him- or herself always a learner, the assessor will quickly become obsolete.

Of course there are many more possible psychological issues and problems in the closure and feedback process. Because all of them cannot be elaborated in this chapter, I can only point out that the closure task is also psychologically an opening task. If the assessor will recognize the critical nature of this process, observe the phenomena of the process carefully, and consciously crystallize his or her own experiences, the assessor will find him- or herself increasing his or her own proficiency with time.

APPENDIX A
INTERVIEW QUESTIONNAIRE
AND WRITTEN QUESTIONNAIRE

To expedite the assessment of current organizational functioning, two methods have been used—the structured interview and a written questionnaire and the organization and job attitude inventory. The structured interview is divided into two components: (a) the detailed interview and the questions themselves, together with the explanatory logic for them and the references points in the outline in appendix D to which they refer; (b) the questions themselves, suitable for easy reproduction and being kept readily at hand. The structured interview will be used throughout the assessment. The third component of this appendix, the organization and job attitude inventory, is keyed to the structured interview. It also is easily reproducible but the assessor may prefer to use other inventories.

INTRODUCTION: STRUCTURED INTERVIEW

The main advantage of the structured interview lies in the presumption that the data are likely to be rich in details, and the validity and appropriateness of the interviewee's verbal and extraverbal responses can be evaluated more easily. Only a personal, private interview, where confidentiality has

---

been ensured, can provide such. The main advantage of the structured interview lies in the presumption that the data are likely to be rich detailed and refined data. Many people will truly "open up," state their opinions, and express their feelings in response to such a situation. However, the structured interview is a form of projective technique. Many people find it difficult to respond to vague questions. The interviewer may have to ask clarifying questions to stimulate further response but must support those people to answer in their own way as much as possible.

The general purpose of the structured interview is to learn about the interviewees' thoughts about the organization and certain of their perceptions about themselves, especially in relationship to the organization. Before undertaking interviews, it is important to obtain clearance from the head of the unit or department, arrange for privacy, clarify with the interviewees the purpose of the assessment and the interview, and ensure confidentiality.

The Structured Interview

(The numbers at the end of each question relate it to the assessment outline in appendix D.)

1. *Tell me about the organization. How did it get to be the way it is?* (Encourage the interviewee to tell you as much as he or she can remember.) The answer to this question usually contains the history of the organization, as the persons know it. The amount of history known by the respondents is some indication of their degree of investment in the organization. However, it is also a function of the degree of orientation and indoctrination carried on by training personnel and the degree to which senior members of the organization regard the newer members as playing a part in the history and tradition of the organization. (IB3ab(1); IB3b; IB3c)

This question also presents an opportunity to talk about how personal needs are provided for, or not provided for, by the organization; the distance or closeness of individuals to the organization, their reactions to changes within it, and their degree of identification with it. The answer can also indicate what the respondents see as the forces within the organization, particularly those affecting them and to what extent they are involved in the realities of the organization that confront them. Their discussion of these forces and the means with which the interviewees cope with them reveals their perception of their own relationship to the organization.

The prodding question, Anything else? may reveal whether the respondents' previous answers are the result of their special preoccupations, and if so, additional facts may be forthcoming. The quantity as well as the quality of this preoccupation may reveal the degree to which a given individual feels pressed by what goes on in the organization.

2a. *What do you do here?* (Try to get the interviewee to be as specific as possible about what he or she does and with whom he or she does it. How significant is this task in the organization?) This question elicits specific information regarding the individuals' tasks. The interviewee's view of tasks as well as his or her feelings about it reveal, in essence, his or her occupational self-image. Does the person see him- or herself as being concerned with details exclusively or also with the larger organizational goals? In this, his or her distance from others and their role conflicts may be revealed. (IIA1c; IIA2e)

2b. *What sort of place is this to do your job?* This pertains more to affect and feeling tone—that is, "How do you like it here?" The answer should reveal what it means to particular individuals to be in the organization; how they fit into the structure; what conflicts, hopes, and aspirations might be engendered through the organization. Will they grow? Will they stagnate? What challenges are present and to what degree do they feel challenged? (IIIA4abc; IIIA5ab)

2c. *Why?* This should abstract from the answers to 2a the important values (or conflicts) to individuals.

3a. *Tell me about the people here.* How are they to work with? This asks for elaboration on questions 2a and 2b and more specifically deals with what the respondents need in their relationships with people. Such needs might be fulfilled by supportive functions, power situations, colleagues, aspirations, models, or rewards and punishments. The "why" part of the question allows them to elaborate on the closeness of their relationships, how their dependency needs are gratified, and how they cope with authority relationships. (III3B1a(3))

3b. *What kind of person would be likely to apply for a job here?* (Ask the interviewee to describe in detail: a part-time farmer; an itinerant casual; a highly trained mechanic; a computer-savvy engineer.) The answer implies the respondents' views of the organizational self-image—that is, the collective "who are we." It also reveals why a given individual came here (his or her self-image), how that individual fits in society, and "what it (the job or organization) takes." This may illuminate a "typical" personality type in the organization. (IIA5bce)

3c. *If you were going to hire someone for a job like yours, what kind of person would you hire?* This extracts an aspect of the respondents' ego ideals—what I should be. It might also suggest what an individual fears in terms of who, or what, kind of person will take his or her job. Sometimes respondents will go on to elaborate particular stresses or conflicts in their job not explained in response to the preceding questions. (IIA6a)

4a. *Tell me what is done here to help a person along once he or she starts to work in this organization?* The question deals largely with the informal type of help present in the organization. It often reveals individuals' needs for support and to what extent their dependency needs are recognized in the organization as well as what their expectations for this are. It may also reveal what mutual coping devices operate between individuals and the organization and what the style of supervision is. (IIA6bcdeg)

4b. *With respect to helping a person along, how does the organization get people started? What happened to you when you started—and when did you start?* This will elicit specific information about question 4a. The second part of the question personalizes the experience and often also elicits the feelings aroused when the person had to cope with his or her initial strangeness and helplessness in the organization. Now that the interviewee is established in the organization, how well-integrated does he or she feel? (IIA6b)

4c. *How much and what kind of training do people get?* This is a more specific inquiry about formal training in the organization. Who does it? Is some done outside the organization? Is there time off for classes? Does the organization subsidize it? Is there recognition for achieving degrees? Added compensation? This question tends to elicit answers regarding what the individual would like to have and how much he or she is depending on the organization to make him or her into something—that is, how much the interviewee sees the organization as a source of his or her adult identity. (IIA6c)

4d. *How do you find out how you are doing?* The answers to this question often list the feedback mechanisms operating within the organization and suggest the nature and quality of manager–subordinate relationships. They deal with such items as the degree and way in which distance or closeness is maintained and how affection and aggression are handled. They also suggest rivalry or openness with peers and where interpersonal gratifications come from. For example, if the chief feedback comes from subordinates or peers, this would suggest that supervisors' or managers' feelings of inadequacy are an issue. If an organization is dominated by strong criticism, this suggests that people will have a great deal of fear regarding wishes and impulses that they regard as unacceptable. Conversely, when the rewards are open and people speak freely for themselves, there will be less fright about such impulses emerging, such as being critical of superiors. (IIA6g)

4e. *What happens when problems come up?* This elicits dependency relationships and to whom persons turn for support. Also involved in the reply are individuals' relationships to their supervisors or managers, which are called for in specific examples. (IIA6hi; IIA7c)

4f. *Every organization does certain things to take care of its people—like having health, safety, or retirement programs. Tell me about what they do here.* This question deals with the broad support functions available in the organization, who needs them, and who gets them. It is another version of question 4e. Vague, uncertain, and misinformed answers to the specific details asked for in this question may mean that there has been poor indoctrination about these facts. On the other hand, they may mean that individuals have confidence in the organization that they will be taken care of and are therefore less concerned about such details. (IIA6jklm; A7c)

4g. *What do people here do for each other if someone gets sick?* Have you ever needed such help or given it? This question deals with the closeness of peers (sibling relationships) to each other—that is, their identification with each other, their feelings about one another, and the degree to which they will mobilize to help one another. (IIIA1a(1)(A) i, ii)

5a. *What are the main rules around here that everyone has to follow?* What rules are unspoken or unwritten? Answers to this question reveal the key issues regarding control within the organization. They suggest taboos and operational values and indicate how much of these values are held by and are acceptable to the employees. Rigidity or flexibility within the organization is also indicated. (IIA6i)

5b. *How well do they work?* What happens if someone violates one of them? This gives the interviewee opportunity to draw contrasts with the previous answer. It may reveal the degree of denial present in response to 5a. (IIIA1c(2))

6a. *What are the busy times around here?* This is to define the external time pressures, their sources, and the realities of such pressures. (IIA8abcf)

6b. *How closely are things scheduled (what does a typical day look like)?* What is done in what order? With what breaks? This deals with how the realities in question 6a are anticipated within the organization. Are they planned for or are they left to occur spontaneously so that the employees must deal with them in the best way they can without help, thus suggesting an attitude of expendability toward the employees. Included in this answer may be a suggestion of how individuals master their world or are mastered by it. (IIA8efg)

6c. *Why?* The respondent will list here the realities of these pressures. Are they necessary or are they weapons used within the organization? This question also deals with how respondents see the operating forces in their work world. (IIA1a(1)(A)i,ii,iii; IIIA1b(1)(A)(B))

7. *What ways are there to find out what is going on around here?* What don't they tell you? Answers to this question will describe communications and their reliability within the organization. Such answers may reveal possible ground for paranoid fantasy (some undefined power up there fouls things up) and helplessness or lack of trust, which lowers self-respect and creates anxiety. The more employees rely on rumor for information, the more ground there is for distrust and anxiety. Conversely, the more data that are shared with individuals, the more they feel trusted and the more they are capable of expressing their own affection and trust to others. The prodding question, Any other ways of finding out what is going on? elicits how relevant and how well-handled the communications may actually be. (IIIA2(a)(1)(A)(B)(C)(D); IIIA2a(2)(A)(B); IIIA2b(2)(A)(B); IIIA2b3)

8a. *What do outsiders think of this organization?* This question allows projection, asking in reality, What do you think others think of the organization? The answer will thus reveal any disparity between the organization's reputation and what the employees actually think of it, possibly in terms of their feelings regarding fulfillment of their own expectations and aspirations. Specific foci of hostility or energy may also be revealed. The "please specify" part of the question deals more with the political aspects and the organization's relationship to competitors, unions, and regulatory agencies. (IIIB1a (1)(2)(4)(f)(7)(9)(10)(11)(12)(13)(14)(15)(16))

8b. *Why?* The second part of the question elicits something about the employees' identifications and attitudes about the issues to be defended, and it yields as well some idea about how isolated the employees may be from the external realities of the organization. It allows further opportunity to focus on the important outside figures against whom the organization must be defended or, perhaps, who must be manipulated in the interests of the organization. (IIIB2e(1)(A)(B))

8c. *How do you know?* This is intended to determine whether the previous answer is based on reality and actual knowledge or on rumor. It also elicits individuals' feelings about the source of their knowledge. (IIIA1a(1)(A)(i))

9a. *How does the organization keep up with what's going on elsewhere?* What does it do to keep up? Answers to this question will elicit the degree to which the organization's interests and perceptions are directed outward, thereby suggesting how much the organization wants to know and how much it listens or, conversely, the degree of withdrawal by the organization. Implicit are such issues as how the organization deals with mastery, curiosity, aggressiveness, progressiveness, innovation, flexibility, security, and change, as well as how it copes with the outside world and how it is coped with. (IIIA2a(1)(A)(B)(C)(D)(E)(F)ii,iii,iv)

9b. *What kinds of things is it most interested in keeping up with?* This is also outwardly directed and deals with the specific direction, or focus, of question 9a. It might reveal the disparity between an individual's expectations and aspirations and reality. (IIIA2a(2)(A)(B))

9c. *How does the organization make use of a person's experience and ideas?* How does it take advantage of what you know and your wish to help it do better? This calls for a more inwardly directed answer, identifying the degree to which the organization makes use of ideas that arise within it. The reply suggests the degree of participation in decision making, stimulation to growth, and respect for the individuals within the organization. (III-A2a(1)(A)(B))

10. *Does the organization make use of the information available?* On one level the response reflects the degree of judgment about what information is available and how well it is used. On another level it will reveal the organization's attitude toward self versus the outside and suggests the quality

of defensiveness or amount of drive within the organization. (IIIA2b(1)(2)(3))

11a. *What does the organization say it stands for?* Does it have a published list of values? What does it tell the outside world about itself? This asks for the organization's idealized expectations around which people are supposed to cohere. It also indicates how much the employees know about the organization. (IIIB1b; IIIB3(a)(b)(c))

11b. *How does it get its message across?* Answers here usually deal with advertising or services and reveal to what extent the collective idealized aspirations are supported by fact and behavior—that is, how much disparity there is between the organization's stated ideals and the degree to which it lives up to them. The converse of this also may be suggested—that is, that employees feel the organization has qualities and ideals that should be, but are not, shown to the outside. (IIIA1b(3)c)

12. *Make believe this organization is a person. . . . Describe that person to me. . . .* This elicits an image of the organization. Taken collectively, such images constitute an organizational self-image. This also personifies the relationship of the employee with the organization. Individuals' replies are an index of the degree of reciprocation in the psychological contract between the organization and employees, saying what employees want from the organization and what they think they actually get. It reveals what individuals experience from the organization and what the organization may experience from individuals, both in reality and as implicit expectations. The prodding question, Is he/she always like this? reveals the consistency and degree of dependability in this relationship. (IIIB1c(1)d2; IIIB2d(2); IIIB2(a)(2))

13a. *How peppy (energetic) is this organization?* This deals with the strength and activity or, conversely, somnolence of the organization. Is it "on the ball," "in the race," an "also ran?" Does the energy vary with realities or with unrealities? The other parts of this question ("b., All the time?" and "c., In what ways is the (pep) useful, or is it just wheel-spinning?") reveal the consistency of this behavior and differentiate between diffuse or goal-directed behavior. (IIIA5a(1)(2); IIIA5b((1)(2)(3)(4)(5))

13b. *Is it like this all the time?*

13c. *In what ways is the pep useful, or is it just wheel-spinning?*

14. *How much do the people here really know about this organization's work?* This question has to do with how much people actually invest themselves in the organization, how much responsible communication and participation there is in the organization's work, and how much the organization is a part of their identity. This differentiates between investment in the "organization

qua organization" versus the industry or broader context—that is, do they see themselves as "locals" or "cosmopolitans?" (IIIB1(b)(1)(2))

15a. *How strong is this organization?* This question complements number 14 and deals with transference issues. What do the employees think of the organization? How much do they depend on it, and how capable do they feel it is? This question deals with the degree of compartmentalization or separation between the organization and themselves. It also deals with the quality of the organization's strength—that is, is it malevolently attacking or benevolently supportive? The degree to which the employees have identified their future with that of the organization and their conception of the organization's enduring quality will be reflected in the answers to this question. (IIIB5d(2))

The second part of this question, Tell me what you mean, delineates the particular areas in which employees will look for strength, such as dependency, aggression, ego support.

15b. *How do you know?* This asks employees to document the sources of their information and thus delineate the solidity of this information. It also elicits how much of their feeling is genuine self-confidence and how much is fantasized trust.

16. *What is he/she (the personified organization) doing?* What is its behavior? Actions? This deals with how the employees perceive the organization to be coping with reality. What are the problems? What are the goals? What are the assets? To what extent is this coping reality-directed; is it aggressive, masterful, passive, manipulative? (IIIA5b(f))

In response to this question the leader (manager, president, chair of the board, foreman) is sometimes personified, which suggests that this leader is the primary focus of trust and power to a given employee. If the employee him- or herself is personified, it suggests that there is no trust in the leader and that the employee is divorced from, or alienated from, the company. His or her lack of investment makes the interviewee unable to personify the company so he or she must personify him- or herself. Conversely, if the company itself is personified, it suggests that there is involvement with the total organization rather than any particular person. A lack of any personification suggests an inability to abstract (concreteness) or the absence of a clear image of self or organization.

17a. *Suppose this organization had to stop doing some of the things it now does. Assuming your job would not be affected, what should not be changed?* How would such a change affect you? This question will elicit what the respondents think are the most important central functions of the organization and reveal how the employees see their relationship to those functions. (IIIB2a)

17b. *Why?* The prodding question deals with the logic to this answer and how much about the realities of the organization a person actually knows. (IIIB32bed)

18a. *Which outside groups does this organization pay attention to? How does it do so?* This question asks where employees see the attention of the organization being focused. Who are the reference groups? Where do the felt pressures come from? How much people know about this suggests the level of their involvement. (IIIB1ab)

18b. *How? Why?* This tests reality further as well as elicits the quantity of collective information. (IIIB1a(1)(2)(4)(6)(7)(10)(11)(16))

19. *What future do you see for this organization?* This deals with what employees see in their own future as well as that of the organization. Where is the organization going, and can the employees go with it? Are the employees' personal expectations and aspirations clearly established, and do they fit with those of the organization? How much confidence do employees have in the organization and in themselves? The "why?" further tests reality. (IIIB3abcd)

20. *Suppose you were the head of this organization and had to make long-range plans for it. What do you think would be the most important things about the organization that you would have to keep in mind in making these plans?* This question is an echo of number 17. It deals with the most important problems that the organization faces and how much they are known, thought about, and realistically assessed. It also asks how much people are involved in the realities of the organization and the interpersonal relationships in it, such as what the employees think about each other's feelings and what the grapevine reveals about each other's complaints. (IIIB4; IIIB2d(1)(3))

21a. *Thinking back over the things we've talked about, do you think most people here would look at these things the same way you do?* This asks how much people feel in tune with, or deviant from, the others in the organization, how much they feel they represent consensus and are a part of what is happening in the organization. The degree of felt alienation will be revealed. (IIIB4a3)

21b. *Why?*

22. *I've asked you a lot of questions. Do you have any you'd like to ask me?* This question allows interviewees to ease their anxiety, satisfy their curiosity, and obtain approval from the interviewer by asking, in indirect ways, how well they did. It also returns interviewees to a more equal level with the interviewer and gives recognition to their mature, adult role, to their being engaged with the interviewer in a joint study effort, and recognizes the interviewer's obligation to the interviewees.

Structured Interview Outline

NAME: _____

JOB TITLE: _____

LOCATION OF INTERVIEW: _____

DATE OF INTERVIEW: _____

INTERVIEWER: _____

Opening Statement by Interviewer

As you know, my colleagues and I from (identify consulting organization if there is an assessment rather than an internal analysis) are doing an assessment of (name of organization). Everyone (will be) (has been) asked to fill out a printed questionnaire. In addition, some people, like you, are being asked to talk with us individually. You were chosen because of the kind of work you do and by chance. The choice has nothing to do with you personally. Some others will be interviewed too. Before we begin, let's review why we are here and what this is all about. Can you tell me your understanding of this assessment? (Correct misunderstandings.) Do you have any questions about it? (Allow time for questions and explanation.)

All right. Now, I'd like to learn as much as I can about how this organization works. To do that I'd like to ask you a number of questions. By the time we're finished, I'd like to feel I know pretty much how things go around here. Whatever you tell me will be confidential.

(It is helpful to put these questions on a computer screen so that the interviewer may refer to them readily.)

1. Tell me about (organization). How did it get to be the way it is? (Anything else?) (IB3ab(1)); IB3b; IB3c)
2a. What do you do here? (IIA1c; IIA2e)
 b. What sort of a place is this to do your job? (IIIA4abc; IIIA5ab)
 c. Why?
3a. Tell me about the people here. How are they to work with? (Why?) (IIIB1a(3))
 b. What kind of a person would be likely to apply for a job here? (Why?) (IIA5bce)
 c. If you were going to hire someone for a job like yours, what kind of a person would you hire? (IIA6a)

4a. Tell me what is done here to help a person along once he or she starts to work in this (organization). (Anything else?) (IIA6bcdeg)

 b. With respect to helping a person along, how does (the organization) get people started? What happened to you when you started—and when *did* you start? (IIA6b)

 c. How much and what kind of training do people get? (IIA6c)

 d. How do you find out how you are doing? (Any other ways?) (IIA6g)

 e. What happens when problems come up? (Give me some examples.) (IIA6hi; IIA7c)

 f. Every organization does certain things to take care of its people—like having health, safety, or retirement programs. Tell me about what they do here. (IIA6jklm; IIA7c)

 g. What do the people here do for each other if someone gets sick? (IIIA1a(1)(A)i,ii)

5a. What are the main rules around here that everyone has to follow? (Specify.) (IIA6i)

 b. How well do they work? (IIIA1c(2))

6a. What are the busy times around here? (IIA8abcf)

 b. How closely are things scheduled? (What does a typical day look like?) (IIA8efg)

 c. Why? (Spell out.) (IIIA1a(1)(A)I,ii,iii; IIIA1b(1)(A)(B))

7. What ways are there to find out what's going on around here? (Any other ways of finding out what is going on?) (IIIA2(a)(1)('A)(B) (C)(D); IIIA2a(2)(A)(B); IIIA2b(2)(A)(B); IIIA2b3)

8a. What do outsiders think of (this organization)? (Please specify which groups have which attitudes.) (IIIB1a(1)(2)(4)(f)(7)(8)(9)(10)(11) (12)(13)(14)(15)(16))

 b. Why? (For each.) (IIIB2e(1)(A)(B))

 c. How do you know? (IIIA1a(1)(A)I)

9a. How does (the organization) keep up with what's going on elsewhere? (IIIA2a(1)(A)(B)(C)(D)(E)(F)ii,iii,iv)

 b. What kind of things is it most interested in keeping up with? (Note "things" is plural.) (IIIA2a(2)(A)(B))

 c. How does (the organization) make use of a person's experience and ideas? (Give examples.) (IIIA2a(1)(A)(B))

10. Does (the organization) make use of the information available? (Why/ Why not?) (IIIA2b(1)(2)(3))

11a. What does (the organization) say it stands for? (IIIB1b; IIIB3((a)(b)(c)))

 b. How does it get its message across? (Both what media and how effectively.) (IIIA1b(3)c)

12a. Make believe (this organization) is a person. Think about that person for a minute. Describe that person to me so I can get a good idea of the picture you have in mind. (IIIB11c(1)d2; IIIB2d(2); IIIB2(a)(2))

b. Is he/she always like this? (If not, what other pictures come to mind?)

13a. How peppy (energetic) is (this organization)? (Tell me what you mean.) (IIIA5a(1)(2); IIIA5b(1)(2)(3)(4)(5))

b. Is it like this all the time?

c. In what ways is the (pep) useful, or is it just spinning wheels? (Give examples.)

14. How much do the people here really know about this organization's work? (IIIB1(b)(1)(2))

15a. How strong is (this organization?) (Tell me what you mean.) (IIIB5d(2))

b. How do you know? (Explain.)

16. A little while ago I asked you to pretend (this organization) was a person and to describe the person. Think about that person again for a minute . . . think of that person doing something. What is he or she doing? (IIIA5b(f))

17a. Suppose (this organization) had to stop doing some of the things it now does. Assuming your job would not be affected, what should *not* be changed? (IIIB2a)

b. Why? (IIIB3abcd)

18a. Which outside groups does (this organization) pay attention to? (IIIB1ab)

b. How? Why? (For each.) (And others? How? Why?) (IIIB1e (1)(2)(4)(6)(7)(10)(11)(16))

19. What future do you see for (this organization)? (Why?) (IIIB3abcd)

20. Suppose you were the head of (this organization) and had to make long-range plans for it. What do you think would be the most important things about (the organization) that you should have to keep in mind in making these plans? (IIIB4; IIIB2d(1)(3))

21a. Thinking back over the things we've talked about, do you think most people here would look at these things the same way you do? (IIIB4a(3))

b. Why?

22. I've asked you a lot of questions. Do you have any you'd like to ask me? Thank you for your help.

INTRODUCTION: WRITTEN QUESTIONNAIRE

The written questionnaire, which may be translated into other languages, is intended to parallel the questions of the structured interview. The main advantage of the written questionnaire is that it can be given to everyone in the organization and yet not consume a great deal of the assessor's time. It provides a means for organization members to express themselves on the issues involved in the assessment. It has the disadvantage of being a one-way communication and one whose validity cannot always be easily assessed. For example, even though the questionnaire is not signed, many individuals will still remain suspicious of the assessor's motives. This is especially true if it is given early in the assessment (as it should be) when the employees have not had a chance to get to know, and trust, the assessor. On the one hand, they more likely will respond to what they think is the "party line" of the organization, or else they will be noncommittal and not disclose their true feelings about many of the issues. On the other hand, if the written questionnaire is given later on in the assessment there are still complicating factors. People in the organization may have come to like the assessor and, therefore, they may respond to the questionnaire by wanting to "do a good job" with it—giving the assessor the answers they think the assessor wants to hear. Needless to say, the reverse can also occur if people in the organization come to dislike the assessor. In such a situation, when answering the questions, they might respond more to their personal feelings about the assessor than to their feelings about the organization.

ORGANIZATION AND JOB ATTITUDE INVENTORY

We would like to learn more about how people feel about the organization they work for and the job. We do not need to know who you are personally, so do not sign the questionnaire. In any event, responses will remain confidential, known only to the assessors.

Most of the questions ask that you check *one* of the answers; however, some questions ask that you write the answer in the space provided. The value of this assessment depends on how honestly and carefully you answer the questions. Remember, *this is not a test*, and there are no right or no wrong answers.

Please answer the questions in order. Do not skip around.

Be sure to answer *all* the questions.

Thank you for your cooperation.

I. Some Things About Yourself

1. What is your job in the organization called? (IIA1c; IIA2e)

_____

2. In what department, section, or unit of the organization do you work?

_____

3. What do you consider to be your usual occupation?

_____

4. How long have you worked for the organization? (check)

(a) _____ Less than 6 months   (e) _____ 5 years to 10 years
(b) _____ 6 months to 1 year   (f) _____ 10 years to 20 years
(c) _____ 1 year to 2 years   (g) _____ More than 20 years
(d) _____ 2 years to 5 years

5. How long have you worked in your present department, section, or unit of the organization? (check)

(a) _____ Less than 6 months   (e) _____ 5 years to 10 years
(b) _____ 6 months to 1 year   (f) _____ 10 years to 20 years
(c) _____ 1 year to 2 years   (g) _____ Over 20 years
(d) _____ 2 years to 5 years

6. How far did you go in school? (check one)

(a) _____ Less than 8th grade   (d) _____ Some college
(b) _____ 8th through 11th   (e) _____ College graduate
(c) _____ High school graduate   (f) _____ Other
(Specify) _____

7. How old are you? (check)

(a) _____ 18 to 21 (e) _____ 41 to 50
(b) _____ 22 to 25 (f) _____ 51 to 60
(c) _____ 26 to 30 (g) _____ Over 60
(d) _____ 31 to 40

8. Gender? (check)

(a) _____ Male
(b) _____ Female

II. The Organization

9. How old is this organization? (check) (IB3ab(1); IB3bc)

(a) _____ More than 100 years old (e) _____ 5 to 10 years old
(b) _____ 50 to 100 years old (f) _____ Less than 5 years old
(c) _____ 25 to 50 years old (g) _____ Don't know
(d) _____ 10 to years old

10. How many people work for this organization at this location? (check)

(a) _____ More than 1000 (e) _____ 50 to 100
(b) _____ 500 to 1000 (f) _____ Less than 50
(c) _____ 250 to 500 (g) _____ Don't know
(d) _____ 100 to 250

11. In the past five years, how much has this organization grown? (check)

(a) _____ A great deal (c) _____ Not at all
(b) _____ Somewhat (d) _____ Don't know

12. How much has the organization changed in the last five years [other than size]? (check)

(a) _____ A great deal (c) _____ Not at all
(b) _____ Somewhat (d) _____ Don't know

13. How would you rate this organization compared to others in the same field? (check) (IIIB1a(1)(2)(4)(6)(7)(8)(9)(10)(11)(12)(13)(14)(15)(16))

(a) _____ The very best (d) _____ Below average
(b) _____ Above average (e) _____ The very worst
(c) _____ Average

14. Compared to other companies in the same field, this organization is? (check) (IIIA5a(1)(2); IIIA5b(1)(2)(3)(4)(5); IIIA2a(1)(A)(B)(C)(D)(E)ii,iii,iv)

(a) _____ Moving ahead faster (c) _____ Falling behind
(b) _____ Holding its own (d) _____ Don't know

15. How does the community feel about this organization? (check)

(a) _____ Very friendly toward it

(b) _____ Neither friendly nor unfriendly

(c) _____ Unfriendly toward it

(d) _____ Don't know

16. Compared to other organizations in this community, how would you rate the employment policies and benefits of this organization? (check) (IIA6bcdeg)

(a) _____ Excellent   (c) _____ Average

(b) _____ Above average   (d) _____ Below average

17. What is this organization's most important product or service?

_____

_____

18. Who is the most important person in the organization and what is his or her title? _____

_____

19. What are the three things that this organization is working hardest for at this time? (IIIB1b; IIIB3(a)(b)(c); IIIAA1b(3)c)

(a) _____

(b) _____

(c) _____

20. What is this organization's greatest strength? (IIIB5d(2)) _____

_____

_____

21. What is this organization's greatest weakness? _____

_____

22. What three recommendations would you make to the organization that would help it achieve its goals? (IIIA2a(1)(A)(B))

(a) _____

(b) _____

(c) _____

III. Your Job

23. What are the main duties of your job? (IIA6a) _____

_____

_____

_____

24. What are the three most important things that the organization wants in a person doing your job?

(a) _____

(b) _____

(c) _____

25. How many people work in your particular department, division, or unit? (check)

(a) _____ More than 100   (d) _____ 10 to 25

(b) _____ 50 to 100   (e) _____ 3 to 10

(c) _____ 25 to 50   (f) _____ Less than 3

26. How many people report to you? (check)

(a) _____ More than 100   (d) _____ 10 to 25

(b) _____ 50 to 100   (e) _____ 1 to 10

(c) _____ 25 to 50   (f) _____ None

27. How important is your job in the organization? (check)

(a) _____ Among the most important

(b) _____ Very important

(c) _____ Necessary, but not particularly important

(d) _____ Unimportant

(e) _____ Don't know

28. How much supervision do you get? (check) (IIA6g; IIA6hi; IIA7c)

(a) _____ A great deal   (c) _____ Very little

(b) _____ A fair amount   (d) _____ None

29. How would you rate the supervision you get? (check)

(a) _____ Excellent   (c) _____ Average

(b) _____ Good   (d) _____ Poor

30. With regard to supervision, would you like to have (check)

(a) _____ More   (c) _____ Less

(b) _____ Same

31. How would you know when you are doing your job well? (IIA6g)

_____

_____

_____

32. How would you know when you are not doing your job well?

_____

_____

_____

33. How would you rate the physical conditions under which you do your job? (check) (IIIA4abc; 5ab)
(a) _____ Excellent   (c) _____ Fair
(b) _____ Good   (d) _____ Poor

34. How would you rate the pay and other benefits you receive, as compared to those of people doing the same kind of work in other organizations in this community? (check)
(a) _____ Above average   (c) _____ Below average
(b) _____ Average

35. How sure do you feel of having a permanent job in this organization? (check) (IIIB3abcd)
(a) _____ Very sure   (d) _____ Rather unsure
(b) _____ Quite sure   (e) _____ Very unsure
(c) _____ Have no idea

36. How much training for your job has the organization given you? (check) (IIA6bcdeg)
(a) _____ A great deal   (c) _____ Very little
(b) _____ A fair amount   (d) _____ None

37. With regard to job training, would you like to have (check)
(a) _____ More   (c) _____ Less
(b) _____ Same

38. How much freedom do you have in planning and doing your work? (check) (IIA6i; IIIA1c(2))
(a) _____ A great deal   (c) _____ Very little
(b) _____ A fair amount   (d) _____ None

39. If problems come up in doing your job, how much help do you get in handling those problems? (check) (IIA6hi; IIA7c)
(a) _____ A great deal   (c) _____ Very little
(b) _____ A fair amount   (d) _____ None

40. Which one of the following would you find most helpful in working out problems connected with your job? (check)
(a) _____ Your immediate supervisor or manager
(b) _____ The person above your supervisor or manager
(c) _____ One of your fellow workers
(d) _____ One of the top executives
(e) _____ Somebody outside the organization

41. In doing your job, how much contact do you have with others in your department? (check) (IIIB1a(3))
(a) _____ A great deal   (c) _____ Very little
(b) _____ A fair amount   (d) _____ None

42. In doing your job, how much contact do you have with others in the organization outside of your department? (check)
(a) _____ A great deal   (c) _____ Very little
(b) _____ A fair amount   (d) _____ None

43. In doing your job, how much contact do you have with people outside of the organization? (check)
(a) _____ A great deal   (c) _____ Very little
(b) _____ A fair amount   (d) _____ None

44. In connection with your job, would you like to have? (check)
(a) _____ More contact with others
(b) _____ The same amount of contact
(c) _____ Less contact with others

45. How well do you like the people in the organization that you work with or have contact with? (check) (IIB1a(3))
(a) _____ A great deal   (c) _____ Very little
(b) _____ A fair amount   (d) _____ None

46. How would you rate the way the people you work with get along? (check)
(a) _____ Very close and friendly   (d) _____ Rather unfriendly
(b) _____ Quite friendly   (e) _____ Very unfriendly
(c) _____ Distant but not unfriendly

47. With regard to yourself and your fellow workers would your prefer? (check)
(a) _____ Closer relationships   (c) _____ Less close relationships
(b) _____ The way it is now

48. If you had a complaint or "gripe" about something connected with your job, whose attention would you bring it to first? (check) (IIA6hi; IIA7c)
(a) _____ Your supervisor or manager
(b) _____ The person above your supervisor or manager
(c) _____ One of your fellow workers
(d) _____ Union steward or representative
(e) _____ One of the top executives
(f) _____ Someone outside the organization
(g) _____ Would keep it to yourself

49. When changes are to be made that affect your job, how much are you consulted? (check) (IIIA2a(1)(A)(B))
(a) _____ Always   (c) _____ Seldom
(b) _____ Good   (d) _____ Never

50. How would you rate the cooperation you get from others in the organization? (check) (IIIB1a(3))
(a) _____ Excellent   (c) _____ Fair
(b) _____ Good   (d) _____ None

51. In a typical day, how much tension and friction is there among the people in your department? (check) (IIA8abcefg)
(a) _____ A great deal   (c) _____ Very little
(b) _____ A fair amount   (d) _____ None

52. How much tension and friction is there between your department and other departments of the organization? (check)
(a) _____ A great deal   (c) _____ Very little
(b) _____ A fair amount   (d) _____ None

53. How would you rate the planning, organizing, and scheduling of the work in your department? (check) (IIIB4; IIIB2d(1)(2))
(a) _____ Excellent   (c) _____ Average
(b) _____ Good   (d) _____ Poor

54. How well does your supervisor or manager and those above him or her understand the technical problems you face in doing your work? (check) (IIIB1(b)(1)(2))
(a) _____ Very well   (c) _____ Not very well
(b) _____ Rather well   (d) _____ Not at all

55. Considering what the organization expects of you in your job and the conditions under which you work, do you think the organization? (check)
(a) _____ Expects too much   (c) _____ Expects very little
(b) _____ Expects about what is right

56. List the three things you like *most* about your job.
(a) _____
(b) _____
(c) _____

57. List the three things you like *least* about your job.
(a) _____
(b) _____
(c) _____

58. How much chance do you have for visiting with others in the organization during or after working hours? (check) (IIIA1a(1)(A)i,ii)
(a) _____ A great deal   (c) _____ Very little
(b) _____ A fair amount   (d) _____ None

59. How many people in the organization do you consider to be your personal friends? (check)
(a) _____ 10 or more   (d) _____ 1 to 2
(b) _____ 5 to 10   (e) _____ None
(c) _____ 3 to 5

60. If you should change jobs in the organization, which job would you like to have? _____
_____

61. How good do you think your chances are for getting a better job in the organization? (check)
(a) _____ Excellent   (c) _____ Fair
(b) _____ Good   (d) _____ Poor

62. How much do you think the organization would help you in preparing for a better job? (check) (IIA6c)
(a) _____ As much as possible (c) _____ Very little
(b) _____ Quite a bit   (d) _____ Not at all

63. How good is the work done by your department compared to other departments in the organization? (check)
(a) _____ The very best   (c) _____ Below average
(b) _____ As good as most   (d) _____ The very worst

64. How would you rate the working conditions in your department compared to other departments in the organization? (check)
(a) _____ The very best   (c) _____ Below average
(b) _____ As good as most   (d) _____ The very worst

65. Who makes the most important decisions in your department? (check)
(a) _____ Your supervisor or manager
(b) _____ The person above
(c) _____ Top management
(d) _____ The department as a whole

66. How much turnover have you had in your department during the past two years? (check)
(a) _____ A great deal   (c) _____ Very little
(b) _____ A fair amount   (d) _____ None

67. Where do you most often learn what is going on in the organization? (check) (IIIA2(a)(1)(a)(b)(c)(d); III2a(2)(A)(B); IIIA2b(2)(A)(B); IIIA2b3)
(a) _____ Official bulletins
(b) _____ Your supervisor or manager
(c) _____ Your fellow workers
(d) _____ People outside the organization
(e) _____ Newspapers
(f) _____ Rumors, the "grapevine"

68. How free do you feel about talking over job problems with your supervisor or manager? (check) (IIA6hi; IIA7c)
(a) _____ Very free   (c) _____ Not very free
(b) _____ Fairly free   (d) _____ Not at all free

69. How free do you feel about talking over job problems with the person above your supervisor or manager? (check)
(a) _____ Very free   (c) _____ Not very free
(b) _____ Fairly free   (d) _____ Not at all free

70. How would you rate the ability of the people who run this organization? (check) (IIIB1(b)(1)(2))
(a) _____ Excellent   (c) _____ Fair
(b) _____ Good   (d) _____ Poor

71. How much consideration are your ideas or suggestions given by the organization? (check) (IIIA2a(1)(A)(B))
(a) _____ A great deal   (c) _____ Very little
(b) _____ Somewhat   (d) _____ Not at all

72. If, because of unusual problems or emergencies, the organization needed you to perform extra duties or work longer hours, would you? (check)
(a) _____ Volunteer gladly   (d) _____ Rather not be asked
(b) _____ Wait to be asked   (e) _____ Refuse, if possible
(c) _____ Not mind being asked

73. If there were a conflict or difference of opinion in which you were involved, how much fairness do you think the organization would show you? (check)
(a) _____ A great deal   (c) _____ Very little
(b) _____ A fair amount   (d) _____ None

74. If you had a serious personal problem that interfered with your work, how much consideration do you think you would get from the organization? (check) (IIA6jklm; A7c)
(a) _____ A great deal   (c) _____ Very little
(b) _____ A fair amount   (d) _____ None

75. How would you rate the strictness of the rules of the organization? (check) (IIA6i; IIIA1c(2))

(a) _____ Very strict   (c) _____ Somewhat easygoing

(b) _____ Average   (d) _____ Very easygoing

76. With regard to strictness of rules, would you like (check)

(a) _____ More strictness   (c) _____ Less strictness

(b) _____ The same

77. How much do you think the organization is interested in your welfare? (check)

(a) _____ Very much   (c) _____ Not very interested

(b) _____ Quite interested   (d) _____ Not at all interested

78. Would you recommend to a friend that he or she work for this organization? (check) (IIA6a)

(a) _____ Yes

(b) _____ No

79. Thinking ahead five years, would you want to be working for this organization? (check) (IIIB3abcd)

(a) _____ Yes

(b) _____ No

80. If you could make changes that would make the organization a better place for you to work, what three changes would be most important to you? (IIIB4; IIIB2d(1)(3))

(a) _____

(b) _____

(c) _____

Date Filled Out _____

Diary Outline

(When the completed questionnaires have been collected, the assessor should complete a diary note, using the topics below as guides. He or she will then be able more easily to recall and review what took place.)

Meeting Location, Date, and Time _____

      Reporter _____

Number present _____ Number of questionnaires distributed _____

      Department _____

1. *Report phase*: attentiveness of audience, evidence of good or poor rapport, mood of reporter (relaxed, tired, tense, comfortable, etc.), comparison with other groups seen.

2. *Discussion phase*: length, questions asked (get as many verbatim as possible), themes emerging from questions or discussion.

3. *Meeting in general*: type of introduction, comparison with other experiences, physical environment (light, heat, noise), degree of time pressure.

4. Other aspects of contact with this group outside the meeting proper but of significance for the study.

5. Rating by reporter:
(a) Degree of rapport
    and understanding: high _____ medium _____ low_____
(b) Degree of acceptance: high _____ medium _____ low _____

APPENDIX B
EXAMPLES OF
PROPOSAL AND REPORT

EXAMPLE OF OUTLINE OF PROPOSAL LETTER

Dear _____

   We are pleased to make this proposal for an assessment . . . focused on. . . . This assessment will allow you to. . . .

Context/Our Experience

   Over the past five years we have undertaken several such assessments on issues of morale, turnover, loss of market share. . . .

Key Issues of Concern to . . .

   Four areas appear to warrant . . . in your effort to . . .

- Effectiveness of . . .
- Impact of . . .
- Ambiguity about, lack of clarity of . . .
- Future . . .

The Assessor's Proposal

This is a good thing for you to do at this time because . . .

For this to be successful, we must develop accurate information and a strong plan to . . . . Attaining these outcomes requires rigorous investigation and the participation of organizational leaders and senior staff in developing a common understanding of the facts.

It is our understanding that a planning committee composed of . . . would be the working group charged with this task. We propose that this committee be an active working group participating in the . . . process. It is our experience that. . . .

We propose three project phases.

The Assessor's Capabilities: Timing and Fees

Our fee for this project would be. . . . We would bill monthly. . . . Expenses would be billed directly. . . .

Conclusion

We believe that we can provide valuable assistance to your organization. I will call you next week to discuss the steps needed to get going. We are extremely pleased that we will have an opportunity to work with you in strengthening Middlesex.

CONTRACT ACCEPTANCE

Example of Proposal Letter

Date

Mr. Paul Liatos
President
Middlesex Software Corporation
110 Summer Street
Boston, MA 02110

Dear Mr. Liatos:

We are pleased to make this proposal for a four-month project at Middlesex Software Corporation to provide a review of the strengths and weaknesses of current operations, a strategy for growth, and an implementable business plan for the future. This long-term plan and clear focus will allow you to enhance already respected products, to provide those to a larger number of customers, and to raise funds aggressively for specific initiatives.

Context

Over the past several years, Middlesex Software has initiated some major efforts in response to identified problems. These efforts have included broadening and strengthening products, diversifying revenue sources, and developing leadership. Initiatives have included,

- Broadening the product range to include more highly focused market niches;
- Adding extended levels of credit;
- Enhancing efforts to obtain more venture capital;
- Recruiting and training a new generation of leaders;
- Adding variants of already established products.

Having responded to both the financial and leadership challenges with these initiatives, we understand that Middlesex is seeking to use this current period of relative stability both to review its underlying strengths and weaknesses and to plan for the future. Although there is a strong belief that the historic mission of Middlesex is still appropriate, the current sense that Middlesex is not capitalizing sufficiently on the potential of its staff and resources raises a host of concerns.

Key Issues of Concern to Middlesex Software Corporation

Five areas, in particular, appear to warrant full examination in your effort to assess current operations and develop a strategy for growth, though no doubt more issues will emerge in the course of assessment.

Review Current Product Lines

Although the targeted customer population is clear, it is not clear whether the products now offered meet all of customers' needs or whether additional or alternative products are needed. An assessment of future customer needs, as well as how current products are doing against the increasing proliferation of other software, including the following data, are required:

- Product use by customers compared to previous use;
- Product effectiveness, including definitions of effectiveness and value of the product to the customers in light of many new ancillary products;
- Cost of producing each product and returns on each over the past three years;
- Analysis of cost-effectiveness of each product.

Middlesex has a unique expertise. An assessment of opportunities to extend that specialized expertise to other customers might also be undertaken.

Effectiveness of Current Marketing Efforts

Given the number of software users and the needs of your customers, the products of Middlesex appear to have substantially greater potential. Assuming Middlesex products meet a significant need, the reasons for that apparent unfulfilled potential must be assessed and understood.

- How are customers developed now? Are there alternative methods of reaching potential customers?
- Is there a systematic marketing plan?
- What is the current cost of identifying and reaching new customers?
- Has Middlesex reached its limit for market share?
- Is there really an untapped pool of potential customers in need of this software?

Effectiveness of Administrative Operations and Management

A review of management practices will identify strengths to be maintained and areas for improvement. This review would include an assessment of the financial, personnel, operations, and strategic management, including the following:

- Allocation of resources to current products and administration;
- Financial management systems;
- Staff management, including staffing patterns, staff development, accountability, and use of technical consultants;
- Product evaluation;
- Managerial effectiveness.

Impact of Growth on Revenue and Expenses

The marginal cost of adding a new customer for each product must be compared to the direct revenue received at current capacity levels. Current data appear to indicate that there is a positive marginal benefit at current use levels.

- Is this true for all products?
- At what point must capacity be increased?
- Does growth place insupportable demands on revenue?

Leadership Development

Unlike some boards in which leaders have a purely policy-making role, most Middlesex board members are integrally connected to the revenue-producing operations of the organization. As a result, it is critical to

- Strengthen the role of the board, diversify its members, and clarify the relationship of leadership to senior staff;
- Develop leadership skills among management and supervision.

Calumet Consultants Project Proposal

Middlesex enjoys a strong reputation in its industry segment. Its current financial stability, together with the goodwill of its customers, provide an opportunity to reinforce underlying organizational strengths and identify and correct weaknesses as the necessary steps to clarifying organizational focus and developing a long-term business plan.

For this project to be successful, we must develop accurate information and a strong plan, as well as reach consensus among those who must carry out the plan. Attaining all three elements requires both **rigorous assessment** and the **participation of organizational leaders and senior staff** in developing a common understanding of the facts and in designing plans and programs.

It is our understanding that a planning committee, composed of both leaders and senior staff, would be the working group charged with this task. We propose that this committee be an active working group participating in the planning process. It is our experience that the information and proposals from this group must be brought forward to ever-widening circles of organization leaders and staff to build the consensus needed for program implementation.

We propose three project phases:

- Phase 1: Assessment and analysis leading to a commonly held understanding of relevant facts.
- Phase 2: Proposal development and program design, including the design of strategies and specific implementable plans to achieve those strategies.
- Phase 3: Broad consensus building, including both the informal sharing of information and plans, as well as formal presentations to a broad group of leadership and staff.

Timing and Fees

Our fee for this project would be $510,000. We would bill monthly in equal installments of $120,750 on signing the contract, and at the beginning of April, May, and June. Out-of-pocket expenses would be billed directly, not to exceed $1000.

Conclusion

We believe that we can provide valuable assistance to your organization. I will call you next week to discuss the immediate work steps needed to get going. We are extremely pleased that we will have an opportunity to work with you in strengthening Middlesex.
Sincerely,

Ephraim Spinelli
Senior Consultant

Please sign below to indicate the acceptance of the terms stipulated in the letter above. This letter will serve as the contract between **Middlesex Software Corporation** and **Calumet Consultants**.

John H. Scott	Paul Liatos
President	President
Calumet Consultants	Middlesex Software Corporation

Date	Date

EXAMPLE OF LETTER TO EMPLOYEES

MEMORANDUM

To: All Employees
From: Fred Saylor
Subject: Forthcoming Assessment

As you all know firsthand, we have been expanding rapidly, adding new people and another shift. Much of our expansion is due to your high standards and increasing productivity. Although we are pleased with our growth, and the respect from our customers that it reflects, we—particularly those who have worked together before the rapid expansion—are concerned lest that growth undermine the family atmosphere that has characterized our work together.

To try to anticipate some of the potential problems and, I hope, counteract them, I have asked a team of consultants from Leverage, Inc., to assess our company and to offer recommendations that will help us grow without some of the growing pains we are all concerned about.

The assessors will develop a schedule of interviews to obtain a representative sample of all parts of the organization. These interviews will be confidential. No person's response will be known to anyone but members of the assessment team. In addition, the team will review our communications, interview some of our customers, and observe some of our work activities to better understand what we do and how we do it. They will also try to help us think about our future and what we might do differently and better.

When their work is done, they will prepare a report that will be presented first to me, then to the top management group, and then to all employees. Except for specific recommendations to me, the report will be the same for everyone. There will be opportunity for questions and discussion. After you review the report, I plan to have all of you, in small groups, discuss its implications and offer recommendations. The comments from the small groups will be summarized for all employees so we can decide collectively how to follow up.

Thank you for your cooperation.

ORGANIZATIONAL ASSESSMENT: THE TREBEL CORPORATION

Conducted by Harry Levinson, PhD
Date: May 14, 2000

CONFIDENTIAL
Trebel Corp.

Introduction

The need to compete more effectively led to an organizational study by Booz, Allen, and Hamilton that resulted in restructuring the company into business units, governed by five directors, each of whom is responsible for a major part of the business. It has also necessitated downsizing and displacing employees. The company must continue to downsize to become the lowest cost producer. Furthermore, the lack of profitability resulted in salary cuts to sometimes painful levels. The contraction and salary reduction, together with the seeming continuous decline as there were no signs of an upturn, led to the current demoralization.

It was this loss of morale that led the board to decide that I be invited to review the situation. This arose because several Trebel executives had attended The Levinson Institute seminars. They felt that the insights gained there were useful and should be shared with other Trebel executives and managers. The subsequent invitation to assess and conduct this feedback seminar is in keeping with the company's tradition of using outside consultants and sending many members of its staff all over the world to take courses and observe paper-making operations.

Method

I interviewed 55 managers and executives in the period from March 23 to April 1 in Plants 1 and 2 and at headquarters in Green Bay. The reason for so many interviews in such a short period was to be able to talk to as many managers and executives as possible. That precluded interviewing in the plants and observing the process of paper making itself, but it allowed for four luncheons with plant management groups.

I found people readily willing to talk with me and I had a sense that they were being straightforward. For some, the interviews were quite painful as they recounted experiences of disappointment and even disillusionment as a result of the downsizing and loss of income. For others, it was hard to imagine Trebel having to do both of those things.

Findings

I had an acute sense that change was overwhelming the organization. Sometimes the sheer number of things that the respondents had to take initiative on was overwhelming. Although the company was becoming more open as a result of the changes, the transition seemed to be taking too much time; the internal changes seemed not to be occurring as rapidly as those taking place in the world outside of Trebel.

Obviously, the directors are very well-trained and capable people. They were thinking positively in that the company was not keeping all its eggs in one basket, but rather thinking of other possible acquisitions.

These were the major problems I found:

Low morale

As had been reported, low morale was the major issue in the interviews. First, there was a sense that not everyone could grasp the magnitude of the problems that the company was facing; and second, the changes occurred so rapidly that people felt that everything was coming down on their heads.

The realities of their situation were that economic rewards were insufficient, and many had to take part-time jobs that then made for additional burdens of stress at home. There seemed to be a total lack of satisfaction and reward that contradicted the widespread company position that it cares about its people. The company that used to be a good payer no longer is. The company sometimes conveys the message that people should be grateful to Trebel, but that is not consistent with reality. People cannot plan their futures. The company seems not to be meeting its moral obligation to solve their career problems. There is no longer any long-term career planning. There is no evidence that the company is worried about them. Guidance and support are among the most important tasks of management, but these are not happening. The company shares its losses with them, but it does not share its profits. The psychological contract is now broken.

None of the changes that has taken place have ever been translated into improvement either for those who made the extra effort or for those who remain in an intolerable economic situation. The company is very demanding, but it has not given corresponding recognition for effort and achievement.

There is no message from the company that managers can incorporate into their lives or communicate to their own people. It is hard for them to give their subordinates good news because the signals they are getting and have to give lead to a greater sense of depression. In some cases, the leadership is antagonistic and uncomplimentary. The company should say what it expects from its people, and what it is ready to give to its people in return. But no one is listening to that need.

It is most important to develop a team spirit, to get people to be motivated, and management should undertake to motivate them better and give them more information about what is going on. However, because that has not happened, a change in management philosophy is urgent; there is no further leeway to absorb the emotional weight; managers feel used up and eroded all the time; they have nothing left to give. There is an experience of "lowering their arms," which I understand is a version of giving up. People cannot stand the situation any longer and wonder what else they have to do to change it. Many feel like abandoning ship. Their experiences are affecting their families.

There is a generalized disbelief in higher management, and a similar feeling on the part of their subordinates. There is a widespread lack of credibility. There is mistrust, distrust, and confusion. There is a request for greater communication with management to alleviate the confusion.

In addition, I do not think the wounds left over from the strike will be healed for a long time. Management may well be going through a period of false calmness with respect to that experience.

Lack of Clear Goals and Objectives

There is a need for a constructive philosophy, a clear policy statement. Furthermore, what the company says is what it should do.

With respect to the first, the company should plan very carefully and set forth its objectives. It needs a strategic plan for performance and accountability criteria because there is no strategic plan now. Even with the problems of dealing with the government, there could be and should be a strategic plan. One has to have clear rules to know how to manage. There is a need to define mission and to establish priorities. The failure to have clear goals, objectives, and priorities makes it difficult to arrive at common views of problems and to establish a single commercial policy.

The company seems to have a good capacity to adapt to short-term problems, but lacks that same adaptive capacity to the longer term issues, reflecting the need for precise plans for the future so that people know what they must do.

The lack of consistency is reflected in too many changes of direction. These occur in part because it seems that each director does not care what the others do or want to do and in part because of the absence of a leadership style that could solve problems as they arise. Sometimes people get decisions after actions are taken. At other times slow decision making made it difficult to adapt rapidly. Because decisions were too highly centralized, very few people really make decisions.

Starting, stopping, starting again does not seem to make for effective adaptation and undermines trust. In sum, the leadership needs to send one message to the organization.

Lack of Common Ways of Doing Things

This is another facet of the preceding section. Not everybody is now playing the same music. Everyone seems to be playing his or her own instrumental solo at the same time. Different managers at different times are in touch with one or another executive. When a manager responds to an executive of his or her own choosing, the manager acts less in a professional manner than in a way that will cement his or her alliance with that executive. Such behavior compounds the inconsistency of direction and conflicting directions.

There seems to be a lack of common decision on the part of the board with the resulting lack of coordination between the top management and the business units. It seems that the information system is not sufficiently sophisticated to tie the management of the corporation and the business units together because it does not provide updated information or adequate data. This contributes to the lack of common decisions and the inability of the leadership to work as a team. Furthermore, the creation of the business units has led to competition among them. That makes for more attention to the rivalries among them than for getting on with the business. The company has not yet achieved that level of cooperation that could be described as having attained horizontality.

Things often are not the way that many executives and directors see them. When members of the board bypass various managers and violate functional boundaries, making for additional confusion, that behavior also makes for a sense of having to start all over again repetitively. It is as if one has to begin anew with every task and project. In turn, that means one seems to have to fight for everything and to explain everything.

Lack of Defined Roles

Without clear goals and objectives and without agreed on ways of doing things, of course, it is difficult to define roles. As a consequence, people do not have a clear idea of how one must behave and where the boundaries of various roles should be. On the one hand, that tends to make for significant bureaucratic problems, and on the other, it impairs the needed effort to become more flexible and thereby more competitive.

The heavy centralization gives rise to the impression that the company is managed from Green Bay, that five people make the decisions, and 4000 people suffer. Higher management should make a religion of pushing responsibility down and establishing guidelines for its exercise, which it seems not to know how to do. Higher management should come closer to the work groups to understand the problems in their situations.

Lack of an Adequate Decision-Making Process

This theme, reflected in the previous sections, indicates that the company is too rigidly structured. In addition, there are endless meetings to which people come unprepared. Furthermore, as indicated earlier, the company has never done what was really needed in the first place, namely to push the responsibility and accountability down.

Lack of Involvement in Decision Making

Decisions are taken too high up, sometimes on the basis of wishful thinking. Those decisions are then difficult to carry out by the people who actually use the equipment and carry out the processes. The change of vision should be developed through people. Management should enlarge the scope and field of action of people lower down in the organization. Opportunity for participation should be extended to all levels of the company and the management should draw as many people as possible, even operators, into the planning process to provide for greater individual initiative.

Lack of Updated Technology

I understand that the company is not at the furthest edge of technology, but that it is the first to apply changes within the industry's structure. However, it seems that it still has a great distance to go in terms of total quality effort.

Lack of Investment

The company could become more efficient with greater investment. With newer technologies, it could reduce costs further. It is in a position to do so because some competitors have lower quality paper and lack some of the technical advantages of Trebel.

Lack of Training

Although the company has fostered a great deal of training, even to the point of sending many people all over the world to learn more, there is a need for a coherent system of training not only to develop employees but also to include management. The heads of business units have not been prepared for those roles to this point. Today, everyone needs to think like a businessperson. The technical level of the operators needs to be increased, as in all businesses, and there needs to be a process of career planning, to incorporate training and development experiences.

Lack of Management Orientation

Good people have left and others may well follow. The company seems not to have tried to save those good people, nor has it rewarded those who work most efficiently. There is a need for new blood, especially because the average age in management has increased as a result of the long-term service and absence of hiring from the outside. Clearly, there is a need for increasing inventiveness, creativity, and competitiveness, while letting those go who are not changing with the changes. To enhance those managers who are to assume more active leadership, there has to be greater autonomy and far less micromanagement.

Public Relations

In the past year, the company has moved out of its low-profile public posture. It now is intensifying its relationship with the government, the media, and the community. This is certainly a big step in the right direction. What happens in the company is heavily influenced by what happens in the government, and progress in resolving the company's problems is closely related to the economic development of the country. Therefore, the company should have frequent constructive relationships with the government, particularly because the reductions in force have necessarily created social problems following the unemployment of those who have been terminated.

Metaphoric Imagery

I asked each interviewee to think of the company as if it were a person and to describe that person to me. Almost invariably the imagery was the same. Almost everybody described that person as a big man, sometimes overweight, sometimes fat, trying to be lighter and healthier, sometimes very strong, sometimes a boxer or a wrestler, sometimes robust, hyperactive, even a giant pushing against a wall. He was described variably as arrogant, proud, overbearing, despotic, impulsive, insensitive, castrating, and suppressive. He was further described as having a confusion of values, as not using his brains, as considering himself as elite, and more concerned with what others say than operating the business, as saying one thing and then another, as being disorganized and not in control of what he does, as being alternately depressed and excited, unstable, and working hard.

On the positive side, there was an occasional comment that at heart he is good, faithful to those he can trust, but feels vulnerable. He is worried lest he fall into a vacuum any minute.

There were only two exceptions to this imagery. One interviewee described the image as that of a middle-aged woman who was going to a surgeon who does not know which part of her body to cut out first. Another described an image of a strong, healthy person going through adolescence. The last was the only optimistic image in all 55 interviews.

Recommendations

The fundamental task of any organization is to perpetuate itself, to make sure that it continues to be in business in the future. That requires two things: (a) productivity and (b) profitability. In an intensely competitive world, one must produce goods and services effectively, efficiently, and of appropriate quality. An organization, of course, must be profitable, because without profitability there is no perpetuation, but often perpetuation can be undermined by short-term profitability.

To achieve these goals, I have recommended a seminar to sustain the focus on productivity and profitability in the interest of perpetuation. To do so requires an understanding of human motivation and underlying assumptions about that motivation, which, if accurate, can contribute to the organization's effective adaptation or, if inadequate, can impair that adaptation.

Perpetuation: Accountability

There is confusion between the roles of members of the family as owners and their roles as executives. To help resolve these differences about roles and functions and modes of decision making, additional consultation probably will be helpful.

I recommend that there be constituted an advisory committee comprising chief executives of other companies who can contribute significantly to the appropriate policies of Trebel. I think, for example, of heads of consumer product companies who have to be market-oriented and could contribute significantly to the development of a marketing orientation in Trebel. There also may have to be other kinds of specialists on such a committee, those who have special knowledge of finance, of international business, and so on. That committee would advise the board.

I also recommend that the company establish a conceptual accountability. I take the position that those with higher level conceptual ability who are responsible for longer range thinking should be able to add value to the work of those reporting to them. If managers do not have greater capacity than their subordinates to think in complex terms, then they cannot add value.

The evolution of such a systematic organization structure will also require behavioral job descriptions. These are ways of describing not only the quantity and quality outcomes of the respective roles but also kinds of behaviors and attitudes required in their relationship to peers, subordinates, superiors, and indeed customers, government officials, and others outside the organization.

The behavioral job descriptions, in turn, should be supported by a performance appraisal system that is based on significant incidents. That is, people should be appraised on the basis of what they do and not merely on the basis of outcomes. The performance appraisal system should lend itself to development of sufficient detail to give adequate consideration to selection and appraisal, as well as training and development.

Perpetuation: Development

It will be important to identify key potential executives in the organization, as well as to develop mentoring relationships for them that will encourage their growth and development. It will be important also to assess their capacity for continued growth and to support that process.

This means that the organization should have an executive development program that would provide both internal courses and arrange for those outside the company, such as advanced management courses in major business schools; special courses in finance, marketing, technology, and strategic planning, with the provision that those who take such courses should be reporting back to their organizations on what they have learned. The latter process, usually not carried out well in most companies, will make it possible to continue to brief those who have not been able to attend those courses to keep them refreshed on contemporary trends and developments.

Of course, there should be a more formal training program that would increase the skills and competencies of all people in the organization. Such a program should rotate them among roles to keep them refreshed. It should also encourage the development of teams that in turn could concentrate on improving products and processes on a continuous basis.

Perpetuation: Functions

Three functions in the organization need special attention. These are the marketing function, the financial function, and the strategic planning function.

Not only does there need to be a shift in the orientation from a technical orientation to a marketing orientation, but also there should be a high-level executive with outstanding marketing skills in charge of such an activity, reporting to the chief operating officer. I am not making a judgment about whether the present marketing staff has such competencies and skills; I simply do not know. I am indicating that that activity should be given appropriate prominence and support.

If the top management in general does not fully understand the marketing function and does not give it adequate support, then inevitably it will fail, as from time to time it has failed in other companies when a company could not make an appropriate shift in orientation. To make that shift will require significant numbers of people in management to learn about the marketing function, to have the opportunity to discuss the shift and its significance for them and their roles, to understand the kinds of support that must be mobilized for such a function to work effectively. In addition, a significant number of managers in the organization, if not most, should be trained in marketing to be effective components of marketing items.

In many companies, there is inadequate recognition of the degree to which active financial management can contribute significantly to profitability. By this I mean that some companies tie themselves to long-term financial arrangements that subsequently impair their flexibility to adapt to changes in currency, inflation, and the economy in general. Too few people in management understand finance sufficiently to grasp this problem and the organization thereby loses the flexibility it could have if significant numbers of its management understood what finance was all about. Those who are not interested in finance should know enough about it to be able to support the function adequately—and that means getting sufficient training to establish a business orientation.

Strategic planning speaks for itself. The company is already engaged in strategic planning, but thinking in those terms seems not yet to be broadly viewed and understood in the organization. Of course, it is difficult to plan for the long term when the short term is so variable, yet the company must continue to use its personnel and resources in the context of whatever political and economic variability it must contend with. There should be plans for various kinds of circumstances: plans for recession, plans for decline in interest in given products, and so forth.

Conclusion

Perpetuation requires aggressive collective attack on the marketplace led by aggressive leadership with a global view. It requires a management team that understands the forces that it must contend with and is unified in its recognition of its need to channel its energies into that effort. Only by collective identification with that task and target will the mobilization and energy counteract the sense of helplessness that results in demoralization.

—Harry Levinson, PhD

APPENDIX C
ADAPTIVE ACTIVITIES

The expression of both affection and aggression is necessary for survival. Nurture and relationships are crucial for most species. So is the capacity for attack. Adaptation is the aggressive attack on self or the environment to master either or both to serve one's own needs. All living organisms must necessarily attack their environments to survive—for example, a tree spreading its roots, drawing moisture and nutrients from the soil; an animal killing another for food; another digging a home out of the ground or making one of branches; a man cutting wood or mining coal to warm himself. Some organisms must, in effect, attack themselves, compelling themselves to sacrifice present pleasures for future gains, learning skills, and competencies. Sometimes adaptive mechanisms or activities lose their effectiveness or cost too much in terms of energy or resources for the results they achieve. Sometimes they achieve short-term goals at the cost of long-term survival. Sometimes they are overreactive, destructive to both the actor and the object of his or her actions. In extreme form aggressive adaptive mechanisms result in the literal destruction of the actor.

Adaptation also refers to equilibrium-maintaining activities that an organism undertakes to sustain its integrity against both internal and external threat. For example, fever reflects the equilibrium-maintaining activity of the body against the threat of infection; flight–fight behavior is defensive against external threat. Many individual and group activities can be used to maintain psychological equilibrium, ranging from rationalization to creating and attacking external enemies.

Activities devoted to mastering the internal and external worlds may be seen as coping behaviors, or mechanisms. Those directed toward protecting the organism against internal or external threat may be seen as defense mechanisms. All behavior necessarily includes both types of mechanisms in varying degrees. The more an organism devotes its energies to defensive behavior, the less it has available for effective and enduring mastery. Similarly, the more an organism devotes itself to its own protection, the more its behavior is stimulated by real or fancied outside forces, and the less it pursues spontaneous mastery efforts. For example, a man who must please others at all costs can hardly be what he wants to be; rather, he is what others want him to be.

Organizations also have coping and defensive behaviors. This appendix lists and categorizes many according to their degree of adaptive effectiveness. These examples are intended to be illustrative, not exhaustive. They may help the assessor weigh more carefully the meaning and cost of the behaviors he or she sees, particularly as the assessor considers organization integrative patterns. The better an organization has integrated its behavior patterns, the more likely it is to adapt and defend successfully. The activities illustrated should be particularly helpful to the assessor in formulating his or her understanding in chapters 9, 10, and 11.

NORMAL ACTIVITIES

These behaviors permit some discharge of energy, presumably toward solving problems and attaining gratification. They may be divided into those having to do with the product or organization per se and those having to do with people.

Having to do with product or organization: processing materials; rendering services periodic reports; quality control revision of tasks and processes; changes in space and schedules; expansion and acquisition; acquaintance with competitors' products and response thereto; acquaintance with changes in consumer's wishes and response thereto; responsiveness to social changes; research: basic, product, market, economic; pilot efforts; proving grounds; testing products; organization planning; projections of future trends; sales promotion and indoctrination; self-laudatory advertising; image-creating efforts, symbolization, publicity public statements by key figures regarding organization's worth.

Having to do with people: building attractive surroundings; functional physical facilities; morale-building activities; encouraging socialization off the job to foster cohesion; company parties and conversational coffee breaks;

background music; encouraging shared fantasies of organizational achievement; providing uniforms and other efforts to foster organization *esprit de corps*; personnel selection, training, benefit, and caring functions; management development; offering seminars, workshops, training not necessarily connected directly with major work goals; participation in professional and trade associations and community activities; seeking support from community and other organizations; exhorting (internal and to community); mild pressure; nagging; expressing overtly internal feelings in advertising ("we like to serve"); complaints of management in public service messages or message seeking public support; protection from arbitrary authority; protection from industrial hazards; care for accidental results; spontaneous and unplanned postponement of tasks (relief); organizational moratorium periods (minimal activity or productivity to repair, recover, reorganize); operation of Parkinson's law (work expands to fill the time for its completion); occasional absenteeism, breakage, flare-up of hostility in reaction to inadequate problem-solving or because of frustration.

FIRST-ORDER ACTIVITIES

These are exaggerations of normal adaptive activities. They are less functional because they tend to cost more in terms of money or energy and to yield proportionately less in results. Usually they increase frustration and anxiety, focus more on short-term than on long-term consequences, and reduce present satisfactions. Therefore, they are indicators of stress and the need for intervention. These activities tend to be of two kinds: denials or more intensive efforts at control. Denials shut out information or pretend the threat does not really exist. More intensive control efforts increase the rigidity of the organization. Both are symptoms. Of course, sometimes increased control efforts are necessary and denials may be temporarily functional. (It does not help the passengers to know that the aircraft pilot is having a difficult time of it in a storm.) The assessor must evaluate whether the activities he or she observes are normal or first-order.

Having to do with product organization: spot audits: PERT systems; time studies; more complex, more frequent reports; more frequent inventory checks; increased security checks, inspections, surveillance of competition, suppliers, operations, processes; reducing intake of information from outside; overtesting; increasing complexity of controls; impulsive revision of tasks and processes

Having to do with people: refusal to recognize threat; minimizing threat; unrealistic optimism; pep talks; unrealistic pessimism; chronic griping;

decreased philanthropy and community service; extended intervention into community affairs; increased stereotyping (competition, labor, community); ignoring own history and effects of own behavior; making political commitments unconnected with organizational business; sporadic efforts: abortive cost-cutting or sales efforts, often short-lived and inappropriate; overexpansion and acquisition; restricting friendships to mainly colleagues; needless overemphasis on cleanliness of equipment, plant; cult of poverty with considerable self-praise for making do; increased absenteeism; waste of time and supplies; bypassing of organizational structure; undermining of organizational caring, training, and growth efforts.

SECOND-ORDER ACTIVITIES

These are disruptive activities that have a high cost in terms of money, stress for individuals, and organizational survival potential.

Having to do with product organization: arbitrary change; sudden cutting of established departments; total rejection of outside information and advice

Having to do with people: withdrawal into organizational self; giving up ties to community, professional associations; unduly risky financial manipulations; sacrificing reputation; employee morale; community relations; failure to live up to guarantees, promises; unrealistic fear reactions; repetitive unimplemented discussions and planning; intense chronic concern with a specific internal issue or problem at the expense of attention to outside realities; repetitive interpersonal or intergroup conflict; scapegoating some member or part of the organization; self-exploitation in failure to collect accounts receivable; excessive rigidity of routine; repetitive self-sacrifice (cutting off parts of organization, narrowing functions, repetitive contraction); great effort to conceal problems; loss of key personnel.

THIRD-ORDER ACTIVITIES

These maladaptive and disruptive activities are characterized by episodic blatant expressions of hostility. They usually require the organization subsequently to effect a resolution of the difficulty its behavior has created or compensation for its destructiveness.

Having to do with product organization: verbal outbursts in advertising against inappropriate targets; seeking the discharge of public officials or spying on opponents; wanton damage to property of others, reputations of persons, or to community; manipulative practices in marketing, motivation, and legal relationships; lying and deception with regard to product; wanton industrial piracy (people, patents); insincere, inadequate, or superficial compensatory efforts for damage previously done—for example, lumber companies that cut the trees, taking the money and run, leaving the people who live there vulnerable to floods; mining companies that compound the slag runoff in rivers; exaggerated speculation; price-fixing; ogilopoly; open violence in labor relations; extreme behavior (panic, catastrophic demoralization, apathy, resignation, hyper excitement for no adequate reason).

FOURTH-ORDER ACTIVITIES

These are self-destructive activities resulting in the demise of the organization or the involuntary surrender of control to another organization.

forced merger;
bankruptcy;
going out of business.

APPENDIX D
ASSESSMENT OUTLINE

This outline lists the individual topics to be covered in the assessment. Chapters 5 through 11 explain the outline. After assessors become familiar with this manual, they are likely to find themselves working directly with the outline and will then refer only occasionally to the text.

I. How the Organization Became What It Is
   A. Identifying Information
      1. Organization name
      2. Location
      3. Type of organization
      4. Organizational affiliation (e.g., part of larger organization)
      5. Size
         a. Financial condition
         b. Stockholders
         c. Employees
      6. Situation of the initial contact
      7. Special conditions affecting validity of the assessment
      8. First overall impressions

B. Historical Data
1. Chief complaint or events leading to the initiation of the assessment
2. Problems of the organization as stated by key figures
    a. Long-range
    b. Short-range
3. Background of the organization
    a. Key developmental phases
        (1) As reported by organizational participants
        (2) As reported by outsiders
        (3) As understood by the assessor
    b. Major crises experienced by the organization
        (1) Natural catastrophes
        (2) Loss of key personnel
        (3) Labor problems
        (4) Financial emergencies
        (5) Technological changes
        (6) Loss of market share
        (7) Major changes in response to information and other technological innovation
    c. Product-service history
        (1) Change and development of organizational goals
        (2) Sequence of development in product or service
        (3) Relative success or failure in various stages of service or product history
        (4) Geographical patterns
        (5) Special skills or competencies of the organization
        (6) Performance reputation and record
    d. Organizational folklore
4. Circumstances surrounding the assessment

II. Description and Analysis of the Organization as a Whole
    A. Structural Data
    1. Formal organization
        a. Chart
        b. Systems concept
        c. Formal job descriptions

2. Plant and equipment
   a. Location: territory covered
   b. Value
   c. Kinds of equipment: size, function
   d. Relative efficiency: age, obsolescence
   e. Special demands plant and equipment make on people
   f. Varieties of work environments
   g. Age, condition, and effectiveness of computer and other technological equipment and systems
3. Ecology of the organization
   a. Spatial distribution of individuals
   b. Spatial distribution of activities
   c. Implications of the data on spatial distribution
4. Financial structure
5. Human resources
   a. Number of employees
   b. Geographical origins and ethnic composition
   c. Educational levels
   d. Average tenure
   e. Range of skills
   f. Absentee rate
   g. Turnover rate
   h. Accident rate
6. Structure for managing human resources
   a. Recruitment
   b. Orientation
   c. Training
   d. Developmental opportunities
   e. Promotion
   f. Compensation
   g. Performance analysis
   h. Kind and intensity of supervision
   i. Rules and regulations for employees
   j. Health maintenance program
   k. Environmental program
   l. Retirement program
   m. Recreation program
   n. Other fringe benefits
   o. Labor contract

7. Policies and procedures

   a. Scope

   b. Mode of communication

   c. Who knows about them?

   d. What discretion is left to lower supervisory levels?

8. Time span and rhythm

   a. Seasonal cycles

   b. Diurnal cycles

   c. Planning spans

   d. Degree activities are regulated by time

   e. Attitudes about punctuality

   f. Urgency

   g. Concern about deliveries

B. Process Data

  1. Communication systems

    a. Incoming: Reception and routing

      (1) Amount and types of materials

      (2) Modes of transmission

        (A) Oral or written

        (B) Formal or informal channels

      (3) Timing, rhythm, urgency

        (A) According to plan

        (B) Erratically or spontaneously

      (4) Source and audience

    b. Processing: Integration, decision

      (1) Amount and types of material

      (2) Modes of processing

        (A) Oral or written

        (B) Formal or informal channels

      (3) Timing, rhythm, urgency

        (A) According to plan

        (B) Erratically or spontaneously

      (4) Source and audience

    c. Outgoing: routing and response

      (1) Amount and types of materials

(2) Modes of distribution

    (A) Oral or written statements

    (B) Formal or informal channels

(3) Timing, rhythm, urgency

    (A) According to plan

    (B) Erratically or spontaneously

(4) Source and audience

d. Processing: Integration, decision

    (1) Amount and types of material

    (2) Modes of processing

        (A) Oral or written

        (B) Formal or informal channels

    (3) Timing, rhythm, urgency

        (A) According to plan

        (B) Erratically or spontaneously

    (4) Source and audience

e. Outgoing: Routing and response

    (1) Amount and types of material

    (2) Modes of distribution

        (A) Oral or written statements

        (B) Formal or informal channels

    (3) Timing, rhythm, urgency

        (A) According to plan

        (B) Erratically or spontaneously

2. Management information systems

  a. Age, condition, and sophistication of computer equipment

  b. Groupware

  c. Availability and distribution of laptops and other communication devices

3. Current and previous studies in, and reports to, the organization

  a. Consultant reports

  b. Special staff studies

  c. Marketing studies

  d. Engineering studies

  e. Accountants' audits and reports

III. Interpretative Data: Inferences Drawn From the Analytic Data

  A. Current Organizational Functioning

1. Organizational perceptions
    a. Degree of alertness, accuracy, and vividness
        (1) To stimuli from within the organization
            (A) From personnel
                i. Employees to management and vice versa
                ii. Supervisor to subordinate and vice versa
                iii. Departments to each other's needs
            (B) From physical plant
        (2) To stimuli from without
            (A) Primary external stimuli
                i. Industry and marketing conditions
                ii. Purchasing conditions
                iii. Labor conditions
            (B) Secondary external stimuli
                i. Legislative (regulatory, tariff, and tax laws)
                ii. Transportation
                iii. Competitors
                iv. Research developments
                v. Economic, social, and political trends
    b. Direction and span of attention (selectivity)
        (1) Dominant foci of interest
            (A) Long-term framework
            (B) Short-term framework
        (2) Significant neglected foci
    c. Assessment of the discrepancy between reality and perceived reality
        (1) Of reality within the organization
        (2) Of reality outside the organization
2. Organizational knowledge
    a. Acquisition of knowledge
        (1) Methods of obtaining new knowledge
            (A) Related to personnel and plant
            (B) Related to products, services, or competitors
            (C) Related to financial resources
            (D) Related to forces and trends affecting the organization
            (E) By whom (sources within and outside the organization)

      (F) Reservoir of intellectual sources

           i. Talents and skills within the organization

          ii. Consultants

        iii. Affiliations with specialized institutions or universities

        iv. Library facilities and services

         v. Computer networks

   (2) Degree of receptivity to new knowledge

      (A) By whom

      (B) To what

   (3) Level and range of knowledge

      (A) Concerning themselves, their products, their services, and related factors

      (B) Outside their immediate area of interest

 b. Use of knowledge

   (1) How is it brought together?

      (A) Who thinks about it?

      (B) Level of abstraction

   (2) How is knowledge organized and systematized?

      (A) Committee system

      (B) Records and storage system

      (C) Other modes of organization and systematization

   (3) Amount and kind of use (retrieval)

   (4) Organizational conditions affecting the use of intellectual sources

      (A) Ability to deal with abstract problems

      (B) Flexibility

      (C) Characteristic style and variations

 c. Dissemination of knowledge

3. Organizational language

 a. Themes and content of employee publications

 b. Organizational ideology

 c. Advertising themes

 d. Organizational symbols and slogans

 e. Language of policies as distinct from the policies themselves

 f. Language of customs, taboos, prohibitions, and constrictions: direct and implied

4. Emotional atmosphere of the organization

a. Prevailing mood and range
b. Overall stability or variability of mood
    (1) Intensity of reactions
    (2) Duration of reactions
    (3) Appropriateness to stimulating factors
c. Intraorganizational variability
    (1) By hierarchical level
    (2) By department
    (3) Other (geographical location, profession)
5. Organizational action
    a. Energy level
        (1) Consistency or variability of application (rate of discharge of energy)
        (2) Points and periods of peak expenditure energy
    b. Qualities of action
        (1) Degree of directness
        (2) Degree of flexibility
        (3) Planning and timing
        (4) Degree of persistence
        (5) Effectiveness
        (6) Constructiveness or destructiveness
B. Attitudes and Relationships
    1. Contemporary attitudes toward, and relationships with, others
        a. Range, diversification, depth, and constancy
            (1) Customers, clients, students, patients, parishioners
            (2) Competition
            (3) Employees
            (4) Occupational associations and representatives
            (5) Stockholders
            (6) Legislative bodies
            (7) Executive and regulatory bodies (governmental)
            (8) Control bodies (internal)
            (9) Suppliers
            (10) Financial community
            (11) Host community
            (12) Dealer organizations
            (13) Plant builders
            (14) Consultants

        (15) Unions

        (16) Others

    b. Major attachments

        (1) Positive

        (2) Negative

    c. Masculine–feminine orientation

        (1) Of organization

           (A) Masculine

           (B) Feminine

           (C) Degree of achievement

           (D) How pervasive?

        (2) In relationship to the industry

    d. Transference phenomena

        (1) Related to the assessor

        (2) Related to the organization

        (3) Related to each other

2. Relations to things and ideas

    a. Quality and intensity of relations to plant, equipment, raw material or supplies, product, and services

        (1) Symbolization

        (2) Unconscious personification

    b. Time: How is it regarded?

        (1) Past, present, future orientation

        (2) How is the future planned for?

        (3) Value of time as an investable commodity

        (4) View of work cycles

    c. Space: How it is conceptualized

        (1) As a local concern

        (2) As a cosmopolitan concern

    d. Meaning of work for organization

        (1) As a device for coping with the environment

           (A) In economic terms

           (B) In terms of skill

           (C) In terms of thinking

           (D) In terms of psychological defense

        (2) As a device for fulfilling psychological contract

        (3) As a device for channeling energy

           (A) Constructively

      (B) Destructively

      (C) As a process of regression

          i. Within the work setting

          ii. In nonwork activities

  e. Authority, power, and responsibility

     (1) How does the organization regard power?

      (A) The power of others

      (B) Its own power with regard to the world outside

      (C) Power internally

          i. Generally

          ii. By ranks

     (2) How does the organization handle authority?

     (3) How does the organization handle responsibility?

      (A) Outside the organization

      (B) Inside the organization

  f. Positions on social, ethical, and political issues

3. Attitudes about self

  a. Who do they think they are and how do they feel about it?

  b. Where do they think they are headed and how do they feel about it?

  c. What are their common aspirations?

  d. How do they look to themselves?

4. Intraorganizational relationships

  a. Key people in the organization

  b. Significant groups within the organization

  c. Implications of a and b

5. Management information systems

IV. Analyses and Conclusions: Interpretations From Inferences

  A. Organizational Integrative Patterns

    1. Appraisal of the effect of the environment on the organization

      a. Historical

        (1) Beneficial

        (2) Harmful

      b. Contemporary

        (1) Beneficial

        (2) Harmful

      c. Anticipated

        (1) Beneficial

        (2) Harmful

2. Appraisal of the effect of the organization on the environment
   a. Historical
      (1) Beneficial
      (2) Harmful
   b. Contemporary
      (1) Beneficial
      (2) Harmful
   c. Anticipated
      (1) Beneficial
      (2) Harmful
3. Reactions
   a. Of the environment
      (1) To the injury
      (2) Toward source of the injury
   b. Secondary reaction from the organization
4. Appraisal of the organization
   a. Special assets
      (1) Material or tangible (financial, patents, physical plant, equipment, geographical distribution, transportation, communication, personnel)
      (2) Functional (including leadership and mental set, or attitude)
         (A) Reality orientation
            i. To external environment
            ii. To internal environment
         (B) Values and ideals
            i. Degree of institutionalization
            ii. Congruence with reality
         (C) Task mastery
            i. Psychological contract fulfillment or violations
            ii. Growth and survival
            iii. Task-directed behavior
   b. Impairments
      (1) Material or tangible (financial, patents, physical plant, equipment, geographical distribution, transportation, communication, personnel)
      (2) Functional (including leadership and mental set, or attitude)

           (A) Reality orientation
                i. To external environment
                ii. To internal environment
           (B) Values and ideals
                i. Degree of institutionalization
                ii. Disparity from reality
           (C) Task mastery
                i. Psychological contract unfulfillment
                ii. Growth and survival
                iii. Task-directed behavior
      c. Level of integration
        (1) Normal adaptive activities
        (2) First-order adaptive activities
        (3) Second-order adaptive activities
        (4) Third- and fourth-order adaptive activities
      d. Overall effectiveness and facade
  B. Summary and Recommendations
    1. Present status
    2. Explanatory formulation
      a. Genetic
      b. Dynamic
    3. Prognostic conclusions
    4. Recommendations

REFERENCES

(To keep the reference list short, it is specific rather than exhaustive. References marked with this ☞ are particularly relevant for the assessment process. These I think the assessor *should* read to round out his or her understanding.)

☞Adizes, I. (1988). *Corporate life cycles*. Englewood Cliffs, NJ: Prentice-Hall.

APA principles of psychiatrists and code of conduct. (1992). Washington, DC: American Psychological Association.

Bertalanffy, L. von (1950). An outline of general systems theory. *British Journal of Philosophical Science*, 1, 134–163.

Black, J. S., & Gregersen, H. B. (1999, March–April). The right way to manage expats. *Harvard Business Review*, 52–63.

Bonisteel, S. (2001). Hewlett heir responds to latest HP merger salvo. Retrieved Dec. 31, 2001, from http://www.washktek.com.

Deming, W. E. (1986). *Out of the crisis* New York: Cambridge University Press.

DetroitNews.com. (2001, Dec. 28). p.1.

Fraker, S. (1983). How DEC got decked. *Fortune*, December 12, p. 83.

Galewitz, P. (2001). Hospitals predict a profit next year. *Palm Beach Post*, December 13, p. B1.

Gannes, S. (1988). IBM and DEC take on the little guys. *Fortune*, October 8, p. 108.

☞Geertz, C. (1973). *The interpretation of culture*. New York: Basic Books.

Goldstein, K. (1939). *The organism*. New York: American Book.

Greenwald, I. (1995, Oct. 30). *Time*, p. 30.

☞Greiner, L. S. (1998, July–Aug.). Evolution and revolution as organizations grow. *Harvard Business Review*, 37–45; *Harvard Business Review*, May-June, 55–68.

Grove, A. S. (1996). *Only the paranoid survive*. New York: Bantam, Doubleday, Dell.

Hafnery, K. (1999). Coming of age in Palo Alto. *New York Times*, June 10, D10.

Harvard Gazette. (2001). Statement from university on student sit-in, April 19, p. 1.

☞Hirschorn, L. (1990). *The workplace within: Psychodynamics of organizational life*. Cambridge: MIT Press.

☞Howard, A. (Ed.). (1994). *Diagnosis for organizational change*. New York: Guilford Press.

Jaques, E. (1955). Social systems as a defense against persecutory and depressive anxiety. In M. Klein, P. Hermann, R. E. & Money-Kryle (Eds.), *New directions in psychoanalysis* (pp. 478–498). London: Tavistock.

☞Jaques, E. (1996). *Requisite organization*. 2nd ed., rev. Falls Church, VA: Cason Hall.

Jaques, E. (2001). Diagnosing sources of managerial leadership problems for research and treatment. *Consulting Psychology Journal, 53*, 67–75.

Jaques, E., & Clement, S. D. (1991). *Executive leadership*. Falls Church, VA: Cason Hall.

☞Kets de Vries, M. F. R. (1996). *Family businesses: Human dilemmas in the family firm*. Boston: International Thomson Business.

Kets de Vries, M. F. R., & Zaleznik, A. (1985). *Power and the corporate mind*. Chicago: Bonus Books.

Kohler, W. (1940). *Dynamics in psychology*. New York: Liveright.

☞Kotter, J. P. (1978). *Organizational dynamics: Diagnosis and intervention*. Reading, MA: Addison-Wesley.

Kotter, J. P. (1998). *What leaders really do*. Boston: Harvard Business School Press.

Labich, K. (1999). Attention shoppers: This man is watching you. *Fortune*, July 19, 131.

Ledeen, M. (1999). The administration quashes truth teller on China. *Wall Street Journal*, June 10, A26.

Lesieur, F. G. (1958). *The Scanlon plan*. New York: Wiley.

Levinson, H. (1971). Conflicts that plague family businesses. *Harvard Business Review, 45*(2), 90–98.

☞Levinson, H. (1981). Seminar on organizational diagnosis. *Consultation, 1*(1), 45–47.

☞Levinson, H. (1984). Management by guilt. In M. F. R. Kets de Vries (ed.), *The irrational executive* (pp. 132–151). New York: International Universities Press.

Levinson, H. (1987). Psychoanalytic theory in organizational behavior. In J. W. Lorsch (Ed.), *Handbook of organizational behavior* (pp. 51–62). Englewood Cliffs, NJ: Prentice Hall.

☞Levinson, H. (1994). Why the behemoths fell. *American Psychologist, 49*(5), 428–436.

Levinson, H., Munden, K. J., Price, C. R., Mandl, H. J., & Solley, C. M. (1962). *Men, management and mental health*. Cambridge, MA: Harvard University Press.

Levinson H., & Rosenthal S. (1984). *CEO: Corporate leadership in action*. New York: Basic Books.

Levinson, H., Sabbath, J., & Connor, J. (1992). Bearding the lion that roared: A case study in organizational consultation. *Consulting Psychology Journal, 44*(2), 2–16.

Lorenz, K. (1966). *On aggression*. New York: Harcourt Brace & World.

LosAngelesTimes.com. (2002). Enron's Lay faces Capitol Hill Hotseat.

Lowman, R. L. (Ed.). (1998). *The ethical practice of psychology in organizations*. Washington, DC: American Psychological Association.

Lublin, J. S. (2001). Place vs. product: It's tough to choose a management model. *Wall Street Journal*, June 27, 2001, l.

Luccetti, A., & Murray, M. (1999). GE unit to stop tracking survey respondents. *Wall Street Journal*, June 10, A2.

Machlup, F. (1962). *Production and distribution of knowledge in the United States*. Princeton, NJ: Princeton University Press.

☞McClelland, D. C. (1975). *Power: The inner experience*. New York: Irvington.

Maruca, R. F. (1988). How do you manage the off-site team. *Harvard Business Review*, 22–26.

Menninger, K. A., Mayman, M., & Pruyser, P. (1962). *Manual for psychiatric case study*. 2nd ed., rev. New York: Grune & Stratton.

☞Menzies, I. (1960). A case study in the functioning of social systems as a defense against anxiety: A report on the study of the nursing service in a general hospital. *Human Relations, 13*, 95–121.

Merrick, A. (2002, March 11). K-Mart is planning to close 284 stores and cut 22,000 jobs. *Wall Street Journal*, p. 32.

☞Mintzberg, H. (1973). *The nature of managerial work*. New York: Harper.

Murphy, K. R., & Cleveland, J. N. (1991). *Performance appraisal: An organizational perspective*. Boston: Allyn & Bacon.

Nadler, D. A., & Tushman, M. L. (1997). *Competing by design*. New York: Oxford University Press.

Parkinson, C. N. (1962). *In-laws and out-laws*. Boston: Houghton Mifflin.

Racker, H. (1968). *Transference and countertransference*. New York: International Universities Press.

Rogers, R. E., & Fong, J. Y. (2000). *Organizational assessment: Diagnosis and intervention*. Amherst, MA: HRD Press.

Schwartz, H. S. (1990). *Narcississtic processes and corporate decay: The theory of the organizational ideal*. New York: New York University Press.

☞Shapiro, E. C. (1995). *Fad surfing in the boardroom*. Reading, MA: Addison-Wesley.

Sherman, H. J. (1998). *Open boundaries: Creating business innovation through complexity*. Reading, MA: Perseus.

Stamm, I. (2002, Jan. 6). Menninger has a distinguished past. *Topeka-Capital-Journal*, p. E1.

Stewart, T. A. (1997). *Intellectual capital*. New York: Doubleday.

Townsend, S. M., DeMarie, S, & Hendrickson, A. R. (1998). Virtual teams: Technology and the workplace of the future. *Academy of Management Executive, 12*(3), 17–29.

☞Trist, E. L., & Murray, H. (Eds.). (1993). *The social engagement of social science: A Tavistock analogy: Thesocio-technical perspective*. Philadelphia: University of Pennsylvania Press.

Vittert, M. (1997). Sewell's "inevitable" depression. *St. Louis Business Journal*, Aug. 4, p. 2.

Waldholz, M. (1999). Bristol-Myers heeds call to bolster war against HIV in Africa. *Wall Street Journal*, May 16, A1.

Waldman, D. A., Atwater, L. E., & Antonini, D. (1998). Has 360° feedback gone amok? *Academy of Management Executive, 12*(2), 86–94.

Weaver, P. H. (1988). *The suicidal corporation*. New York: Simon & Schuster.

Weyrich, S. (1992). Prelude: Steve Jobs and making jobs. *Apple History, Part 8*. Winston-Salem, NC: Duke University.

Wilcox, J. (2001). Microsoft, Kodak settle XP dispute. *CNET News.com*, August 12, p. 2.

BIBLIOGRAPHY

(To keep the bibliography list short, it is specific rather than exhaustive. References marked with this ☞ are particularly relevant for the assessment process. These I think the assessor *should* read to round out his or her understanding.)

Berg, B. L. (2000). *Qualitative research methods for the social sciences*. 4th ed. Boston: Allyn & Bacon.

Charan, R., & Colvin, G. (1999, June 21). Why CEOs fail. *Fortune*, 68–80.

de Geus, A. (1997). *The living company*. Boston: Harvard Business School Press.

☞Deal, T. E., & Kennedy, A. A. (1982). *Corporate cultures: The rites and rituals of corporate life*. Reading, MA: Addison-Wesley.

Denzin, N. K., & Lincoln, Y. S. (Eds.). (2000). *Handbook of qualitative research*. 2nd ed. Thousand Oaks, CA: Sage.

Duncan, W. J., Ginter, P. M., & Swayne, L. E. (1998). Competitive advantage and international organizational assessment. *Academy of Management Executive*, 12(3), 6–16.

Dunham, K. J. (2001). Employers seek ways to lure back laid-off workers when times improve. *Wall Street Journal*, June 19, B1.

Eisenberg, D. (2001). Where people are never let go. *Time*, June 18, 2001, 40.

Greenwald, J. (2001). Rank and fire. *Time*, June 18, 2001, 38–40.

Gummesson, E. (2000). *Qualitative methods in management research*. Thousand Oaks, CA: Sage.

Hill, J. M. M., & Trist, E. L. (1953). A consideration of industrial accidents as a means of withdrawal from the work situation. *Human Relations*, 6, 357–388.

☞Hirschorn, L. (1984). *Beyond mechanization.* Cambridge: MIT Press.

Hormuth, S. E. (1986). The sampling of experiences in situ. *Journal of Personality, 54,* 262–293.

Kehoe, J. E. (Ed.). (2000). *Managing selection in changing organizations.* San Francisco: Jossey-Bass.

☞Kets de Vries, M. F. R., & Balazs, K. (1997). The downside of downsizing. *Human Relations, 50,* 11–50.

☞Kilburg, R. R. (2000). *Executive coaching: Developing managerial wisdom in a world of chaos.* Washington, DC: American Psychological Association.

Kotter, J. P. (1982). *The general managers.* New York: Free Press.

☞Kotter, J. P. (1985). *Power and influence.* New York: Free Press.

Kraut, A. I., & Korman, A. K. (1999). *Evolving practices in human resource management.* San Francisco: Jossey-Bass.

Kubler-Ross, E. (1960). *On death and dying.* New York: Macmillan.

☞Levinson, H. (1972). Easing the pain of personal loss. *Harvard Business Review, 50*(5), 80–88.

Levinson, H. (1976). Appraisal of what performance? *Harvard Business Review, 54*(4), 30–46.

Menninger, K. A., Mayman, M., & Pruyser, P. (1963). *The vital balance.* New York: Viking.

Menninger, W. C. (1936). Psychoanalytic principles applied to the treatment of hospitalized patients. *Bulletin of the Menninger Clinic, 1,* 35–43.

☞Mintzberg, H. (1979). *The structuring of organizations.* Englewood Cliffs, NJ: Prentice-Hall.

Peterson, D. B., & Hicks, M. D. (1996). *Leader as coach: Strategies for coaching and developing others.* Minneapolis, MN: Personnel Decisions International.

Rigby, D. (2001). Don't get hammered by management fads. *Wall Street Journal,* A22.

Rosenzweig, S. (1951). Idodynamics in personality theory with special reference to projective methods. *Psychological Review, 58*(3), 213–223.

☞Ross, C., & Gubbels, P. (2000). *From the roots up: Strengthening organizational capacity through guided self-assessment.* Oklahoma City: World Neighbours.

☞Schein, E. H. (1985). *Corporate cultures and leadership.* San Francisco: Jossey-Bass.

Schein, E. H. (1987). *The clinical perspective in field work.* Beverly Hills, CA: Sage.

Senge, P. M. (1990). *The fifth discipline.* New York: Doubleday.

Stake, R. F. (1995). *The art of case study research: Perspectives on practice.* Thousand Oaks, CA: Sage.

Surowiecki, J. (2001). A good CEO is not hard to find. *New Yorker,* July 2, 97.

☞Tomasko, R.M. (1987). *Downsizing: Reshaping the corporation for the future.* New York: Amacom.

AUTHOR INDEX

Numbers in italics refer to listings in the references and bibliography.

Menzies, I., 205, *303*
Mintzberg, H., 91, *303, 306*
Munden, K. J., 57, 205, 222, *302*
Murphy, K. R., 138, *303*
Murray, H., 158, *304*
Murray, M., 149, *303*

Nadler, D. A., 126, *303*

Parkinson, C. N., 198, *303*
Peterson, D. B., *306*
Price, C. R., 57, 205, 222, *302*
Pruyser, P., *306*

Racker, H., 22, *303*
Rigby, D., *303*
Rogers, R. E., 5, *303*
Rosenthal, S., 174, *303*
Rosenzweig, S., *303*
Ross, C., *306*

Sabbath, J., 10, *303*
Schein, E. H., *306*
Schwartz, H. S., 200, 206, *303*

Senge, P. M., *306*
Shapiro, E. C., 152, *303*
Sherman, H., 87, *304*
Solley, C. M., 57, 205, 222, *302*
Stake, R. F., *306*
Stamm, 170, *304*
Stewart, 174, 177
Stewart, T. A., *306*
Surowiecki, J., *306*
Swayne, L. E., *305*

Tomasko, R. M., *306*
Townsend, S. M., 95, *304*
Trist, E. L., 158, *304, 305*
Tushman, M. L., 126, *303*

Vitter, M., *304*

Waldholz, M., 148, *304*
Waldman, D. A., 138, *304*
Weaver, P. H., 5, *304*
Weyrich, S., 5, *304*
Wilcox, J., 188, *304*

Zaleznik, A., 207, *302*

SUBJECT INDEX

Education levels, 133–134
Ego ideal, 112, 206
Emotional atmosphere, 55, 185–188
    overall mood stability, 186–187
    prevailing mood and range, 186
Employee
    assessor interactions, 67–68, 83,
        233–237
    regarded by management, 56, 193
    skills, 134
    tenure, 134
Emporia (KS) State University, 183
Engineering studies, 158–159
Enron Company, 198
Enterprise resource planning, 146
Environmental effects, 217–219
Environmental program, 140–141
Equilibrium-maintaining activities, 283
Ethical issues
    authority, 16–18
    avoiding harm, 36
    integrity, 14–16
    obsolescence, 13–14
    organizational positions, 210
    See also Professional concerns
Executive and regulatory bodies, 194–195
Expectations, 63–64, 105, 111–112
Explanatory formulations, 59–60, 227–228
External stimuli, 164–168
Exxon, 204

Federal Emergency Management Adminis-
    tration, 189
Feedback
    to client executive, 233–234
    to employees interviewed, 67–68
    postconsultation, 20–21
    process, 233–236
    report, 106–107, 232–238
    360°, 138
Feminine organization, 198–199
Financial community, 195
Financial condition, 110
Financial emergencies, 119
Financial resources, 173
Financial structure, 46–47, 131–133
Firestone, 172
First-order adaptive activities, 225–226,
    285–286
Florida Atlantic University, 166, 188, 195

Florida Power and Light Co., 136, 171
Focus groups, 158
Folklore, 122–123
Ford, Henry, 170
Ford Motor Company, 6, 172, 196
Formal contract, 111
Formal organization, 125–128
Formal statement, 111
Fourth-order adaptive activities, 226, 287
Freeing process, 35–36
Fringe benefits, 142
Functional assets, 221–223

Gainsharing, 150
General Electric, 136, 171, 183, 204
General Motors, 120, 162, 189
Genetic data, 41–44, 109–123
    background, 116–123
    categories of contact, 111–113
    chief complaint, 114–115
    consultant reports, 48–49
    financial structure, 46–47
    first impressions, 42–43, 113–114
    historical data, 114–123
    human resources, 47–48, 53
    identifying information, 109–114
    major crises, 44–45, 119–120
    organization background, 43
    organization description, 44–54
    plant and equipment, 45–46
    problems viewed by key figures,
        115–116
    product service history, 49–53
    seasonal cycles, 53–54
    special conditions, 113
Globalization, 167–168
Goals, 6, 120
Good Samaritan Hospital, 169, 170, 195
Governmental executive and regulatory
    bodies, 194–195
Group-process consultant, 14
Groupware, 156
Guilt, 26, 139, 236

Harvard Business School, 141
Harvard University, 163, 178, 195, 197,
    209
Health Maintenance Program, 140
Heimbold, Charles A., Jr., 148
Helyar, John, 119

Organizational major crises, 44–45,
    119–120
    financial emergencies, 119
    labor problems, 119
    loss of key personnel, 119
    market share loss, 120
    natural catastrophes, 119
    technological changes, 119
Organizational perceptions, 162–170
    alertness/accuracy/vividness,
        162–168
    assessment, 169–170
    external stimuli, 164–168
    from personnel, 163–164
    from physical plant, 164
    primary external stimuli, 164–165
    selectivity, 168–169
Organizational planners, 168
Organization and job attitude inventory,
    253–262
Organization chart, 86
Organizations
    background, 116–123
    described, 3–5
    descriptive data, 125–159
    ecology, 130–131
    genetic data, 109–123
    growth phases, 117
    hierarchy, 115–116
    historical data, 114–123
    identifying information, 109–114
    interpretive data, 161–190, 191–214
    mission and vision, 6
    purpose, 5–6
    reactive, 53
    size, 110–111
    strategy and goals, 6
Outsider interviews, 85–86, 118
Overidentification, 28

Paternalistic management, 84, 121
Perception, 162
Performance appraisal, 84, 96, 137, 138–139
Performance Record, 122
Personal effectiveness, 138
Personification, unconscious, 201–202
Personnel
    knowledge acquisition, 172
    loss of key people, 119
    organizational perceptions, 163–164

Plant and equipment
    in descriptive data, 128–130
    example of, 45–46
    initial tour, 73–77
    knowledge acquisition, 172
    location, 128
    organizational perceptions, 164
    relative efficiency, 129
    size and function, 129
    special demands, 129
    technological systems, 130
    value, 128
    work environments, 129–130
Plant builders, 196
Policies and procedures
    communication mode, 143–144
    flexibility, 144
    knowledge of, 144
    scope, 143
Policies, language of, 184–185
Positive developmental phase, 117
Power, 58, 207–208
Present status statement, 227
Presentation, 111
Prime Computer Co., 176
Process data, 146–159
    communications systems, 146–156
    management information systems,
        156
    studies, 156–159
Procter and Gamble, 136
Product service history, 49–53, 120–122
    development sequences, 120–121
    geographical patterns, 121
    organizational goals, 120
    performance reputation, 122
    special skills or competencies, 122
    success or failure effects, 121
Professional concerns
    assumptions and cautions, 21–23
    consultant responsibility, 23–25
    contract formulation, 18–20
    data interpretation, 36–37
    internal consultation, 37–39
    intervention, 30–35
    keeping track, 36
    management helplessness, 33
    ordering information, 25–30
    postconsultation feedback, 20–21
    simultaneous consultations, 19–20
    termination, 35–36, 105–107

Prognostic conclusions, 60–61
Projection, 235
Promotion, 136–137
Proposal letter, 18, 265–266, 267–270
Psychoanalytic theory, 10
Psychological contract, 57–58, 111–113,
   205–206, 222–223
Psychological distance, 28, 112, 113
Psychological testing, 137
Purchasing conditions, 165

Qualities of action, 189–190
   constructiveness or destructiveness,
      190
   degree of directness, 189
   effectiveness, 190
   flexibility, 189
   persistence, 189–190
   planning and timing, 189
Questionnaires, 87–88, 253–262

Range, 192
Rationalization, 235
Reactive organization, 53
Reality orientation, 222, 223
Reception and routing, 146–149
   formal and informal channels, 148,
      150–151
   hotlines, 148
   material amount and types, 147
   modes of transmission, 147–148
   sources and audience, 148–149
   timing/rhythm/urgency, 148
Recommendations, 10, 61–62, 226–230
Records and storage system, 178
Recreation program, 141–142
Reengineering, 173
Regression, 206–207
Relative efficiency, 129
Research developments, 167
Responsibility
   attitudes toward, 209–210
   defined, 207
   organizational, 58
Retirement programs, 141
Reviews, 106, 156
RJR Nabisco, 119
Roman Catholic Church, 120, 149, 208
Rules and regulations, 139–140

Safety programs, 140–141
St. Mary's Hospital, 169, 170, 195
Salvation Army, 205
Sampling errors, 99
Scanlon plan, 150
Sears, Roebuck, 183, 195
Seasonal cycles, 53–54
Second-order adaptive activities, 226,
   286
Securities and Exchange Commission,
   131, 198
Selectivity, 168–169
Self-image, 210–211
Setting
   accessibility, 88–91
   difficult or denied, 89–90
   dispersed, 95–96
   on-site contacts, 94
Short-range problems, 116
Short-term framework, 168–169
Significant groups, 212
Six Sigma, 173
Skills, employee, 134
Social contract, 58
Social influence, 209
Social science theory, 8
Sociological temperature, 129–130
Southwest Airlines, 186, 207
Space, concept of, 203–204
Special assets, 221–223
Splitting phenomenon, 200
Staff studies, 156, 157, 158
Stockholders, 194
Strategy, 6
Structural data
   ecology, 130–131
   financial, 131–133
   formal organization, 125–128
   human resources, 133–135
   human resources management,
      135–145
   plant and equipment, 128–130
   policies and procedures, 143–144
   time span and rhythm, 144–146
Structured interview
   described, 239–240
   example of, 241–248
   outline, 249–252
Subsystems, 4
Summary section, 226–230
   explanatory formulation, 227–228

ABOUT THE AUTHOR

Harry Levinson, PhD, is chair of The Levinson Institute and clinical professor of psychology emeritus in the Department of Psychiatry, Harvard Medical School. Beginning his innovative work in 1953, he played a key role in the widely acclaimed reformation of the Kansas state hospital system. In 1954 he created, and for the next 14 years directed, the Division of Industrial Mental Health of The Menninger Foundation. He was a visiting professor in the Sloan School of Management at the Massachusetts Institute of Technology and in the School of Business at the University of Kansas. From 1968 to 1972 he was the Thomas Henry Carroll–Ford Foundation Distinguished Visiting Professor in the Harvard Graduate School of Business Administration. He is a consultant to and lecturer for many business, academic, and government organizations. He has received extensive awards for his outstanding contributions to the field of psychology and for the understanding of human motivation and behavior in the workplace. In addition to numerous articles, he is the author of 16 books, several of which have received major awards. He lectures regularly both at the On Leadership seminar and at organizational meetings. He writes articles and books and continues to make major contributions to the knowledge of human behavior and organizational effectiveness.